THE END
OF LIBERALISM

Ideology, Policy, and the Crisis

of Public Authority

THE END
OF LIBERALISM

Ideology, Policy, and the Crisis

of Public Authority

THEODORE J. LOWI
UNIVERSITY OF CHICAGO

W · W · Norton & Company · Inc ·

NEW YORK

TO

Alvin Lowi, Jr.

Library of Congress Catalog Card No. 69-14704

ALL RIGHTS RESERVED
Published simultaneously in Canada by
George J. McLeod Limited, Toronto

SBN 393 05365 9   Cloth Edition
SBN 393 09835 4   Paper Edition

PRINTED IN THE UNITED STATES OF AMERICA
5 6 7 8 9 0

Contents

PART III. WHY LIBERAL GOVERNMENTS
CANNOT ACHIEVE JUSTICE

PART IV.   BEYOND LIBERALISM

Preface

The End of Liberalism is a deliberately ambiguous title intended to convey at least two purposes. First, it is an inquiry into the actual character of contemporary liberalism, its tenets, its origins, and the state and policies it is responsible for. That is to say, it is an analysis of the end or ends of the liberal state in the 1960's. I have for this purpose tried to write a textbook, in which the reader will find enough data and exposition through which to make analyses and draw conclusions for himself.

Second, the book is a polemic. It is a textbook with a point of view, a strong point of view. As a polemic, its principal target is the modern liberal state itself, its outmoded ideology, and its self-defeating policies. But the polemic is addressed, too, to academic political science and its fellow disciplines of history, sociology, and economics. The tie between the modern liberal state and political science parallels the older tie between the capitalist system and laissez-faire economics. Like classical economics, contemporary political theory is good theory elevated into bad ideology through repetition of its hypotheses as though they were inviolable principles. And, like criticisms of laissez-faire economics, criticisms of political science theory often make difficult reading. But there is a need to break the thirty-year moratorium on consideration of first premises that has characterized modern political science. Controversy must be opened on questions of theory and ideology, not merely on questions of methodology and practice.

Almost exactly thirty years ago the contemporary liberal state was founded on the basis of two overwhelming national elections and a series of Supreme Court decisions that seemed to validate new constitutional principles. But in United States history there have always been two dimensions to the problem of what constitutes acceptable constitutional government. The first has concerned the actual scope of governmental power; the second, the forms by which governmental power, whatever its scope, could be exercised. The Roosevelt Revolution conclusively settled only the first, by establishing the principle for all time in the U.S. that in a democracy there can be no effective limit to the scope of governmental power. The idea of government limited to a specific set of activities had been a characteristically American invention which, characteristically, was discarded once it became too confining. The second issue —essentially the issue of due process of law—was not settled in the 1930's. Instead, the new theory and jurisprudence of the liberal state defined it away. This was done by borrowing from political science the pluralist notion that the pulling and hauling among competing interests is sufficient due process. Pluralism became the model and the jurisprudence of the good society. In the liberal state all formalisms were effectively set aside, as though formalism were the enemy of democracy.

The result—which only at first exposure appears paradoxical —was not the strong, positive government of which the pluralists spoke but impotent government, no less impotent because it was getting bigger. Government that is unlimited in scope but formless in action is government that cannot plan. Government that is formless in action and amoral in intention (i.e., *ad hoc*) is government that can neither plan nor achieve justice.

Two images of contemporary liberal government will probably emerge from the ensuing pages. In some instances it will appear as a gigantic prehistoric beast, all power and no efficacy. In other instances it will appear as another case of Casey at the Bat, power with purpose but without definition, finesse, discrimination, ending in disappointment. Together the two images capture the essence of contemporary liberal government.

It should thus be clear that the issues with which the book deals are remote from the mere question of more government or less government. We already have more, and twentieth-century democracies will tolerate nothing less. It is my hope that such a question will be completely discarded, along with a great number of the other intellectual burdens of the past several decades. Instead, the issues will be the still older and almost forgotten ones of what kind of government, what ends of government, what forms of government, what consequences of government—for our time and for the future, as the United States faces the revolution of human relations. Since these are the questions to which contemporary liberalism has refused to address itself—and in so refusing has failed to found a potent or a just regime—perhaps the way out of the crisis might be discovered by returning to such questions. Therefore they are the primary sources of my polemic, the primary subjects of my textbook, and the primary goals of the alternative ideology—juridical democracy—proposed at the end of the volume.

A polemic poses special problems for the members of the intellectual community who helped shape it. I am therefore especially grateful for the goodnatured assistance of my colleagues, and must with greater than usual emphasis absolve them all of any responsibility for my errors. However, they are responsible for many improvements in the draft. My only regret is in not having followed their advice more carefully and more frequently. Wallace S. Sayre of Columbia University and Winston Fisk of Claremont Men's College read the entire manuscript and provided a view of the whole without which many important revisions would not have taken place. Many colleagues read parts of the book and were most generous in giving me the benefit of their skills. It is impossible to overestimate the value of the community of scholars of the University of Chicago, but it is possible to single out a few of those who made the environment so productive for me: David Easton, Richard Flathman, David Greenstone, Morris Janowitz, Grant McConnell, Paul Peterson, and, from the Law School, Kenneth C. Davis. There were many excellent students at Chicago and also at Cornell, among whom the most influential were Isaac Balbus, Elliott Feldman, Warren Olson, Lawrence Pierce, L. John Roos, and Peter Sharfman, by virtue of their research or their disagreement, or both. I am also indebted to a great many professional associates in other universities. Among them I must single out a few: Alan Altshuler, Massachusetts Institute of Technology; Daniel Bell, Columbia; Jean Blondel, Essex, England; James Davis, Wisconsin; L. A. Froman, Jr.,

University of California (Irvine); E. Pendleton Herring, Social Science Research Council; Henry Kariel, Hawaii; Anthony King, Essex, England; Walter LaFeber, Cornell; George LaNoue, Teachers College; Paul Oren, Centre Universitaire International; Annick Percheron, Foundation National des Sciences Politiques; Austin Ranney, Wisconsin; Randall Ripley, Ohio State; James Rosenau, Rutgers; Charles Roig, Grenoble; Edward V. Schneier, College of the City of New York; Harry Scoble, University of California at Los Angeles; Nicholas Wahl, Princeton; William Wallace, Manchester, England.

I would also like to take this opportunity to thank the editors of the following reviews and presses for having given me the opportunity to publish articles that became trial runs for the book: *American Political Science Review, The Reporter, Challenge*, The Free Press, and the University of Chicago Press.

Without institutional assistance all possible individual assistance might have been wasted. A Social Science Research Council Fellowship in 1963–64 and a Guggenheim Foundation Fellowship in 1967–68 made it possible for me to undertake the long-range analyses of public policies of which the present volume is the second installment. The first, *Private Life and Public Order* (W. W. Norton, 1967), is a companion book of readings and bibliography. The third, in progress, entitled *Arenas of Power*, is a somewhat less normative study of the processes of policy formulation and implementation in the United States and France. The University of Chicago, Social Science Division, and the Centre Universitaire International of the University of Paris are two other institutions whose assistance has been invaluable.

Among all my many debts, however, my strongest is to my brother, Alvin Lowi, Jr. In a real sense, this book is merely an episode in an argument that began over a decade ago. I dedicate it to him in full knowledge that it will only cause a temporary quiet between rounds.

THEODORE J. LOWI

Paris
August, 1968

Prologue

A crisis is a time when leadership and ideologies begin to falter. It is a time when established standards fall and customary procedures yield unexpected results. It is a time when all alternatives, including no choice at all, become calculated risks.

We are living in a decade of crisis. The crisis is so serious that it poses a graver threat to the nation than the last great domestic crisis, the Great Depression of the 1930's. It has already eroded the values which arose out of the Great Depression and shaken the regime based upon its memory.

The crisis of the 1960's is at bottom a political crisis, a crisis of public authority. During the Depression, stability was regained after a spectacular but unrevolutionary turn to government. Confidence was restored long before economic conditions had returned to normal. But today government itself is the problem. Public morality has become involved. The institutions of the state have become implicated. There is serious doubt about efficacy and justice in the agencies of government, the processes of policy-making, leadership selection, and the implementation of decisions. The crisis deepens because its nature has not even been discovered as yet. Scholars, contract researchers, presidential commissions, and legislative and administrative committees continue assiduously to sift every socioeconomic fact. But they have looked everywhere except at the very structure of authority within which they are operating. The entire *modus operandi* of power must be called into question. The kitbag of political technique needs emptying. Until then the crisis will deepen.

Indications should have been clear enough. Protests and militancy, black and white, are the outward signs of decaying respect for public symbols and destroyed trust in public objects. Governmental effort on a scale unknown in the Western world seems to offend more beneficiaries than it ingratiates. The emergence of hostilities long suppressed reveals the awesome possibility that the national political system is no longer capable of maintaining the ideal of one nation indivisible. The cry for black power and student power, the cry against the power structure, and the cry for participation and decentralization constitute political rhetoric because the problems are basically political.

The crisis of public authority was not caused by the Vietnam war. It did not begin with the assassination of John F. Kennedy and it was not changed appreciably by the assassinations of Martin Luther King, Jr., or Robert F. Kennedy. The root of the problem is the liberal state. The seeds of crisis were sown by the crumbling of the American caste system; they germinated while governmental and political institutions failed to cope with the social revolution.

During the 1930's the old nineteenth-century liberalism and the regime it had created became almost universally confirmed as an anachronism. Out of the ashes of the old liberal state emerged another type of liberal state, but now, after thirty years, it too is coming to be appreciated as an anachronism. We too will soon have our Herbert Hoovers to ridicule. We too will soon have an Old Guard who live undernourished on the diet of their memories of New Deals, Fair Deals, Great Crusades, New Frontiers, and Great Societies.

PART I

THE ORIGIN AND DECLINE OF LIBERAL IDEOLOGY IN THE UNITED STATES

". . . the ideas of economists and political philosophers, both when they are right and when they are wrong, are more powerful than is commonly understood. . . . Practical men, who believe themselves to be quite exempt from any intellectual influences, are usually the slaves of some defunct economist. Madmen in authority, who hear voices in the air, are distilling their frenzy from some academic scribbler of a few years back."

Lord Keynes

CHAPTER 1

THE OLD PUBLIC
PHILOSOPHY

Capitalist Ideology
and the Automatic Society

The United States is a child of the Industrial Revolution. Its godfather is capitalism and its guardian Providence, otherwise known as the "invisible hand."

Capitalism is an ideology because it is a source of principles and a means of justifying behavior; that is, it is something Americans believe in. It is a liberal ideology because it has always participated in positive attitudes toward progress, individualism, rationality, and nationalism. It is capitalism because its foundation is a capitalistic economic theory and because its standards of legitimacy are capitalistic. It was the public philosophy during the nineteenth century because it dominated all other sources of belief in the formulation of public policy. It is the old public philosophy because it no longer dominates other sources of belief.

In a very important sense, of course, capitalism is not an ideology at all. It is a bundle of economic and technological processes. In this sense capitalism is not something one be-

3

lieves in but rather something one does. One simply amasses wealth and tries to make it produce in the most rational manner by ruthlessly submitting it to the principles of human organization, machines, and double-entry bookkeeping.[1] Objectively it can be done by private or by public means; capitalistic practices are adopted whenever and wherever rational economic order is sought. But when these objective capitalistic practices are successfully employed privately for many years, as in the United States, institutions develop around them, classes of wealth emerge, power centers organize. Then words are spoken on behalf of these patterns. When repeated often and spread widely these justifying words become the ideology of the thing. When these words end up coloring the Constitution, influencing policies of government, and shaping the very criteria of worth as well as wealth, they constitute a public philosophy.

Capitalism as public philosophy had an immensely strong theoretical core. Karl Marx as economist is an amateur and an imitator in comparison to Adam Smith. Smith's kind of economics appealed to the nineteenth-century American builders for a number of obvious reasons. The most important reason, it seems in retrospect, must have been the reliance of his theory on an automatic, self-regulating society. The second most important reason was, obviously, that it was purely commercial at a time when "being in trade" was still something relatively despicable. In sum, left entirely to their own devices, commercial interests could provide the greatest possible wealth for a nation: When the enterpreneur "intends only his own gain . . . he is . . . led by an invisible hand to promote an end which was no part of his intention. . . . By pursuing his own interest he frequently promotes that of the society more effectually than when he really intends to promote it. . . . The

[1] *Cf.* Max Weber, *General Economic History* (New York: Collier Books, 1961), pp. 207 ff. Reprinted in my *Private Life and Public Order* (New York: W. W. Norton, 1968). *Cf.* also Herbert Muller: "Few have heard of Fra Luca Pacioli, the inventor of double-entry bookkeeping; but he has probably had much more influence on human life than has Dante or Michael Angelo." *The Uses of the Past* (New York: Oxford University Press, 1952), p. 257.

statesman, who should attempt to direct private people in what manner they ought to employ their capitals, would not only load himself with a most unnecessary attention, but would assume an authority which could . . . nowhere be so dangerous as in the hands of a man who had folly and presumption enough to fancy himself fit to exercise it." [2]

There were other reasons for its appeal. Laissez faire, as the theory became identified during its elevation to ideological status, made a happy fit with the native American fear of political power. Smith gave systematic reasons for opposition to government, but his reasons merely supplemented and confirmed reasons already widely embraced before and during our Revolution. And why not such confirmation? American grievances were as much against mercantilism as against colonialism. Smith was known and debated during the formative years of the Republic perhaps better in the new country than among the educated classes in England at that time. Hamilton in his *Report on Manufactures* (1791) must have had good reasons to spend the bulk of his first section attempting to refute Smith as regards the application of laissez-faire principles to the new country.[3] Hamilton won his battles but lost his war. If the principles of nineteenth-century economics had not existed the Americans would most certainly have invented them. The Americans accepted the view that there was a natural economic harmony which could only be harmed if touched. The dismal laws of Smith's colleagues Malthus and Ricardo made little difference, for any effort to repeal them could only do still greater injury.

This was the underlying dynamic. Strongly and logically related to it at the level of behavior were the sanctity of property and the binding morality of contract. These notions were justified by the classical economics and were, at one and the same time, additional bulwarks against tyranny. Already imbedded in common law, property and contract were flexible enough to survive the changes in actual property and actual contract

[2] Adam Smith, *The Wealth of Nations*, Book IV, reprinted in Lowi, *op. cit.*, p. 12.

[3] Reprinted in part in Lowi, *op. cit.*, pp. 111 ff.

as corporations split the property atom into millions of anonymous parts and anonymous corporate giants entered into sacred contracts with tiny suppliers and individual laborers.

Insofar as it also shaped objective constitutional practices and governmental life, capitalist ideology can also be said to have constituted the public philosophy during the same period. Beliefs about popular rule, decentralization of power, and the evils of government were strong; but the case for capitalism as the stronger doctrine can be fairly convincingly documented. Happily for both, the tenets of popular rule and of capitalism generally reinforced each other; but in instances of conflict, American government and public policy were decidedly unresponsive to popular rule ideology. The issue could be *Dred Scott v. Sanford,* in which slaves were incorporated into the system by confirmation that they are property under the Fifth Amendment. Or the issue could be popularly enacted state regulatory laws, invalidated as unreasonable restraints on contract; many were invalidated as interference with even the process by which contracts are made. Or the issue could be that of the corporation itself, which was given two advantages in nineteenth-century jurisprudence; taken together they strain heavily upon one's sense of logic. On the one hand corporations were merely property, for which the owners, the shareholders, received for themselves total protection and full claim to all profits. On the other hand corporations were defined as persons separate from their owners, so that the death of a corporation affected no owner beyond his shares—because stockholders are not responsible for the debts of the corporation—and yet this "person" was held to enjoy almost all the rights of citizenship under the Bill of Rights and the Fourteenth Amendment.

Following the Civil War, conflicts between capitalism and popular rule increased. But whatever the issue during all of the nineteenth-century and part of the twentieth, capitalism won out in a straight fight. In his famous dissent in *Lochner v. New York,* Justice Holmes proclaimed: "The Fourteenth Amendment does not enact Mr. Herbert Spencer's Social Statics. . . . [A] constitution is not intended to embody a particular economic theory. . . ." This doctrine makes Justice Holmes one of the better prophets and one of the worst historians of his day. Spencer was extreme, but his vision of laissez faire fairly represented an ideology of capitalism that shackled popular-rule ideology, ordaining in effect that popular rule was all right so long as popular institutions chose to do nothing. As soon as state assemblies and Congress became captured by majorities favorable to regular and frequent state intervention, the inconsistencies between the demands of capitalistic ideology and the demands of popular-rule ideology became clear. By the end of the nineteenth-century the two were no longer reinforcing at all, and the entire constitutional epoch of 1890–1937 can, and will in Chapter 3, be characterized as a dialogue between the two.

In the course of that dialogue, capitalism declined as ideology and died as public philosophy. It came to be called conservatism, but that is an incredibly obtuse misnomer that in no way contributes to an understanding of the decline. Capitalism never became conservative. It went into a decline because it became irrevelant and erroneous. The intellectual and theoretical core of the ideology became weakened by generations of belief in itself. Smith and the nineteenth-century liberal economists who followed him were not wrong; in fact, they still hold up for the phenomena with which their theories deal. Capitalist ideology became irrelevant and error-ridden because capitalist ideologues became disloyal to the intellectual spirit of liberal economics. Rather than risk incorporating the new facts of twentieth-century economics and society they closed their minds.

CAPITALISM AS ECONOMIC THEORY AND SOCIOLOGICAL MONSTROSITY

How did nineteenth-century capitalism view society? It necessarily had social views, for no mere economic theory was broad enough to provide ideological support for the new social classes, the new sources of power. What were its weaknesses?

Weaknesses it must have had if it lost its place as public philosophy.

The competitive, or "supply-and-demand," or market model of capitalist economics has been criticized from a number of points of view. No criticism has ever satisfactorily cracked the logic of the theory or its applicability to the cases that lie within its assumptions. Successful criticism takes the form of arguing toward a larger frame of reference. Theories of imperfect competition, macroeconomics, national income, "systems," and notions of that sort suggest the different dimensions from which twentieth-century criticisms are hurled back at nineteenth-century truths.[4]

There is, however, still another dimension of the problem which is of greatest relevance to the connection between nineteenth-century liberal economics and the rise and fall of capitalist public philosophy. This dimension is the more strictly social views of capitalism. Based upon the same dynamic of competition, the notion spread from Smith that the market produced extremely important social as well as narrowly economic benefits. The "equilibrium" of which such economists spoke came to mean not merely stability of prices near actual costs but also to mean social stability—i.e., harmony, felicity, public order.[5] Smith was optimistic. Perhaps the gloomy political economists who followed him also believed that it would be difficult to improve upon a society governed largely by the principle that selfish interests produce the public interest. But it is equally clear that their economics did not commit them or us to the sociology developed in their name in succeeding gen-

[4] The relevant literature is too vast to sample here. A clever review of Keynes and his American disciples can be found in a review article of John Kenneth Galbraith, reprinted as "Came the Revolution" in Lowi, *op. cit.*, pp. 142 ff. For a well-balanced assessment of many other features, written with particular regard for social scientists other than professional economists, see R. A. Dahl and C. E. Lindblom, *Politics, Economics, and Welfare* (New York: Harper and Brothers, 1953), esp. Chapters 6 and 7, including their most helpful bibliography.

[5] The most brilliant as well as most orthodox contemporary version of *laissez-faire* theory is Ludwig von Mises, *Human Action* (New Haven: Yale University Press, 1949). Note the title. To Mises, market economics is a science of society. *Cf.* passages reprinted in Lowi, *op. cit.*, pp. 70 ff.

erations. Herein lies the key to understanding the success and eventual decline of laissez-faire ideology. Four great political economists captured the basic developmental truths about their century. But the clear implications of their laws of development lead in directions irrelevant to or inconsistent with the model of the automatic society erected by the laissez-faire ideologues. Review of these laws of development reveals that the society they anticipate is not automatically provided for by market competition. Review shows a contrary feature that the market mechanism in the economy assumes a society whose institutions have adjusted themselves to the market mechanism. Modern society must become capable of controlling, suppressing, and absorbing market forces or the market becomes menace rather than good provider.

THE LAWS OF DEVELOPMENT

The division of labor: Adam Smith began his great classic, *The Wealth of Nations* (1776), not with a disquisition about market competition but with an inquiry into the division of labor. To Smith the division of labor was the cause of "improvement in the productive powers of labour." It would spread if men were free to apply rationality to their self-interest, and there would be an immense increase in productivity, far beyond anything public policy might try to ordain.

Smith expected the division of labor to spread toward every aspect of industry because it was the only rational way of organizing. But how far would the division of labor actually spread and how extremely would it be applied? On Figure 1.1 the tendency is expressed as an S-curve, which suggests that the rate of application of the principle of the division of labor is very high but then slackens up after a certain point. That makes the phenomenon appear to be naturally harmonious with other needs, suggesting, for example, that the principle would not be applied to such a runaway extreme that workers completely lost touch with their product. But in truth there is no naturally harmonious tendency to be found here. The division of labor curve has been given an S-shape because it is a ratio, and the tendency of all such ratios may be an S. Operationally, the division of labor is a ratio of the actual number of different tasks in a given work force to the total personnel in the work force. The *rate* by which a given task is broken into two or three separate tasks will probably decline as the ratio approaches 100 per cent. But that is only for a given size of work force at a given level of technology. Smith himself, for example, observed that the full potential of specialization can begin to be realized only as a work force or market reaches large size and is growing. Moreover, new machines and processes open new possibilities for specializing labor in a given work force. This means that even if the division of labor tendency is an S-curve, the rate of specialization may not slow up until society is submerged in specialties. Economic rationality and market pressure may dictate this, but those same factors do not specify when society—mankind—is suffering under the weight. Specialization may, therefore, reach an automatic equilibrium, but not necessarily at a level that other social needs will tolerate.

The law of population: Thomas Malthus in his *Essay on the Principle of Population* (1798) produced one of the most influential and clearly the most dismal of the laws of industrial society: as the supply of food goes up at an arithmetic rate, the population goes up at a geometric rate. Consequently, poverty, pestilence, and war are inevitable unless society learns "moral restraint." Population growth is expressed as an S-curve on Figure 1.1 although it is not a ratio subject to statistical tendency. It is drawn as an S-curve because that has been the actual history of population growth in the West.[6] However, again we have a tendency that does not relate in any naturally harmonious way with society at large.[7] In the first place, reduction of the population growth rate by poverty and pestilence, and at least a few of the wars, must represent a malfunctioning rather than a proper functioning of the economic sys-

[6] For an interesting discussion of the population S-curve and its significance for society, see David Riesman *et al., The Lonely Crowd* (Garden City: Doubleday, 1953), pp. 21 ff.

[7] Von Mises, *op. cit.,* argues forcefully that an unfettered market is the best natural birth control, but it is only an hypothesis logically derived from restating the market model in more general terms. *Cf.* reprinted portion in Lowi, *op. cit.*

tem. Secondly, the market economy depends upon th
pressure of the Malthusian law for the proper operatio
labor market. That is where Ricardo comes in.

The iron law of wages: David Ricardo's formulation (in
Principles of Political Economy and Taxation, 1817) is an extension of Smith and Malthus. In Ricardo's hands the two

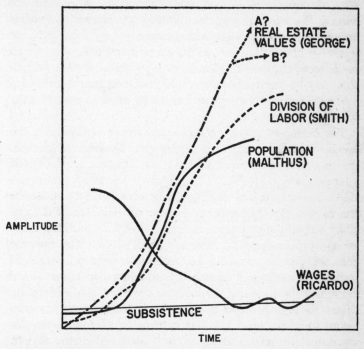

FIGURE 1.1. The Nineteenth-Century Laws of Political Economy:
A Diagrammatic Survey

tendencies, division of labor and population growth, support
each other not in the harmonious way seen by Smith but in a
vicious relationship due to insufficiently expanding productivity. The amount of product available for distribution is never
enough; moments of prosperity are either short-lived or create
new population pressure which, through competition for
work, reduce the price of labor. This was a close relationship,
not dependent upon lengthy birth cycles, because new supplies
of labor came into cities from the countryside, and they came

with only slight incentive once the feudal relation to land
ended. A fluid and expansive labor supply has been a major
factor in the development of commerce and industry.

To Ricardo the tendency toward declining wages was limited only by the absolute necessities of survival.[8] The curve
takes its S-shape (upside down) from the assumption that the
rate of population growth will directly affect pressure on
wages. The bottom horizontal is drawn to suggest fluctuation
around subsistence, with the tendency always toward subsistence—*if other things are left equal and no deliberate effort is
made to interfere.* Here is another equilibrium, or leveling off,
that may be natural but is certainly not necessarily reached at
a level supportive of equilibrium in all other realms of social
life.

The explosion of real estate values: Henry George, although
less appreciated, ranks with the others in the importance of his
insights into industrial society. In *Progress and Poverty*
(1879), George attempted to grapple with the apparent paradox of a large class of unattached poor in a society of increasing prosperity. Pauperism as a mass phenomenon was something virtually unknown to the pre-industrial world, but it was
recognized by many of George's predecessors. The factor of
rent was also appreciated by economists before George; Ricardo's criticisms had already helped convert it into a weapon
by which the capitalists could attack the old landholders. But
Henry George brought to these issues their fullest socioeconomic meaning, much the way Ricardo had fused the implications of Smith and Malthus. George observed simply that the
value of real estate increases in some proportion with increased
population density or urbanization, and that this increased
value is never distributed to the population whose growth
produced it. Instead, the increased value goes as an "unearned
increment" to those fortunate enough to own the land before
urbanization. As a result, "in the new city you may have a
luxurious mansion, but among its public buildings will be an

---

[8] On Figure 1.1, subsistence level is drawn on a slight upward slant
to suggest historical changes in the level considered to be bare subsistence.

almshouse." Unquestionably there were many exceptions to his thesis. Real estate bubbles could burst; prices could tumble to earlier levels. However, George's book had hit a responsive chord in world opinion, probably because he had hit upon such a strong underlying basis of truth.

What is the shape of the curve of real estate values? Because of its relation to population growth it may be an S-curve; but due to speculation, anxiety, and many other non-demographic factors, rent may bear some geometric relation to the population curve. Would its equilibrium be reached, if rent were left to its natural course, in time to avoid revolution? When we add to rent the costs of other factors of production, the phenomenon about which George concerned himself is seen to be fundamental, fully worthy of consideration in the context of revolution. We do not have to believe with George that rent is original sin. We need only take his thesis as cause for inquiry into possibly self-destructive aspects of capitalism.[9] Capitalism produces industrialization and urbanization. These two phenomena are the sources of stresses and strains that will not necessarily be solved by more capitalism, industrialization, and urbanization. Yet to have less of them would require interference with the natural tendency of a market-governed economy to expand.

AUTOMATIC ECONOMY VERSUS AUTOMATIC SOCIETY

These four basic tendencies do not represent runaway factors. Industrial societies have had, despite their many problems, impressive histories. But the problems are as often as not attributable to the very same forces that produced the impressive histories. As has already been suggested, these tendencies, expressed in the four curves, have an aggravating effect on each other. Once industrialization began there seemed to be no stopping Western societies from the fullest pursuit of all its implications: Advances in the division of labor demanded

[9] Only the social consequences are explored here. For a fascinating speculation into certain self-destructive economic features, see Joseph Schumpeter on capitalism in his classic *Capitalism, Socialism and Democracy* (New York: Harper & Brothers, 1942).

more population; increased productivity made greater population possible as well as necessary, but populations were badly
affected as productivity brought on concentration. Increasing
concentration of population put great pressure on for still more
output, but productivity rates declined as the price of real estate and other factors of production went up. Inventions only
postponed the moment when more masses of labor were
needed, because new levels in the division of labor required
more workers, and more population pressure was needed to
keep the price of labor down and consumption up. The price
of labor was of special importance because it was far easier to
manipulate than the price of real estate and capital.

This is only a partial statement of the system but it suggests
how the parts of the system related to each other. It takes
something of an optimist to believe that such relationships, if
left alone, produce nothing but felicity.

In the modern city we can observe without difficulty how
these forces must have worked themselves out. The growth
curves on Figure 1.2 suggest that once a society enters upon
industrialization—or, in the terms of W.W. Rostow, begins its
"takeoff"—its central cities become creatures of these forces.
The population of Old London had reached 225,000, according
to the best estimates, by 1600. Two centuries later, on the eve
of the Industrial Revolution, London had grown only to about
900,000.[10] By 1800, in fact, a rather small proportion of the
population of England or the United States lived in cities.
From that point the story is one of incredible urban-industrial
growth, despite slow progress in public health and the ame-
nities in cities. For example, between 1800 and 1890 the proportion of the U.S. population living in cities of 8,000 or larger
increased 87 times, while the general population increased 12
times. But the story is more vividly told in Figure 1.2. Sepa-

[10] Figures for London (1800–1841) are taken from Adna F. Weber,
The Growth of Cities in the Nineteenth Century (Ithaca: Cornell
University Press, 1899, republished 1963), p. 46. His figures include
territory in the county that is not included in the official definition of
Registration London. The differences are negligible. They are noted
here only to avoid confusion over the slight lack of correspondence with
figures on London taken from other sources, cited below.

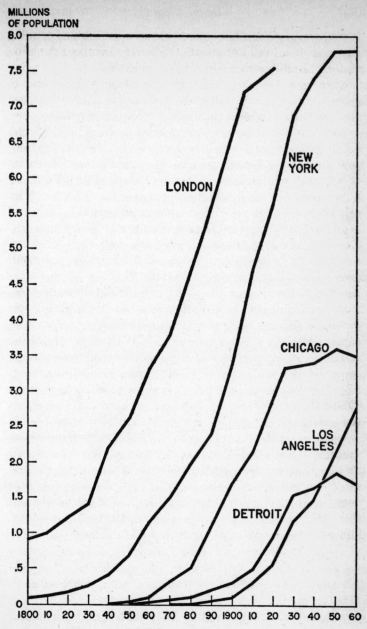

FIGURE 1.2. Growth Profiles of the Great Industrial Cities

rated by a time lag of about 20 years, New York and London show enormous rates of growth. Following by about the same time lag are three other large industrial cities.

Even more striking than the consistently high rates of growth is the fact that all five cities grew at almost *identical* rates once their takeoff had begun. Every industrializing city seems to be under the same intensity of pressure to realize the fullest potential of its resources and culture. The extreme and parallel rates of growth seem to confirm the universality of aggravating relations among the developmental tendencies of industrialization. This is further confirmed by the very structure of those large cities that were built after the advent of capitalism. The structure of each reveals that it was built fundamentally as a producing and marketing unit. Only Washington, which was designed to be a capital city, shows any influence of noncapitalistic values in the building of the great American cities. It was designed and built with defense of the White House and Capitol buildings in mind. Its back is the Potomac, and one side is the "Eastern Branch" (Anacostia River), with the Capitol on a hill above the fork. The street layout is a nearly perfect grid cut across by major arterials that converge on each other to form sixteen intersections (now called circles) at strategic points in every direction around the White House and Capitol. This was an ideal defense against the movement of cavalry and heavy artillery. However, no other major modern city bears the stamp of such noncapitalist preoccupations. New York has its Battery, but New York's development was overwhelmingly toward encouraging movement, not defending against it. Still more have inland cities been, even according to their boosters, gateways to this and that. The same tracings can be made in England and France although they may be somewhat confused the fossil remains of precapitalist values in old cities. Paris is the exception proving the rule: Paris is a royal city, an anticapitalist city. Not only are most cities in other countries now built for access, they, like the American cities, were created as economic capitals, not government or esthetic capitals. They were built for functional specialization. They were and are still built for efficiency. One particularly antisocial form of this is the practice of building for a life expectancy of around 40 years. Once the structures are "amortized" they can be destroyed or abandoned to other uses, the most important of which is the very profitable entity called the slum. Manchester, England, might as well be in New Jersey. How many times have capitalist economies renewed and recreated the slums that Engels saw? Contemporary France, even with its stronger statist tradition, displays most of the same values today. If not in Paris, this is true even of the Paris suburbs, where so much of the industry and industrial proletariat were relocated. French cities rebuilt after World War II damage suggest that capitalist values are still preeminent.[11]

The trend lines on Figure 1.2 suggest that the cities have, except for Los Angeles, reached their upper levels of expansion. But this does not mean equilibrium, and certainly not natural, felicitous, and self-maintaining equilibrium. In the first place, expansion continues toward a scale and complexity impossible to imagine. It does not show up in the population curves simply because the population living beyond the city's legal boundaries erected *political* barriers to further city expansion. Each metropolitan region continues in its pace. Soon most of the land east of the Mississippi and west of the Divide will be megalopolis. Half the population of France will someday live in the region of Paris.[12] In the second place, the processes of specialization and amortization, as well as progress and poverty, continue as the pace of invention makes these changes possible without local population increases. The end is not in sight, though the forms may change.

What of the capitalist vision of the automatic society? The structure and life of industrial cities, as well as the logic of the tendencies of industrial development, suggest that the market system is *simply one and only one adjustment industrial society made to the demands of industrialization.* Market systems

---

[11] Max Weber's essay *The City* and Lewis Mumford's *The City in History* are useful corroborative studies. However, the most fascinating, due to the richness of the data, is Adna F. Weber, *op. cit.,* esp. Chapter 3.

[12] See below, Chapter 7.

were vital to industrialization, they remain indispensable, and they clearly do generate benefits beyond the mere provision of rational information and control among entrepreneurs. But the market system falls far short of including within its sphere all of the fallout of industrialization. It, moreover, makes its own distinct contribution to those pressures: In history, competition tended to reduce prices toward the irreducible costs of production. Such reduction put irresistible pressures upon the entrepreneur to reduce his costs wherever he could. That meant reduction of production costs. Population pressure gave the entrepreneur no control over the price of land, but it gave him a great opportunity in his relation to labor; hence, increased pressure for more population and cheaper labor costs. Pressure, too, for more invention; free competition probably did produce many of the technological advances of the epoch. But invention is a postponement, not a repeal, of the workings of industrial forces.

If the U.S. and other industrializing societies maintained some semblance of public order during their developmental ordeals, it could not have been due entirely to some self-correcting characteristic of the very factors in the process of development. The capitalistic assumption that capitalistic processes produce their own social solutions is sheer mythology— that is, it bears no necessary relation to the truth. Since there is some truth to it—since the economic forces of capitalism produced some social benefit—the influence of capitalist ideology was strengthened and spread, ultimately to become accepted by an entire governing class. But in the extension of this image of an automatic society lay the seeds of its decline. As capitalist society galloped into the twentieth century its intellectual weaknesses strained belief. At some undetermined point capitalism ceased to constitute the public philosophy, although it remains a strong ideological force.

AUTOMATIC SOCIETY VERSUS THE VISIBLE HAND

The intellectual core of capitalist public philosophy became corrupted by complacent insistence upon its own universal applicability. It reinforced itself largely in a manner resembling primitive magic—when it did not seem to be working the answer lay in some devilish outside interference with the long run, just as the medicine man might explain drought as the wages of insufficiently passionate rain dancing. The fact of the matter is that capitalist theory assumed society would somehow adjust to take up the social slack created by the market. Society did in fact adjust, but it did not do so in patterns remotely explicable in terms of self-regulating commercial mechanisms. Quite the contrary; modern industrialized society can be explained as an effort to make the "invisible hand" as visible as possible. The tendencies represented by the curves on Figure 1.1. are laws of development in societies that operate according to capitalist principles. But the capitalistic principles alone will only guarantee that production will be maximal and that prices will tend toward their lowest levels; that says nothing about the society except that its average members will probably enjoy improved comforts and choices. The question of whether and at what point the curves become S-curves is representative of the social problems left unsolved. As long as the laws of development cannot be repealed, the aggravating and unpredictable interrelations among them suggest that they must be taken not as problems somehow automatically solved but rather as "functional prerequisites" that must somehow be regularly fulfilled in industrial societies if such societies hope to maintain themselves at all. That is to say, the industrializing societies had to develop institutions that would, as a regular matter, adjust themselves and their members to the requirements of capitalism.

If the adjustment was successful, it was due to the successful application of a trait essential to market economies—rationality. But rationality was used *on* markets as well as *in* them. Rationality came to be set above all other values. Smith unassailably attributed the market and the division of labor to man's "faculties of reason." But it is hard to imagine rational man happy to submit under all conditions to so nonrational and mechanistic an expression of rationality as a self-regulating market. Man did not, of course, submit; and his universal application of rationality created a history which stands in strong contrast to the claim to universality of capitalist theory, ideology, and public philosophy.

Rationality was product as well as prerequisite of industrialization, but it was at no point limited to markets. Rationality can be seen in virtually all the larger forms of social activity. While we cannot actually see a thing called rationality, we can see its most important application. This is *differentiation,* which is simply rationality in the organization of conduct.

Differentiation can be defined as the articulation of parts, or, with Herbert Spencer, the "unlikeness of parts." It can be thought of as the principle of the division of labor applied to any and all aspects of life. However differentiation is defined, two critical things can be said of it. First, it is immediately and intimately bound up in the process of development in the West. And second, it is, or quickly becomes, a phenomenon whose workings and consequences are far removed from anything resembling a market mechanism.

There are at least four forms of differentiation: (1) Multiplication of individual roles; (2) Multiplication and specialization of the units of production and distribution; (3) Multiplication of the units of social control; and (4) Spatial differentiation. A brief treatment of each will reveal the significance of differentiation as the prime response to the curves of development and the primary means by which the curves are leveled out into S's.

(1) The division of labor, despite its undoubted importance, is but a part of the process of multiplication of individual roles in industrial society. For, in addition to the separation of men by tasks, there is also subdivision of the individual according to his various realms of life. The week is divided into employment, family life, church, association; and in each realm a man varies in role, status, and identity. Early in industrial development work is separated from the home. Men become involved in workplace associations that are separate from neighborhood associations, and there is little continuity among these and the roles of father, husband, deacon, and son. The "urbane person" is one who is admired for the ease with which he lives with and passes easily among a large number of separate roles.

Sociology in an advanced society can with justification define a human being as a bundle of roles. Sir Henry Maine's evaluation of society as passing "from status to contract" captures with incredible efficiency a society whose roles are so conscious and so well defined as to provide a basis for specific, contractual fulfillment.[13]

(2) The multiplication and specialization of the units of production is as important an economic phenomenon as the division of labor into specialized tasks for individuals within the units. There is probably a period of years in every industrializing country when the total number of producing units declines, because the evolution of industry usually passes through and destroys such preindustrial systems of production as the household or family system, the guild or handicraft system, and the domestic or cottage system.[14] But once production becomes more centralized in factories, the actual number of separate units within factories increases, these units specialize, and the likelihood of any one unit producing a whole item for a market goes down accordingly. Countless firms grow deliberately larger in order to be able to differentiate sufficiently to provide for their own specialized services. But an equally important type of unit specialization is the growth of autonomous special service firms. One of the vital functions of central business districts has become provision of the most highly specialized economic services. The best known examples are communications, information, advertising, legal and stenotyp-

---

[13] Developments in the medical profession show clearly that even a narrowly economic multiplication of roles is not merely a phenomenon of centralized and bureaucratized big industry. Most professional specialization in medicine has occurred in the last 100 years, during which time it passed from a simple profession to one in which, by 1942, there were 23 basic medical specialties available for the prospective resident. Here is a dramatic case of differentiation in the free professions. See Victor A. Thompson, *Modern Organization* (New York: Alfred A. Knopf, 1961), pp. 49 ff.

[14] See, for example, Adna F. Weber, *op. cit.*, p. 185. Weber's statistics show, for example, that in Germany between 1882 and 1895 (the period of Germany's greatest industrialization) the number of persons working on their own account dropped by 5.3% while the number working in establishments rose as follows: Establishments of 5 or fewer, +23%; of 6 to 50, +76.3%; of more than 50, +88.7% (p. 188).

ing services, professional employment agencies, and consulting firms. Still another form of specialization of units is in the legal and capital structure of the firm itself. A most important example during the past 50 years is the separation of ownership and control. As stock became a basic means of accumulating capital, ownership spread to many, while operating control of policy and management was necessarily retained by a few. Ultimately control and management become split too, so that many top managers of large firms are no more than highly paid professional employees. Even the fullest exercise of every stock option would give few managers the dominant voice in policy-making on the board of directors.

(3) Of equal importance in the rational adjustment to the incessant forces of industrialization is the specialization of the units of social control. This applies to virtually every institution in society that is not included under "units of production" above. The decline of the family as a producing unit was accompanied by the loss to the family of other functions as well. The family no longer functions as an agency of self-defense, or as a holder of property in perpetuity. It does little even to educate children beyond the age of five. As a unit, the family narrows down to the dual functions of procreation and childrearing, and even these receive narrower and narrower definition with expansion of hospitals and day-care centers, kindergartens and nursery schools, the folkways of babysitting at one end of life and institutions for the aged at the other end. Mosca and others note the parallel development of separation of public and private roles and institutions, and an extreme narrowing down of the functions performed by any one of them. Mosca's distinction between the "feudal state" and the modern state rests largely upon this type of differentiation.[15] In the feudal state "all the executive functions of society—the economic, the judicial, the administrative, the military—are exercised simultaneously by the same individuals, while at the same time the state is made up of small social aggregates, each of which possesses all the organs that are required for self-sufficiency." [16] In the modern

---

[15] See Gaetano Mosca, *The Ruling Class* (New York: McGraw-Hill, 1939), Chapter 3. This is a classic essay in the politics of development.
[16] *Ibid.*, p. 81.

bureaucratic state, the military becomes a totally public instrument, but all administrative and judicial powers are withdrawn from it. Administrative and judicial functions become separated. Offices become separated from holders of office; "*L'état c'est moi*" becomes an impossibility even in modern absolutisms. Specialization of political functions among administrative, elitist and elective elements makes the modern system of representative government "the most complex and delicate type of political organization that has so far been seen in world history." [17] Meanwhile, many nongovernmental institutions have displaced or supplemented family *and* government. Obvious examples are philanthropic and social service organizations, unions and trade associations, political parties, fraternities, and social registers. Specialization leaves the church as simply one more example.

(4) Finally, there is spatial differentiation, which contributes its own advantages and disadvantages. A famous analysis shows how Chicago developed its concentric circles of land uses emanating from the central business district through warehouse and skid rows to lower-, middle-, then upper-income housing districts.[18] If Chicago's concentric circle pattern is not universal, it is at least an interesting case of a universal—the specialization of land uses in one form or another. This, like the other forms of specialization, is a rational ordering of things. Jane Jacobs has argued that along with such rational use of space we run the risk of grave social problems, but that only points immediately toward the general problem created by all differentiation.[19] This is that *the rational organization of conduct produces new social problems, and these in turn require a rational approach to social control.*

Thus, differentiation in all its forms was productive of responses appropriate to industrialization, but at what cost? There

[17] *Ibid.*, p. 389.

[18] E. W. Burgess, in Robert E. Park *et al.*, *The City* (Chicago: University of Chicago Press, 1925).

[19] For a fascinating account of some of the serious problems of spatial differentiation in cities, see Jane Jacobs, *The Death and Life of Great American Cities* (New York: Random House, 1963). Ponder with Jacobs the consequences of the simple fact that large parts of the city go empty and unattended for several hours each day.

seem to be at least three regular and intimate consequences of differentiation. They need little explication beyond what is evident in the mere listing: (1) Multiplication of dependencies (interdependence); (2) Multiplication of statuses; and (3) Multiplication of interests.

(1) When a man is able to produce a surplus due to the increased productivity of his own specialization, he also becomes unable to live without the many who provide him with his other needs. Observers from Smith to Durkheim have celebrated this interdependence as the basis of a new kind of social solidarity. But, as we shall see, other conclusions are equally supportable. The only unassailable generalization seems to be the truism that men lose their independence and their autonomy. When President Eisenhower left public life, he faced two ordinary but irritating problems—learning how to drive again and learning how to tie his shoelaces. It is difficult to imagine a modern American housewife plucking her own chicken. Workers no longer have the family plot to return to and would not know how to use it if it still existed.

(2) One form of differentiation earlier noted was the multiplication of roles. Each role defines a particular set of functions and an obligation to carry out the functions. But inevitably, statuses also come to be involved; persons are indentified by their roles, and some roles are considered more important than others. The more roles there are, the more occasions for individious distinctions among roles, among types of roles, and among the people who are identified with each role. There are still some social values, such as wealth, social standing, popularity, around which major pecking orders are established. But there has nevertheless been a great increase of special status orders, so much so that a given individual may enjoy many different status positions during one waking day.[20]

(3) Finally, it seems almost unnecessary to say that as men become separated by their specialties and by the roles and statuses that develop around the specialties (without mentioning the many nonoccupational roles and statuses), their view

[20] For the effect of this on general social class stratification, see Sir Ernest Barker's observations in Chapter 2.

of the outside world and of their own relation to it is bound to be shaped accordingly. The more complex is the society, the more numerous and complex will be the distribution of interests. There are enormous varieties of relations to the market. There are proportionate numbers of economic and noneconomic groupings.

By this route we are led to a confrontation with the two central sources of disequilibrium in industrial societies. They cannot be eliminated but rather must somehow be controlled. These are 1) alienation and 2) conflict. They seem to be as much a part of capitalistic practice as is the market. Moreover, they seem to increase along with the expansion of the market system, a factor which bears heavily against the argument that markets solve their own social problems.

Some may define alienation as the narrow issue of work and its meaning; but the problem is obviously broader than that. Specialization reduces a man's chances of developing a whole personality; it can twist and depersonalize him. Men thus become alienated from themselves; they become *anomic*. Men also become alienated from other men—from their own families, from friends, from the community. Work becomes a mere matter of compulsion. A man no longer owns his own tools. His labor, therefore *he*, becomes a commodity. Work can become separated from life, and life can become so divided and subdivided that one loses the human meaning of living. To any Marxist, the Smithian and the Ricardian curves (on Figure 1.1) are the curves of alienation. But such interpretations are not the exclusive invention of Marxist ideologues. Thoreau, for example, objected "to the division of labor since it divided the worker, not merely the work, reduced him from a man to an operative, and enriched the few at the expense of the many." Tocqueville, as we shall see, was equally concerned.[21]

Increased potential for conflict is hardly more than another way of looking at alienation. Specialization, extreme mobility, large markets, enormous ranges of choice (far greater for the

[21] Quoted in C. Wright Mills, *White Collar* (New York: Oxford University Press, 1951), p. 225. See an analysis of de Tocqueville, in Chapter 2, below.

commoner today than to the king of antiquity), discontinuities
between each generation, renewal every forty years, vastly increased scale—these are a few of the things one usually has in
mind when one tries to capture the difference between modern
and premodern communities. No longer do people grow up
together, know exactly what to expect of one another, move in
easy interactions by unconscious cues. Yet they must somehow
interact, indeed more frequently and over a wider range of infinitely more complex expectations. Many conflicts settle themselves if they are at all subject to an economic calculus. But the
others, the majority certainly, are either settled by informal,
individual endeavor, or, increasingly, are dealt with administratively. It is clear that neither of these methods of settlement
depends upon automatic forces.

Karl Mannheim best captured the meaning of alienation and
conflict with his formulation, "displacement of self-regulating
small groups." [22] To Mannheim, society literally entered into a
process of disintegration when it expanded from "a parochial
world of small groups . . . into a Great Society [sic] in a com-
paratively short time." [23] Mannheim was strongly confirmed
by on-the-scene observers, as suggested already by Marx,
Maine, and de Tocqueville. Jefferson was another, a man far
less optimistic than his French, British, or American contem-
poraries that some sort of commercial calculus would be sufficient in the dreaded urban society. To Mannheim—and others
—self-regulation could not work beyond families, local markets, traditions. The very requirements of the expanded markets of commercial societies prevent them from being fully
sufficient as social forces.

We need not go all the way with Marx and Mannheim—and
many like-minded theorists during the years between them—in
order to accept their hypotheses. We do not have to use the
term *alienation* to see that differentiation, interdependence,

[22] Karl Mannheim, *Freedom, Power and Democratic Planning* (New
York: Oxford University Press, 1950), p. 11.

[23] *Ibid.*, p. 4. Many a modern antisocialist agrees wholly with Mannheim's diagnosis. See, for example, a fascinating field study by Baker
Brownell, *The Human Community* (New York: Harper & Brothers,
1950).

multiplied statuses and interests, etc., etc., might tend to weaken the automatic or self-regulating social mechanisms. Yet those same factors—all of the forces discussed in this chapter —increase the number of situations in which people with different goals must deal with each other. Thus we run into the final dilemma: *There is an inverse relation between the need and the availability of informal and automatic social controls. Those societies most in need of automatic social controls have fewer of them to bank on.*

The fact of the matter seems to be that the immense complexities of development and control in the industrial society are too powerful for thoughtless institutions. Leaders, seeking to reap the incredible benefits of technology, apply rationality to production and exchange. But it seems impossible to imagine that the effort to reap such benefits would stop there. The various forms of differentiation suggest that rationality quickly comes to be applied to virtually every personality, institution, group, and function in the social process.[24]

To suppose that rationalization stops merely with tasks, units of work, and markets is to suppose that modern society, after one revolutionary round of organizing, is just as mindlessly automatic as ever. In such a case our distance from the medieval would merely be a step from the organic to the mechanistic. Far newer arrangements must be accounted for. The modern method of social control involves the application of rationality to all social relations. In production we call it technology. In exchange it is called commerce or markets. In social structure we have here called it differentiation. *Rationality applied to social control is administration.* Administration may indeed by the *sine qua non* of modernity.

Administration is a necessary part of capitalism and capitalist society. But it never was incorporated into capitalist ideology. In fact, the idea of conscious and systematic application of legitimate controls on conduct, by public or private institu-

[24] It is applied even to our concept of time, according to Lewis Mumford, to whom "the clock, not the steam-engine, is the key-machine of the modern industrial age." The clock fathered the notion of orderly nature and regularity of behavior. See Mumford's *Technics and Civilization* (New York: Harcourt, Brace, 1934).

tions, is rejected altogether by orthodox capitalist theoy. Here
was a gap between myth and reality that would inevitably
weaken the myth. At a minimum it meant that public leadership would have to have a new public philosophy. Capitalist
ideology could not last as the public philosophy because it
could not accept capitalism in any other except the most orthodox commercial world. Orthodox capitalist theory recognized
only one legitimate type of modern social control—competition. Yet capitalism is third only to the Church and warfare in
its contribution to the rational approach to control, administration. Obviously an orthodox capitalist position that society
must cease to change after an entrepreneurial revolution is no
less absurd than an orthodox Marxist position that society must
cease to change after a proletarian society is established.

CHAPTER 2

PLURALISM AND THE TRANSFORMATION OF CAPITALIST IDEOLOGY

Administration presents two basic dilemmas to capitalist theory. First, the predominance of administration proves that conscious control rather than mechanistic, automatic, self-control is the predominant fact about modern conduct. Second, it proves that even the remaining self-regulating mechanisms, still a substantial factor, have shifted in very large part from market competition to group competition—from self-regulation through economics to self-regulation through politics. These two factors became a sort of one-two punch. The first led finally to an acceptance of *statism;* i.e., the overwhelming proportion of leaders embraced positive government. With its rise began a long dialogue with laissez faire over the value of public control that led to the reclassification of laissez faire as a conservative doctrine. The second led to *pluralism,* the intellectual core of the new liberalism which would eventually replace capitalism as the public philosophy by a process of absorption. The new public philosophy, interest-group liberalism, is the amalgam of capitalism, statism, and pluralism. The amalgam is evaluated in Chapter 3 and beyond. Here it is necessary to see how the parts could possibly fit together.

The Administrative Component and
the Inevitability of Government

Administration is a process of self-conscious, formal adaptation of means to ends. Administered social relations are all those self-conscious and formal efforts to achieve a social end, whether expressed as a general condition like predictable conduct, legality, productivity, public order, or as a more concrete organizational goal. Many traditional social patterns continue to fulfill vital control functions in society. Economic and political competition are also vital controls. But the modern overlay upon all this is not so automatic. It is administration.

Many influential observers maintain that technology is the key to what is modern in the revolutionary Western civilization.[1] But this seems to beg the question, which is how and with what result men come to live peacefully and productively with each other in the presence of this technical complexity and scale and yet in the absence of complete familiarity. Karl Polanyi provided an appropriate riposte:

Social not technical invention was the intellectual mainspring of the Industrial Revolution. . . . The triumphs of natural science had been theoretical in the true sense, and could not compare in practical importance with those of the social sciences of the day. . . . The discovery of economics was an astounding revelation which hastened greatly the transformation of society . . . while the decisive machines had been the inventions of uneducated artisans some of whom could hardly read or write. It was both just and appropriate that not the natural but the social sciences should rank as the intellectual parents of the mechanical revolution which subjected the powers of nature to man. [2]

This is not to deny technology. It is only to ask for the social inventions through which a technical invention became revolu-

[1] *Cf.* Michael Harrington, *The Accidental Century* (New York: Macmillan, 1965), and John Kenneth Galbraith, *The New Industrial State* (Boston: Houghton Mifflin, 1967), for recent expressions of this view.

[2] Karl Polanyi, *The Great Transformation* (Boston: Beacon Press, 1957), p. 119.

tionary instead of a museum curiosity. Administration takes a machine and makes it a "man-machine" system. The increased pace of technological change in our epoch seems only to make the need for administration more intense—or else the technological change would be wasted.

In a sense, the administrative component is a fifth form of differentiation to go along with the four earlier identified. This fifth form is a differentiation of social units that perform "system maintaining" functions. Moreover, there are several dimensions. Units within groups are separated out to administer to the internal needs of the group. In the literature of administrative science these are usually referred to as staff, auxiliary, or overhead functions. Then there is a large category of groups and institutions whose entire function is to administer services to nonmembers and groups, services once performed automatically—or not at all. Thirdly, while most groups and institutions are not founded especially to do these good works, they tend just the same to spend a great deal of their time and resources administering against some possible social disequilibrium. Some may call these "latent functions."

ADMINISTRATION BY GOVERNMENTS

By far the most important mechanism of administered social relations is modern government. The rise of large government with a large administrative core came relatively late in the U.S., but its coming is undoubted. Per capita dollar outlays by Federal, State, and local governments are impressive when 1878 and 1908 are compared to 1938 and 1968. Also of great significance is the rise in administrative personnel in government. But of far greater significance is the nature of the outlays of dollars and the activities of the administrative personnel. Neither budgets nor bureaucrats will measure the importance of such agencies as the Federal Reserve Board, the ICC and its sister public service commissions in all the States, the rest of the "alphabetocracy" begun in the 1930's, and the research, service, and fiscal components added largely since then. Their administrative role in the fate of persons and properties is important beyond measure.

Perhaps even more indicative of the administrative importance of modern government is the scale and purpose of expenditure at local and State levels. In 1962, local and State
governments spent $500 per capita ($88 billion) as compared
to $460 per capita spent by the Federal government. Over 22
per cent of all State and local government expenditures went
for education. Another 5 per cent went for public welfare.
These figures compare very meaningfully with such traditional
State and local functions as highways (10 per cent) and police
and fire protection (4 per cent). The comparison indicates that
the overwhelming proportion of government responsibility is
administrative operation of facilities and services that a century ago were left primarily to family, neighborhood, local
church, guild, and individual initiative.[3] Public schools have
expanded downward to kindergarten and then to nursery
school, toward further and further incorporation of family
functions. They have expanded upward to take over more and
more of the preparation for life that once was done in the
labor market by the "School of Hard Knocks." And they have
expanded outward, toward subjects and types of training
never thought of as the province of school or anything else
very public—sex hygiene, family finance, psychological and
occupational guidance, and so on. (One of the basic under-
graduate courses at Michigan State University for many years
was Effective Living.) Along with this, the expansion of public
welfare administration, with the Federal social security programs, suggests the extent to which many other problems outside the realm of rudimentary socialization have ceased to be a
normal part of the everyday life of traditional social units. The
"problem of the aged" is a simple and poignant expression of
the almost total disappearance of the extended family. We are

[3] Even as late as 1900 public education was slipshod and far from
universal. There were no standards or administrative controls regarding
teacher recruitment, and every school and local district was an operation
in and of itself. Only around 71 per cent of the children between 5 and
17 years of age were enrolled (compared to 84 per cent in public schools
alone in 1964), and an overwhelming proportion of these were attending
part-time, one-room schools. These and many other significant figures
are reported in Thomas R. Dye, *Politics, Economics, and the Public*
(Chicago: Rand-McNally, 1966), Chapter 4.

faced here with two quite different methods of performing one of society's natural and inevitable duties. Obviously the contemporary form is administrative.

PRIVATE ADMINISTRATION

The governmental response to industrialization was very late in the United States, but when it did come it was swift, massive, and administrative. However, since the rise of modern administrative government was so late, it would be too easy to come to the erroneous conclusion that for most of our modern history public order was being maintained by the self-regulating mechanisms. On the contrary, it would be closer to the truth to propose that at no time in the past century or more was there a period when society in the United States was anywhere nearly self-regulating. Allowing for a time lag during the early consolidation of capital, the administrative component has developed in hand with the technological, the commercial, and the pluralistic components. The development was simply taking place in the private sector.

The rise of administration in the private sphere began early and has been dramatic. One measure of its importance can be seen in the employment figures below. In less than half a century, administrative employees in the United States increased from below 6 per cent to nearly 25 per cent of all production employees.[4] The rise of this aspect of the administrative component has been even more extreme in Sweden and Great Britain. The rate of change has been a good deal less extreme in Germany (from 5 to about 12 per cent) and in France (a rate which was static at the relatively high level of over 12 per cent). However, these two latter cases are significant because France and Germany have had the largest and most authoritarian public sectors among the five. Perhaps the quantum of administrative need, public and private, was close to the same in all five.

A look inside the larger corporations in the United States

---

[4] The source for the following statistics and the graphs is Rinehart Bendix, *Work and Authority in Industry* (New York: Harper Torchbooks, 1963), pp. 216 ff.

helps specify the elements of the private administrative component. Pricing and production decisions have long been removed from the market by an immense planning, program-
ming, and research apparatus. Undoubtedly many an American giant had the equivalent of a Five-Year Plan earlier than
did the Soviet government. Bell reports that as of 1956 white-
collar workers outnumbered blue-collar workers. While not all

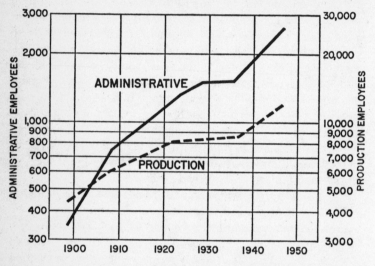

FIGURE 2.1a. Increase of the Number of Administrative and Production Employees in Industry, the United States, 1899–1947 (in
thousands)

white-collar workers are administrative, they do reflect the extent to which production works by shuffling papers, handling
routines, and supervising or facilitating the conduct of others.[5]

As much as the administrative employee and internal bu-

[5] Daniel Bell, "Notes on the Post-Industrial Society," *The Public
Interest* (Winter, 1967), 28. In this fascinating essay Bell also suggests
that the post-industrial society will be typified by even the administration of knowledge and innovation: "In one sense, chemistry is the first
of the 'modern' industries because its inventions—the chemically-created
synthetics—were based on theoretical knowledge of the properties of
macromolecules, which were 'manipulated' to achieve the planned production of new materials." (P. 29.)

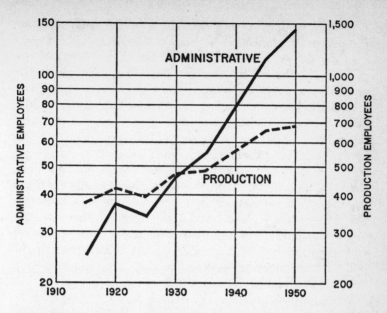

FIGURE 2.1b. Increase in the Number of Administrative and Production Employees in Industry, Sweden, 1915–1950 (in thousands)

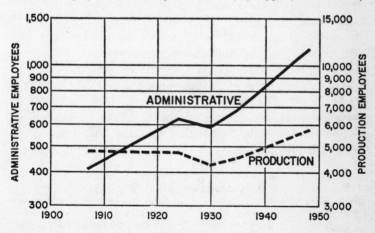

FIGURE 2.1c. Increase in the Number of Administrative and Production Employees in Industry, Great Britain, 1907–1948 (in thousands)

reaucratic apparatus help to measure the administrative component in production, so does the *trade association* indicate the degree to which the commerical dimension of the system—i.e., the market economy itself—has come also to be an administrative process. The trade association is basically an administrative structure whose most important mission is regularizing relations among participants in the same industry, trade, or sector. Where the market seeks competition, the trade association seeks to administer. Trade associations have been widely defined erroneously as pressure groups first and foremost. While they are ubiquitous in Washington and the State capitols, their basic function is administering to their members.[6] For example, Bauer and associates were struck by the amount of time and energy trade associations spend informing and consulting their own members relative to the time spent in political bargaining and coalition-building, even when they are involved in a highly political issue.[7]

The population of trade associations began to mushroom in the late nineteenth century. From a few guilds and rate bureaus, formalized economic cooperation expanded to at least 12,000 national, state, and local trade associations in 1940, when an official census was taken.[8] Taking a complete contemporary census would be extremely difficult; but it is difficult to imagine any product, process, or service in the U.S. whose operatives are not represented and served by at least one of these agencies of private administration. Single firms of more than modest size usually find it desirable to belong to several associations. Imagine the total number of associations if General Electric claims among its active affiliations a Porcelain Enamel Institute.[9]

[6] *Cf.* Melvin Anshen and Francis D. Wormuth, *Private Enterprise and Public Policy* (New York: Macmillan, 1954), p. 319. Their entire Chapter 11 is an excellent discussion of the various devices of "business self-government" administered by trade associations.

[7] Raymond Bauer *et al.*, *American Business and Public Policy* (New York: Atherton, 1963), esp. pp. 315 ff.

[8] Trade Association Survey, TNEC Monograph No. 18 (Washington: U.S. Government Printing Office, 1941).

[9] For good treatments see Robert A. Brady, *Business as a System of Power* (New York: Columbia University Press, 1943), pp. 189 ff.; and David B. Truman, *The Governmental Process* (New York: Alfred A.

Trade associations cannot be cast off as evils of overbureau-
cratized, overcentralized, and oligopolistic business that would
disappear if some semblance of competition could be reintro-
duced. The fact is, the administrative functions of trade associations become even more necessary in decentralized markets.
The number of firms is greater, the fear of competition is
stronger; and the need for research and marketing services,
trained personnel, and so on turns smaller firms to outside
forms of administration where bigger firms can provide much
of this internally. Three of the most famous trade associations
—the National Association of Real Estate Boards, the National
Association of Retail Druggists, and the American Medical
Association—administer to highly decentralized markets.

The rise of private administration is not manifested only in
economic phenomena. In the first place, many of the functions
of all trade associations are noneconomic. Moreover, many
thousands of groups that are not trade associations perform
administrative services vital to the stability of the society. For
example, regular social service becomes attached as a "latent
function" to most groups. Robert Merton observes best how
the old-time urban machine was rooted not merely in control
of office but more solidly still in its displacement of impersonal
controls with informal and personalized, yet systematic, controls.[10] Then there is the proliferation of groups—"do-gooder"
groups—manifestly dedicated to ministering to one problem or
another of socialization or social control. Between church
school and public school and all related activities, almost nothing is left to the family, clan, neighborhood, or guild—or to
chance. Even sand-lot baseball has given way to Little
Leagues, symptomatic of an incredible array of parental
groups and neighborhood businesses organized to see that the
child's every waking moment is organized, unprivate, whole-
some, and, primarily, oriented toward an ideal of adjustment
to the adult life of rationality that comes all too soon.

All of the larger voluntary associations, as well as most of

Knopf, 1951), pp. 55–62. Note particularly the second level of administration, the "peak association," an organization whose members are
mainly other organizations.

[10] Robert Merton, *Social Theory and Social Structure* (New York:
Free Press, 1957), Chapter 1.

the smaller ones have given up their sponteneity for a solid administrative core. The study of groups limited to capitols and city halls tends to exaggerate the political over the socio-administrative. Life in the cities would be hard to imagine without the congeries of service and charitable agencies that, systematically, help keep our streets clean of human flotsam and jetsam. Of growing importance are the family service agencies, agencies for the elderly, for adoption, and for maternal and child care, all of which in turn draw financial support from still other (e.g., Community Chest, United Fund) agencies that are still more tightly administrative. To repeat, all such groups naturally possess potential political power, but only occasionally are they politicized. The rest of the time they administer.

Another all-too-little appreciated example of private administration is the nonprofit sector of our economy and its phenomenal expansion in the past generation. In other countries many of these units are governmental, but that only emphasizes the administrative importance of their function in the United States. This sector includes mutual insurance companies, savings and loan associations, professional societies, foundations, cooperatives, health insurance programs, research organizations, private universities, and so on. Each deals administratively with some vital element of social relations. Each receives special privileges in tax law and in other ways precisely because as a category they are all considered to be dedicated more to community than to competitive goals. Together they employed 3.3 million people, or 4.9 per cent of the labor force, in 1960. The growth of these organizations between 1950 and 1960 accounted for nearly one out of every two net new jobs, one in three of *all* new jobs.[11] These jobs are administrative, as are the organizations.

Perhaps the most unappreciated service in that sector, although by no means all of it is classified as nonprofit, is insurance. Most studies have catalogued the impressive rise of insurance as a mere part of the general phenomenon "concen-

11 Eli Ginzberg *et al.*, *The Pluralistic Economy* (New York: McGraw-Hill, 1965), pp. 22, 61, 139.

tration of economic power." [12] Or they give it no treatment at all.[13] But the insurance companies are far more socially significant in that we rely upon them to administer our conflicts, with each other or with nature, rather than leave these to spontaneous confrontation or traditional litigation. Companies set up to run death benefits and pensions have helped further to replace the family. Fire, automobile, theft, weather, travel, title, and other insurance is provided by companies that administer our liabilities.[14] The liability lawyer may not be so highly regarded as he goes after the big settlement and makes our premiums rise; but he is, for all that, no less important a functionary in the modern social apparatus. Ponder just for a moment the social implications of "liability insurance." Recall, for example, your last traffic jam. It will then be impossible to imagine that an interdependent society could exist without the *socialization of risk*. Keeping these social accounts requires an incredibly large and intricate administrative apparatus. The insurance industry is precisely that.

Finally, there is that category called interest groups, in the most orthodox pluralistic sense. Interest groups do compete and coalesce, as political scientists say. Yet they also possess an important administrative dimension. They would have no "staying power" at all if they did not have an efficient bureaucracy. This is particularly true of the large groups most frequently noted for their national political importance. Unions, like trade associations, administer and reduce competition within their own ranks. Job classification alone, despite such occasional absurdities as the electrician's helper who is forbidden to move a rug or a broom, is vital to industrial peace; and it is no less an administrative process because unions rather than government civil service commissions participate in the

[12] This approach was inspired by the TNEC research of the late 1930's. For example, David Lynch, *The Concentration of Economic Power* (New York: Columbia University Press, 1946), pp. 122–23.

[13] For example, W. W. Rostow, *The Stages of Economic Growth* (London: Cambridge University Press, 1960); and J. K. Galbraith, *American Capitalism* (Boston: Houghton Mifflin, 1962).

[14] *Cf.* Edgar S. and Jean C. Cahn, "What Price Justice: The Civilian Perspective Revisited," *Notre Dame Lawyer* (1966), pp. 936–38.

classification. Even when trade unions square off against employer groups the relationship is, at least since the 1930's, one in which the labor market is replaced by an administrative process. General demand affects collective bargaining, and together these two competitive mechanisms comprise part of the relationships. However, general demand and collective bargaining are most often marginal; in "labor-management relations," collective bargaining has become a brief, albeit critical, moment in a long process of administering the terms of the labor-management contract. In the strictly political realm fewer intergroup relations may be so strongly institutionalized; but the many notable examples suggest that the pattern is significant and increasing. From the NAM and the U.S. Chamber of Commerce and all the state chambers, to the Farm Bureau Federation, to the Federation of Jewish Philanthropies and the Council of Churches, to the AFL-CIO, we have layer upon layer of "peak associations," which exist to institutionalize relations among constituent groups. Each peak association and every major interest group started out as a coalition that eventually perpetuated itself by the development of a central administrative core.[15]

Stress on the administrative component is not an attempt to deny the existence of the self-regulating mechanisms of markets and pluralism. It is rather to stress what is still more modern about social control, including those very mechanisms. Groups, federations, insurance companies, corporations, and government agencies share at least one common trait; they impose an administrative process on as much of their internal structures and on as much of their environments as they possibly can. Whether one looks first at the Little League, the bureaucratization of philanthropy, or community psychiatry; or whether one comes first to appreciate the cheap insurance

[15] *Cf. Truman, op. cit.,* Chapters 2–4. See also Robert Michels, *Political Parties* (New York: Collier Books; first published 1915). His general theory of parties and pressure groups is based largely on this sort of development among European unions and democratic socialist parties. See also Wallace Sayre and Herbert Kaufman, *Governing New York City* (New York: Russell Sage Foundation, 1960), pp. 497 ff., for the composition of typical large groups in cities.

which is the real secret of farm bureaus and many other societies; or whether one starts with awareness of the indenturing
of the middle classes in career and salary plans and retirement
plans; or whether one looks at the staff of a powerful pressure
group or the headquarters of a national trade association: one
way or the other the true image of modern society emerges. In
hardly more than two peaceful generations the great American
prototype has passed from Andrew Carnegie to Dale Carnegie.

Pluralism, Its Influence, Its Fallacies

Central to capitalist theory is the belief that power and control
are properties of the state and, therefore, should be feared and
resisted. This proposition, while hard to deny, is patently one-
sided; in fact it covers only one of at least three sides. It says
nothing about who controls the state; and it says nothing about
institutions other than the state that possess the same properties of power and control.

The Marxist critique of capitalism is overwhelming on the
question of control of the state, especially when applied to the
very period of industrial growth when fear of the state was so
pervasive in the U.S. Up to a point capitalist values were so
directly expressed in the activities of Federal and State governments that it would have been impossible to say where the
one ended and the other began. The very idea of capitalist
public philosophy can be accurately termed a euphemism for
capitalist political power during most of the nineteenth century. It was not a question of influence *on* the policy-maker;
capitalism was so pervasive because it operated as an influence
in the policy-maker.

Important as the Marxist analysis has been, American history suggests that it, like capitalist theory, presents one-sided
truths. The side left untouched by capitalism and falsely
treated by Marxism is that of the nature and significance of the
institutions other than the state in an industrial civilization.
Here the pluralist model is overwhelmingly superior, at least
for American society.

Pluralist theory begins with recognition that there are many sources of power and control other than the state. In our differentiated society, there will be many basic interests represented by organizations able and willing to use power. This is why the pluralist can accept government expansion with equanimity. But the significance of the pluralistic organization of the society goes beyond that. Since there are so many well-organized interests, there is, in pluralist theory, no possibility that a unitary society, stratified in two or three simple, homogenized classes, could persist. The result, however, is not the Marxist revolution where the big class devours the small, but an evolution in which the unitary society becomes a pluralistic one—i.e., where the addition and multiplication of classes tends to wipe out the very notion of class stratification.[16] Stratification in two simple classes, bourgeoisie and proletariat, seems to have been a passing phase of early industralization. Perhaps that is the reason why it figured so large in the sociology of Marx.

PLURALISM AS THEORY: UBIQUITY OF CONTROL,
AUTONOMY OF POLITICS

Alexis de Tocqueville, over a decade before Marx, identified many of the fundamental features of the industrial society. He expressed strikingly similar concern about the sort of society which was emerging. In his essay "How an Aristocracy May Be Created by Manufactures," Tocqueville went to the core of the matter. He began by recognizing the importance of the division of labor and proceeded immediately to a consideration of what it does to human beings and social classes:

While the workman concentrates his faculties more and more upon the study of a single detail, the master surveys an extensive whole, and the mind of the latter is enlarged in proportion as that of the former is narrowed. . . . [I]n proportion as the mass of the nation turns to democracy, that particular class which is engaged in

[16] For a well-balanced discussion of the weakening of social class stratification in the United States and other industrializing societies, see Sir Ernest Barker, *Reflections on Government* (New York: Oxford University Press, 1942), pp. 108 ff.

manufactures becomes more aristocratic. Men grow more alike in the one, more different in the other; and inequality increases in the less numerous class in the same ratio in which it decreases in the community.[17]

However, unlike Marx, Tocqueville provided more than a theory of alienation within simple social classes. He also paid attention to the composition of this industrial aristocracy. Tocqueville saw this new aristocracy as quite peculiar in comparison to its predecessors. While there are and will be extremes of wealth and poverty, the members of the new aristocracy do not constitute a unitary social class, for there develop no feelings of class, no consciousness of shared status:

To tell the truth, though there are rich men, the class of rich men does not exist; for these rich individuals have no feelings or purposes, no traditions or hopes, in common; there are individuals, therefore, but no definite class. . . . [T]he rich [are] not compactly united among themselves. . . .[18]

This was the very basis of James Madison's argument half a century before—and nothing had happened between Madison and Tocqueville to alter the fact—that industrialization produces social diversity along with extremes of wealth and poverty: "A landed interest, a manufacturing interest, a mercantile interest, a moneyed interest, with many lesser interests." [19] Developments in the generations since Federalist 10 would only require that we lengthen Madison's list. Pluralists do not have to deny the Marxian proposition that there is a conflict between those who own and those who work for those who own. They need only answer by adding to Marx's the other equally intense conflicts. Exporters cannot love importers, except perhaps on the Fourth of July—and, in fact, many people may still have misgivings about the patriotism of importers. Renters cannot love owners. Borrowers cannot love lenders, nor creditors debtors, and this is particularly interesting in our day, when the biggest debtors are not the poor but the rich.

[17] Alexis de Tocqueville, *Democracy in America.* Reprinted in Lowi, *op. cit.,* p. 15.

[18] *Ibid.,* p. 15.

[19] *Ibid.,* p. 19.

etailers cannot love wholesalers. The black middle class loves
neither the black lower class nor the white sellers of middle-
class housing.

In this context the existence of the administrative component merely confirms the reality of the pluralist model of society. Groups amount to far more than a façade for a class.
Administration gives each basic interest an institutional core,
renders each interest less capable of being absorbed or neutralized, gives each interest the capacity to articulate goals,
integrate members, provide for leadership and succession, in
short, to perpetuate itself. The organization of interests is the
first step, but after rudimentary organization comes staff, procedures, membership service, internal propaganda, addition of
more permanent personnel, salaried help, files—corporate existence, staying power.

As alluded to above, the pluralist model cuts equally against
capitalist theory. It renders absurd the capitalist notion that
government is the only source of power and control. It rightly
rejects any and all notions of a natural distinction between the
functions of government and the functions of nongovernmental institutions. Power and control are widely distributed. They
are in fact ubiquitous.

Sayre and Kaufman introduce a useful game for pursuing
the problem of government and nongovernment.[20] Try to
identify a governmental activity for which there is not an important counterpart in some private institution. The judiciary?
Mediation and arbitration play a widespread and increasing
role. Police? Pinkertons are famous in our history; today every
large company and school has its own security force, and private eyes continue to be hired for peephole duty; many highly
innovating industries have their own secret service working in
the world of industrial espionage. Welfare? Any listing of private, highly bureaucratized and authoritative welfare systems
would be as long as it is unnecessary. Armies? It is difficult to
overestimate the significance of private armies in the past, or
such present private armies as those possessed by the Mafia
and other syndicates, not to mention the neighborhood gangs
and Minutemen. Society highly prizes the function they per-

[20] *Cf*. Sayre and Kaufman, *op. cit.*, pp. 57–58.

form in administering the acceptable vices and keeping the violence associated with these vices subterranean. Obviously the game need not be carried into every realm.

Some activities may be found universally among modern governments; but they will not be found *only* in governments. Moreover, the complete pattern of functions associated with any given government is the result of time, chance, culture and politics. Government is only one institution of social control, as it was and always will be. Government is distinguishable from other institutions, as we shall soon see. But the distinction is not the one upon which the American Constitution and the nineteenth-century liberals erected their defenses.

This in turn reflects critically still further upon the Marxist model. Central to the pluralist model of power is the anti-Marxist hypothesis that with the flowering of the system of autonomous groups the monopoly hold of capitalism, or of any other class, passes. Control of the state does not pass from the capitalists to another class but rather is dispersed. This breaks the deterministic link between economics and politics: *In the pluralist system, modern developments have brought about a discontinuity between that which is socioeconomic and that which is political.* Politics in the pluralist model ceases to be an epiphenomenon of socioeconomic life. Politics becomes autonomous as the number of autonomous and competing social units multiplies.

In these simple propositions, reaching back to James Madison, lies the pluralist critique of capitalism and of Marxism. To summarize: (1) Groups, of which corporations are merely one type, possess power directly over a segment of society and also a share of control of the state. (2) Groups, rather than entrepreneurs and firms, are the dominant reality in modern life. (3) As long as even a small proportion of all interests remains strong and active, no unitary political class, or "power elite," will emerge. That is, in the pluralist system it is highly improbable that a consensus across a whole class can last long enough to institutionalize itself.[21]

[21] The best treatments of the theory, even though limited to cities, will be found in Robert A. Dahl, *Who Governs?* and Nelson W. Polsby, *Community Power and Political Theory* (New Haven: Yale University

PLURALISM AS IDEOLOGY: ITS STRENGTH

A good social theory is always but a step away from ideology. The better it is as theory, the more likely it is to become ideology. The bigger the scope of the theory the greater the likelihood of becoming the public philosophy. Pluralism became a potent American ideology. It did not become the public philosophy, but it is the principal intellectual member in a neocapitalistic public philosophy, interest-group liberalism.

Short and few are the steps in the reasoning procedure by which pluralist theory becomes pluralist ideology: (1) Since groups are the rule in markets and elsewhere, imperfect competition is the rule of social relations. (2) The method of imperfect competition is not really competition at all but a variant of it called bargaining—where the number of participants is small, where the relationship is face-to-face, and/or where the bargainers have "market power," which means that they have some control over the terms of their agreements and can administer rather than merely respond to their environment. (3) Without class solidarity, bargaining becomes the single alternative to violence and coercion in industrial society. (4) By definition, if the system is stable and peaceful it proves the self-regulative character of pluralism. It is, therefore, the way the system works and the way it ought to work.

A closer look will show how potent these principles are in a country so traditionally concerned about power. Most obviously they show pluralism to be very much in line with the realities of modern life. Groups and imperfect competition are impossible to deny. Second, the reasoning suggests that pluralism can be strongly positive toward government without relinquishing the traditional fear of government. Since the days of Madison the pluralist view has been that there is nothing to fear from government so long as many factions compete for its favor. Modern pluralism turned the Madisonian position from negative to positive; that is, government is good because many

Press, 1961 and 1963). For a review of the issues and bibliography at the national level, see my "American Business, Public Policy, Case Studies and Political Theory," *World Politics,* July, 1964.

factions do compete for its favor. A third and obvious fea
of pluralist reasoning is that with pluralism society rema
automatic. Pluralism is just as mechanistic as orthodox Smit
ian economics, and since the mechanism is political it reinforces acceptance of government. Pluralists believe that pluralist competition tends toward an equilibrium, and therefore
that its involvement with government can mean only good.
Use of government is simply one of many ways groups achieve
equilibrium. Pluralist equilibrium is really the public interest.

Pluralism's embrace of positive government first put it at an
ideological pole opposite capitalism. This is the foundation of
the liberal-conservative dialogue that bridged the gap between
the old public philosophy and the new. On the basis of these
opposing positions, debate over great issues took place in the
United States, even without socialism, for many years following 1890. But this situation was only temporary. The two
apparent antitheses ultimately disappeared. The rhetoric continued, so that even today one may occasionally feel that the
two poles represent substantial differences. But in reality they
have come to represent a distinction without a difference.
Capitalism and pluralism were not actually synthesized, how
ever; in a sense, they absorbed each other.

The transformation, rather than the replacement, of capitalist public philosophy was made possible by two special features of pluralist ideology. First, pluralism shared the capitalist
ideal of the automatic society. Second, the pluralist embrace of
government turned out to be, in its own way, as antigovern-
mental as capitalism. Ultimately this shared mystique, despite
differences along other lines, made some kind of fusion possible. The hidden hand of capitalist ideology could clasp the
hidden hand of pluralism, and the two could shake affirma-
tively on the new public philosophy, interest-group liberalism.
Here lies the foundation of the Consensus of 1937–67.

PLURALISM AS IDEOLOGY: ITS FALLACIES

Here lies also the source of the weakness and eventual failure of interest-group liberalism, which has led us into a crisis
of public authority in the United States more serious than any

other in the twentieth century. Pluralism had helped bring American public values into the twentieth century by making the state an acceptable source of power in a capitalist society. Pluralism had also made a major contribution by helping to break down the Marxian notion of solidary classes and class-dominated government. But the zeal of pluralism for the group and its belief in a natural harmony of group competition tended to break down the very ethic of government by reducing the essential conception of government to nothing more than another set of mere interest groups.

The strength of pluralism rested in very great part upon the proposition, identified earlier, that a pluralist society frees politics by creating a discontinuity between the political world and the socioeconomic world. However, there is a related proposition that present pluralist theories either reject or miss altogether: *In a pluralist society there is also a discontinuity between politics and government.* The very same factors of competition and multiple power resources that frees politics from society also frees government from both society and politics. This is precisely why pluralism appealed to such constitutionalists as Madison. Group competition could neutralize many of the most potent power centers sufficiently to keep all of them within the formal structure of government. This was the Madisonian method of regulating groups and protecting the governmental authorities from control by any "majority," which could mean a class elite, a capitalist group, or a mass social movement. In contemporary pluralism this aspect of the pluralist argument has gone by the boards. Groups become virtuous; they must be accommodated, not regulated. Formalism in government becomes mere formality. Far from Madison, they could say, as the disappointed office-seeker is supposed to have said to President Cleveland, "What's a Constitution among friends?"

It should thus be evident that pluralist theory today militates against the idea of separate government. Separate government violates the basic principle of the automatic political society. This was reinforced by the scientific pluralist's scientific dread of such poetic terms as "public interest," "the state," and "sovereignty" that admittedly cannot be precisely defined and are closely associated aesthetically with the notion of separate government. But by such means pluralism gained a little and lost a lot. Only three of its losses are pursued here: (1) Pluralist theory achieved almost no additional scientific precision by insisting that government was nothing but an extension of the "political process." (2) It could maintain this fiction, and the fiction of the automatic political society, only by elimination of *legitimacy*. (3) It could maintain those fictions only by elimination of *administration*.

(1) In 1908, Arthur F. Bentley fathered the scientific definition of the state as an interest that could be thought of "as an interest group itself." [22] Despite preference for the immaculateness of the formulation, modern pluralists have ever since felt the tug of limitation more than the leverage of precision. Along the way concessions have been made, so that "we must reckon with the inclusive set of relationships that we call the state." [23] The fact that this institution did not seem to operate quite like a pressure group led Truman to the concept of a "potential interest group" whose interest is the "rules of the game." [24] These formulations did not introduce precision. They simply constituted an invitation to disregard those aspects of the political system not susceptible to group interpretation and the hypothesis of natural equilibrium. Even to the most sophisticated, government became "the political process." We shall see the results in Chapter 3.

(2) Competition and its variant, bargaining, are types of conflict distinguishable by the existence of rules. Rules convert conflict into competition. But rules and their application imply the existence of a framework of controls and institutions separate from the competition itself. Whether we call this a *public* or not, *there is a political context that is not itself competition* within which political competition takes place.

A good way to approach the problem of the distinction is to return momentarily to the game of counterparts. It must have

[22] Quoted in Truman, *op. cit.*, p. 51.
[23] *Ibid.*, p. 52.
[24] *Ibid.*, pp. 51–52.

occurred to many already that something was missing. Once while participating in the exercise a student found the missing dimension by identifying prisons and imprisonment as a public activity without private counterpart. Leaving aside a quibble over the question of whether the Mafia has a prison system, it is easy to spot the essential point implied to the student in his choice of governmental activity. The practice of imprisonment suggests simply that the intrinsic governmental feature is *legitimate use of coercion.*

Legitimacy is not easy to operationalize, but its problems are actually easier to solve than those the pluralist solution offers, because our interest is not in measuring the behavioral attribute in question but only in using the fact of its existence as a criterion. It justifies our treating the state as a real thing apart and not merely a group or a poetic figment. Thus, while governments can rarely if ever perform any function that a nongovernmental institution cannot also perform, governmentalization of a function—that is, passing a public policy—is sought because the legitimacy of its sanctions makes its social controls more surely effective. This is what activates and motivates politics in the pluralist system, but it is far from being part and parcel of pluralism.

(3) Finally, rules and their enforcement do not merely exist. They must be applied with regularity and some degree of consistency if pluralist competition is to exist at all. This is administration. Administration is necessary to construct and to change the system within which pluralism is to operate, yet pluralism presupposes the existence of that favorable structure, just as laissez faire presupposed a social system favorable to itself. To pluralists, social change in a pluralist system works in small increments. "Incrementalism" is what moves the successful polity, and by definition that is how the successful polity ought to be moved. This means that social oscillation in the pluralist ideal is and ought to occur at a very narrow range around some point of equilibrium. But note how susceptible all of this is to the criticisms earlier heaped upon capitalist theory. First, it takes a certain predefined equilibrium as good and presupposes it in order to work the theory. Second, recall the

problem of market perfection: Even if you get your economic equilibrium it may not be at anywhere near full employment. The political variant of this would be equilibrium at something far less than an acceptable level of participation, or satisfaction, or even "public interest." Let us take a simple dimension to illustrate both points: expansion of membership in the system. This usually comes from critical, as distinct from incremental, changes, and is usually imposed administratively. One need only ponder the case of the Negro, who was kept out of the pluralist system for ages, and who is being only now introduced into it not only by fiat but by a fiat with force, accompanied by intricate and authoritative processes of administration.[25]

One of the most influential pluralist scholars, Robert A. Dahl, has made the following proposition about the political system: "When two individuals conflict with one another . . . they confront three great alternatives: deadlock, coercion, or peaceful adjustment."[26] Deadlock is "no deal"; there is no change of demands or behavior on either side. Coercion to Dahl means forcible change of behavior by physical imposition. This he feels is an extremely exceptional alternative, rarely involved even in governmental acts, all the more rarely involved in the affairs of popular governments. Everything else, including all other methods of government, comes under the rubric "peaceful adjustment," by which he means consultation, negotiation, and the search for mutually beneficial solutions.[27] Obviously this cannot possibly exhaust the alternatives. It relies on an extremely narrow definition of coercion, giving one to believe that coercion is not involved if physical force is absent. And it depends on an incredibly broad and idealized notion of what is peaceful about peaceful adjustment. A slight readjustment of Dahl's categories will reveal what is missing. It will also reveal the ideological element just

[25] This will be further developed in Chapter 3, below; and Chapter 7 is a case of the unanticipated consequences of pluralistic influences on administration in racially significant areas of policy.

[26] Robert A. Dahl, *Modern Political Analysis* (Englewood Cliffs: Prentice-Hall, 1963), p. 73.

[27] *Ibid.*, p. 71.

underneath the skin of pluralist theory. What Dahl is really dealing with here are the logical relations between two continua —the extent to which coercion is involved and the extent to which adjustment is involved in any response to conflicting interests. This slight formalizing of his scheme yields the following results:

TABLE 2.1

THE PROPERTIES OF POLITICAL RELATIONSHIPS

		Likelihood of Peaceful Adjustment	
		LOW	HIGH
Likelihood of Coercion:	Remote	Deadlock	Negotiation
	Immediate	"Coercion"	?

What goes in the fourth cell of the four-cell table of properties of political relationships? It is a vast category. It must include virtually all of the public and private "governmental processes" in which people have internalized the sanctions that might be applied. The element of coercion may seem absent when in actuality the participants are conducting themselves in a certain way largely because they do not feel they have any choice.[28] Since it is well enough accepted to go unnoticed, this coercion can be called legitimate. Since it is regular and systematic, is can be called administration because an administrative component must be there if the conduct in question involves a large number of people making these peaceful adjustments. This immense fourth "great alternative" is missing from Dahl's scheme because it is beyond the confines of the theory of the perfect, self-regulating pluralist society. That fourth cell is actually the stable regime of legitimacy and effec-

[28] Grant McConnell, in a brilliant analysis of the myth of democracy in trade unions, aptly refers to the group phenomenon as "private government." *Private Power and American Democracy* (New York: Alfred A. Knopf, 1966), Chapter 5. This phenomenon is neither all "peaceful adjustment" nor all coercion. It seems to belong in the fourth cell, and it applies to many relations among groups and between groups and government, as well as to relations within the big groups.

tive administration without which neither the reality nor the theory of pluralism has any meaning.

THE PRINCIPLE OF SEPARATE GOVERNMENT AND
THE CONSEQUENCES OF ITS REJECTION

Many social theorists earlier in the century stressed the distinction between nongovernment and government. Weber's definition of government is founded on the distinction.[29] Mosca based his classification of modern and traditional systems upon the distinction.[30] Robert McIver and many others based their liberal response to syndicalism upon the same distinction, passionately affirmed:

> The extreme insistence of the guild socialists on functional representation becomes an attack on the state itself . . . A nation is not simply composed of crafts and professions. These might logically elect an economic "parliament," but if it possessed also political sovereignty it would be a denial of the whole process which has differentiated economic and political centres of power. The state is retained in name but disappears in fact . . . Political representation is real only because it is not based on any function but citizenship.[31]

E. Pendleton Herring, although one of the key figures in developing pluralist political science, was still able to warn in the 1930's that while the "government of the democratic state reflects inescapably the underlying interest groups of society . . . the very fact that the state exists evinces a basic community of purpose." [32]

These authors were defending the notion of a distinguishable government from the doctrines of fascists, syndicalists, corporativists, and guild socialists because it was these doctrines and experiments that sought to destroy the distinction.

[29] A. M. Henderson and Talcott Parsons, *Max Weber: The Theory of Social and Economic Organization* (New York: Oxford University Press, 1947), p. 156.

[30] See Mosca, *op. cit.*, esp. part quoted above, chapter 1.

[31] Robert M. McIver, *The Modern State* (New York: Oxford University Press, 1964; first published 1926), pp. 465–66.

[32] E. Pendleton Herring, *Public Administration and the Public Interest* (New York: McGraw-Hill, 1936), p. 397.

Not very much later American liberalism began to develop in the same direction, but these features of it tended to escape attention precisely because American pluralists had no explicit and systematic view of the state. They simply assumed it away. Such negative intellectual acts seldom come in for careful criticism.

Concern for government was an American culture trait. Yet, ironically, once the barriers to its expansion were broken, government ceased almost altogether to be a serious issue. Destruction of the principle of separate government, the coerciveness of government, the legitimacy of government, the administrative importance of government, was necessary if capitalist ideology was to be transformed rather than replaced. The fusion of capitalism and pluralism was a success; destruction of the principle of separate government was its secret.

As this aspect of pluralism becomes dominant in the new public philosophy its more repulsive features can more easily be seen. The new liberal public philosophy was corrupted by the weakness of its primary intellectual component, pluralism. The corrupting element was the myth of the automatic society granted us by an all-encompassing, ideally self-correcting, providentially automatic political process. This can hardly be more serviceable than the nineteenth-century liberal (now conservative) myth of the automatic society granted us by the total social equilibrium of freely contracting individuals in the market place. The pluralist myth helped bring about the new public philosophy, but the weaknesses of the myth made certain the degeneration of the public philosophy. What has it degenerated into? What kind of liberalism can be formulated to take its place?

CHAPTER 3

THE NEW PUBLIC
PHILOSOPHY

Interest-Group Liberalism

The decline of capitalist ideology as the American public philosophy took the form of a dialogue against a more public view of society. Many elements made up the opposition. By far the most important element was pluralism, as already defined and as presently to be seen in greater detail. But progressivism and related notions of direct democracy were also important elements of the new left at the turn of the twentieth century. It was in fact progressivism that gave the new left its real antagonism to nineteenth-century liberalism; but it gave way to pluralism as pluralism and capitalism began their process of mutual absorption in the 1930's. Early in the century even socialism may have made up a small part of the new left amalgam. Due to the emergence of these views on a rather large scale, capitalism became redefined, perhaps redesignated, as conservatism.

The dialogue between the new liberalism and the old liberalism, or new conservatism, comprises the constitutional epoch immediately preceding our own, ending in 1937. During this period there was no prevailing public philosophy but rather two bodies of competing ideology. Liberal and conservative regimes derived their rationalizations of government and policy from their general positions. Modal differences between the two national parties were for the most part quite clear in these terms, particularly between 1896 and 1914 and again between 1932 and 1936. The perennial issue underlying the dialogue was the question of the nature of government itself and whether expansion or contraction best produced public good. Expansion of government was demanded by the liberals as the means of combating the injustices of a brutal world that would not change as long as one's fate were passively submitted to it. The mark of the liberal was his assumption that the instruments of government provided the means for conscious inducement of social change, and that without the capacity for such change no experimentation with new institional forms would be possible. Opposition to such means, but not necessarily to the proposed forms themselves, became the mark of the contemporary conservative.

Among the adversaries there was unanimity on the underlying criteria. All agreed that a man's position was determined by his attitude toward government and his attitude toward social change, or "planning." All agreed, and many persist in agreeing, that these two attitudes are consistent and reinforcing both as a guide for leaders in their choices among policies and as a criterion for followers in their choices among leaders. For example:

> Conservatism is committed to a discriminating defense of the social order against change and reform (liberalism). . . . By the Right, I mean generally those parties and movements that are skeptical of popular government, oppose the bright plans of the reformers and dogooders, and draw particular support from men with a sizable stake in the established order. By the Left, I mean generally those parties and movements that demand wider popular participation in government, push actively for reform, and draw particular support from the disinherited, dislocated and disgruntled. As a general rule, to which there are historic exceptions, the Right is conservative or reactionary, the Left is liberal or radical.[1]

[1] Clinton Rossiter, *Conservatism in America* (New York: Alfred A. Knopf, 1955), pp. 12, 15. The term "conservative" came to be attached

These two criteria arose out of a particular constitutional period, were appropriate to that period, and provided a mutually reinforcing basis for doctrine during that period. After 1937, the Constitution did not die from the Roosevelt Revolution, as many had predicted; but the basis for the liberal-conservative dialogue did die. Liberalism-conservatism as the source of public philosophy no longer made any sense. Once the principle of positive government in an indeterminable but expanding political sphere was established, criteria arising out of the very issue of the principle itself became irrelevant.

The old dialogue has passed into the graveyard of consensus. Yet it persists. Old habits die hard. Its persistence despite its irrelevance means that the liberal-conservative debate has become almost purely ritualistic. However, its persistence in this form has not been without many evil effects. This persistence has blinded the nation to the emergence of a new and ersatz public philosophy. The coexistence of a purely ritualistic public dialogue with an ersatz, unappreciated, uncriticized, but quite real new public philosophy has produced most of the political pathologies of the 1960's. The empty rhetoric of liberalism-conservatism has meant the decline of meaningful adversary proceedings in favor of administrative, technical, and logrolling considerations—or, if you like, questions of equity rather than questions of morality. It has meant little, if any, conflict among political actors at the level where each is forced regularly to formulate general rules applicable to individuals and at the same time ethically plausible to individuals. The tendency of individuals to accept governmental decisions simply because they are good has probably at no time in American history, save during the Civil War, been less widely distributed and less intensely felt. Political cynicism and dis-

---

to the nineteenth-century liberals—as they are described in Chapter 2— because they favored the entrepreneur's government and social order that had become the established fact, the very Constitution, of the nineteenth-century United States. There is other conservatism in America—racial, aristocratic, ethnic, perhaps even monarchic and feudalistic. But the major part of it is nineteenth-century liberalism gone cold with success. This already suggests the narrow span of the ideological gamut in the United States.

trust in everyday political processes have never been more widespread. The emerging public philosophy, interest-group liberalism, has sought to solve the problems of public authority by defining them away. This has simply added the element of demoralization to that of illegitimacy. Interest-group liberalism seeks to justify power and to end the crisis of public authority by avoiding law and by parceling out to private parties the power to make public policy. A most maladaptive political formula, it will inevitably exacerbate rather than end the crisis, even though its short-run effects seem to be those of consensus and stabilization.

LIBERALISM-CONSERVATISM: THE EMPTY DEBATE

It is necessary to look directly at the problems inherent in the old liberal-conservative dialogue, but fortunately a brief look at a few hard cases is all that will be required. Table 3.1 shows at a glance how irrelevant are the old criteria to present policies.[2] In Table 3.1 there are a number of selected public policies and private policies, or widely established private practices, that have been arranged in two dimensions according to the two basic attributes of liberalism-conservatism. Above the line are public policies; below the line are private policies or examples of established business and group practices. This vertical dimension is a simple dichotomy. Therefore, above the line is the "liberal" dimension and below the line the "conservative" dimension. The horizontal dimension is a continuum. Each policy or practice is placed along the line from left to right roughly according to its real or probable impact upon the society. To the left is the liberal direction, where policies are placed if they are likely to affect a direct change in things. To the right is the conservative direction, where policies and practices are placed if they tend directly to maintain one or another status quo.[3]

[2] *Cf.* Dahl and Lindblom, *op. cit.,* Chapter 1.
[3] Placement along the continuum is gross and informal. However, it is clear that no basis for placing these policies according to impact could reduce their spread. And, differences of opinion as to the placement of

TABLE 3.1

SELECTED PUBLIC AND PRIVATE POLICIES ARRANGED ACCORDING TO PROBABLE EFFECT ON SOCIETY

GRADUATED INCOME TAX (POTENTIAL)						KENNEDY-FREEMAN FARM PROPOSALS
Social Security programs based on graduated income tax	Luxury taxes	Growth fiscal policies	Counter-cyclical fiscal policies	Social Security programs based on insurance principles (U.S.)	Existing farm programs	High tariffs
Civil rights package	Real antitrust	Graduated Income Tax (United States)	Sales taxes	Direct regulation (e.g., FCC, ICC, CAB, etc.)	Restraint of competition (NRA, fair trade, anti-price discrim.)	Import quotas
Low tariffs	"Yardstick" regulation (TVA)		Aids to small business	Antitrust by consent decree	Tax on colored margarine	Utilities
						Group representation on boards
						Strict gold standard with no bank money
Competition in agriculture	Competitive business	Oligopoly with research competition	Oligopoly without competition (steel, cigarettes)	Trade associations		Monopoly
New interest groups	Corporate philanthropy		Brand names	Pools		Old interest groups (NAM, AFL-CIO, TWU, etc.)
	Merit hiring and promotion		Ethnic appeals of political campaigns	Basing points		
				Price leadership		
				Fair trade policies		
				Union unemployment and automation policies		

Above the line: Public policies ("liberal")
Below the line: Private policies or practices ("conservative")

Toward the left side: Policies likely to produce change ("liberal")
Toward the right side: Policies likely to maintain existing practices ("conservative")

If the two criteria—attitude toward government and attitude toward change—were consistent, and if together they described and justified programs, then liberal policies would be concentrated in the upper left corner, and conservative policies would be concentrated below the line to the right. In reality they obviously range all across the continuum. Little study of Table 3.1 is therefore necessary to discover that the inconsistencies between the two criteria are extreme. And little reflection is necessary to see that policy makers are being guided by some other principles, if principles do guide them at all. Obviously, the liberal-conservative dialogue made no sense after the establishment of the principle of positive government.[4]

The distance above or below the line in Table 3.1 is not meant to convey additional information about the degree of public involvement. The horizontal line merely separates what is governmental (above) from what is nongovernmental (below). But let us consider that dimension. We can cross-tabulate the actual degree of government involvement characteristic of each public policy against the probable degree of social change expected or experienced with that policy. (See Table

specific policies (should antitrust go in the middle or over on the left?) would lead to the very kind of policy analysis political scientists need to get involved in.

[4] Some, especially "liberals," might object, arguing that the true basis of the distinction is public versus private but that it involves much more than merely change versus maintenance. Equality and welfare as well as change are the liberal attributes of public policies. Adding dimensions to the one diagram would overly complicate it, but some response to the objection can be made: (1) A strong element of the equality dimension is already present in the sense that those policies on the left do represent change and "change toward equality." However, (2) note the fact that, at least to this observer, "equality" is present among public but also among private policies and practices. Furthermore, (3) many public policies aim at the reduction of the forces of equality (as well as change) in the private sphere. Those in the upper right area of the chart serve as examples. Thus, "equality" is not a basis for distinguishing positions any more than is "change," with or without consideration of the equality aspects of change. I will not attempt to defend the absence of the "welfare" dimension except to say that no definition of welfare could possibly show that it is strictly within the province of the public or the private sphere. Any diagram based on *any* definition of "welfare" would show policies above and below the line and to the left and the right.

3.2.) This particular look at government should be most unsettling to liberals, and especially to Negro leaders who, socialized by white liberals, have assumed that political power is all one needs in order to achieve important humanitarian goals. It is most important to note here, as in Table 3.1, how many government policies seem to congregate in cells labeled with a minus sign (hypothesized as likely to "militate against change"). It is even more important to note that government's relation to social change does not increase as government involvement increases from one to two to three pluses. On the contrary, there almost seems to be an inverse relation, suggesting that *government is most effective and most frequently employed when something in society has been deemed worthy of preservation.* This is why the notion of "maintaining public order" may be a more suitable definition for contemporary government than any current liberal is prepared doctrinally to accept.

Analysis of the real or potential impact of public policies shows how incomplete is the fit between the earlier public philosophy and the policies it is supposed to support and justify. It shows that those who espouse social change in the abstract, especially government-engineered social change, are seldom peddling policies that would clearly effect any such change. Conversely, it shows that those who harangue on principle against government and change are frequently in real life pushing for strong doses of each. If these criteria do not really guide the leaders, they offer almost no plausible justification for the intelligent follower. A few examples in detail follow.

(1) The income tax. All taxes discriminate. The political question arises over the kind of discrimination the society desires. The graduated or progressive income tax is capable of effecting drastic changes in the relations among classes and between man and his property. According to the two criteria in question, then, the steeply progressive income tax is "liberal" both because it is governmental and because it effects social change. Our own income tax structure can be called only mildly, if at all, progressive, allowing as it does full exemption

TABLE 3.2

SELECTED PUBLIC POLICIES, TABULATED BY DEGREE OF SOCIAL CHANGE AND DEGREE OF GOVERNMENT INVOLVEMENT

Impact of Policy:
Likelihood of Significant Social Change

Degree of Government Involvement	CHANGE VERY LIKELY +++	CHANGE PROBABLE ++	+	–	MILITATES AGAINST CHANGE	– – –
+++ Sustained and active intervention	Title VI of 1964 Civ. Rts. Act; Civ. Rts. Act, '65; Fully Progressive Inc. Tax (Hypoth.)	Walsh-Healy; Civ. Rts. of '64; Reciprocal Trade	TVA; 1964 Tax cuts	Counter-cyclical fiscal policy; Manpower Training; Tax Revision; 1961–62 Tax Cuts	AEC-type corp.; FTC; Area Redev'nt; Nationalized industry	Defense construction; Public Housing; Farm Parity; Old tariff; ICC; Utilities
++ Substantial involvement	1962 Trade Act	Aid to Education	COMSAT; Appalachia	Patents; Urban redevelopment	FCC; CAB; Social Security; French & Ital. public corps.; War on Poverty	Farm extension; NRA codes; Robinson-Patman of FTC; Monopolies
+ Low but measurable involvement	Head Start; Free trade (Hypoth.)	Education grants-in-aid; Title I Housing; Research Subsidy			SEC	

on interest from public debt, fast write-offs, depletion allow-
ances, hosts of "Louis B. Mayer Amendments," [5] privileges on
real estate transactions, and so on *ad nauseam*. It is generally
understood that the effective ceiling on taxes is not 91 per cent
or 75 per cent but a good deal less than 50 per cent. And considering all taxes together, it seems fairly clear that they comprise a bastion against rather than a weapon for fluidity among
classes and channels of opportunity. This is not an argument in
favor of one tax structure or the other, but rather one in favor
of the proposition that no trace of a sign can be found of
liberal-conservative principles underlying taxation, not even as
a guide to compromise. During the legislative action in 1963–
64, there was much discussion and debate on the technical
question of the impact of the tax cut on the rate of aggregate
economic growth. But there was almost no consideration of the
significance of the tax structure or the tax cut to the society. In
fact, plans for large-scale tax reform were withdrawn altogether before the tax bill was ever formally proposed. As a
consequence, taxation in the United States is a government
policy to preserve the established economic relations among
people and classes.

(2) The social security system. This is, of course, a bundle
of policies, and accuracy would require classification of each.
On balance, however, they are "liberal" only because they are
governmental; they are conservative in their impact on social
structure and opportunity. If they promote welfare, then, indeed, it is important to be able to say that a conservative
policy *can* promote welfare. Above all else, old age insurance,
unemployment compensation, and the like are techniques of
fiscal policy. They are initially important as countercyclical devices, "automatic stabilizers," that work systematically to maintain demand and existing economic relationships without
dislocation throughout the business cycle. In this dimension,
"liberals" are a good deal less willing to take chances than
"conservatives."

[5] Amendments can be so cleverly phrased that they grant enormous
tax relief to only one or a few persons, as in the case of Mr. Mayer upon
his retirement a few years ago.

At another dimension, social security in the United States is an even more interesting case of the gap between the old liberal criteria and the real impact of established programs. For social security programs are techniques of social as well as fiscal control, and as such they are clearly conservative. The American system of social security is based fairly strictly on a principle of the socialization of risk through forced saving. Government's role is essentially paternalistic; speaking roughly, government raises the minimum wage by the amount of the employer's contribution, takes that (for unemployment) plus about an equal amount from the employee's wages (for old age), and says, "This much of your income we'll not trust you to spend." This principle of contributory social security does not affect the class structure, the sum total of opportunity, or anything else; on the contrary, it tends to maintain existing patterns. It helps make people a little happier to be where they are doing what they are doing. The social security system is consistent with the criteria of liberalism only to the extent that it is based on a graduated income tax or to the extent that it supports those who did not contribute before entering the rolls. And that is a small and very unpopular extent indeed.[6]

The Medicare program is significant as an addition to the scope and scale of social security, but in no important way does it change the social significance of social security. After President Kennedy proposed a medicare bill limited to the aged and based on "actuarial soundness," there was not even any need to debate the social significance of the bill. Actuarial soundness was a sufficient message that social security would remain altogether what it had been, except for the temporary addition of people who were already old and had made no contribution before entering the rolls. The only surprise in the Medicare case was the difficulty of passage. But that was due to a stalemate not between liberalism and conservatism but between the unorganized and apathetic elderly and the intensely felt and highly organized trade union interests of the

[6] *Cf.* below, Chapter 8, on the "public assistance" features of the Social Security Act.

American Medical Association. A program that originated with
Bismarck was simply a while longer being needed in the
United States.

(3) The farm programs provide an equally good case of the
irrelevance of policy to the old criteria. High price supports
with crop controls, the center of farm policy for a generation,
are supported by "liberals"; but these policies are "liberal" because and only because they are governmental. The entire establishment escaped death in 1949–50 only with urban-labor
support, but that support proves nothing about liberalism.

What has been the purpose and what is the impact of such a
program? Basically, the aim was to restore and to maintain a
pre-1914 agriculture in face of extremely strong contrary finan-
ical, industrial, and technological developments. The effect of
the program has clearly been implemented as intented, for far
larger numbers of farmers and subsistence farms remain than
are supportable in strictly economic terms. And the program
perpetuates the established sizes of farms and relationships
among farmers by basing present quotas and controls upon
past outputs, state by state, county by county, and farm by
farm. The New Frontier and Great Society proposals must be
ranked as even more "conservative," despite their governmental base (or perhaps because of it). They would have delegated to a few leading farmers or farm group leaders in each
surplus commodity area the power to determine the quotas,
thus allowing those most involved to decide *for themselves* just
what there is about agriculture worth conserving. This is elevation of government-by-conflict-of-interest to a virtuous principle. Early in his presidency, Lyndon Johnson called on the
leaders of the major agriculture interest groups to formulate
new policy solutions to agriculture. This was the beginning of
the Johnson round. In music, a round is a form in which everything is repeated over and over again.

(4) Business practices. The "conservative" side of the argument is no more consistent. Competitive business enterprise is
a highly dynamic force that usually makes change normal, innovation necessary, and influence by ordinary individuals over

economic decisions possible. For these reasons many forms of competitive enterprise should be thought of as supported by real liberals despite the fact that government is only in a marginal way responsible for it. But, except for martyrs from Thurmond Arnold to Walter S. Adams who have sought vainly to use government to decentralize industry, the net impact of attitudes toward business from conservatives as well as liberals has been to restrain the system.

One might say that the only difference between old-school liberals and conservatives is that the former would destroy the market through public means and the latter through private means. This is very largely due to the fact that, lacking any independent standards, all politicians depend upon those organized interests that already have access to government and to the media of communication. Following the second criterion of liberalism-conservatism, *all established interest groups are conservative.*[7] Government policy is one of many strategies organized interests feel free to pursue. In this respect it is useless to distinguish between the NAM and the AFL-CIO. Trade associations, as observed in Chapter 2, exist to "stabilize the market," in other words, to maintain existing relations among members despite any fluctuations in their respective sectors of the economy. They, in turn, are the primary determiners of private as well as public policies toward business and business competition. Holding companies, pools, market sharing, information sharing, interlocking directorships, price leadership, competition through advertising and not prices, and collusion in bidding are typical nongovernmental policies which become inevitable if they are not illegal. On the other hand, they are in no way functionally distinguishable from such governmental

---

[7] They are so placed in Table 3.1. Interest groups are not policies, strictly speaking. However, individuals and corporations belong to and support trade associations and other groups as a matter of policy; and each such group formulates relatively clear policies supported by the members. Placing "old interest groups" to the right in Table 3.1 is meant to convey two hypotheses: (1) that the existence of the group is itself conservative, and (2) that it is highly possible that the policies formulated by such old groups will be conservative. New groups represent pathology in society. Old groups represent status quo of some sort or another.

policies as basing points laws, fair trade laws, anti–price-discrimination laws, NRA codes, and so on. To the extent that liberalism-conservatism is taken seriously as the source of public philosophy, liberals-conservatives become hemmed in by it, too rigid to withdraw their sentiments as new needs become old, vested interests. They are inevitably betrayed by the very groups that profited most by their support.

The enormous inconsistency between what public policy really is and what the old doctrines suppose it to be may turn out to be merely true but still inconsequential. This might be the case if it could be shown that American public men were the original pragmatists and were never in need of any doctrine other than the loose social code that binds us all. This possibility must be rejected. Stable countries with their highly rationalized political order, have great need of legitimizing rituals, perhaps more so than transitional societies where expectations are not so high. Moreover, the very persistence of the old criteria so far beyond their appropriate hour can be taken as an index to the need American elites have for doctrinal support.

The old public philosophy became outmoded because in our time it applies to the wrong class of objects. Statesmen simply no longer disagree about whether government should be involved; therefore they neither seek out the old criteria for guidance through their disagreements, nor do they really have need of the criteria to justify the mere governmental character of policies. But this does not mean that public men are not now being guided by some other, widely shared, criteria that do apply to the relevant class of objects. The good functionalist must insist upon being guided by the hypothesis that some political formula or public philosophy does exist. If it is obvious that public men are no longer governed by their older public philosophy, then the next logical proposition is this, that there is some other public philosophy with which their public policy behaviors are consistent, but it may be one not clearly enough formulated to be well known yet beyond public men themselves.

INTEREST-GROUP LIBERALISM

The weaknesses of the old liberalism-conservatism were not altogether clear before the 1960's. This tardiness is due simply to the intervention of two wars and then an eight-year period of relative quiescence in policy-making. Truman's Fair Deal agenda, already left over from the end of the New Deal, held fire for over a decade until it became a major part of the Democratic agenda of the 1960's and comprised a very large proportion of the successful record of the 89th Congress, the most actively legislating Congress since 1933. Even the historic *Brown v. Board of Education* decision failed to bring about noticeable expansion and intensification of political activity until the Little Rock debacle of 1957. With increasing pace thereafter, new pressures began to be placed upon political institutions, and another round of governmental activity was in the making. In many ways the period that began in 1957 with Little Rock and Sputnik was as much a constitutional revolution as that of the 1930's. In this decade—as measured by Federal budgets, personnel, the sheer proliferation of service and other agencies, or the expansion of public regulatory authority —there have clearly been a civil rights revolution, an educational revolution, and a scientific and technological revolution.

All of this activity proves that there is no end to government responsibility. It is not possible to automate all the stabilizers. The new activity in the 1960's also proves that the political apparatus of democracy can respond promptly once the constitutional barriers to democratic choice have been lowered. However, that is only the beginning of the story, because the almost total democratization of the Constitution and the contemporary expansion of the public sector has been accompanied by expansion, not contraction, of a sense of illegitimacy about public objects. Here is a spectacular paradox. We witness governmental effort of gigantic proportion to solve problems forthwith and directly. Yet we also witness expressions of personal alienation and disorientation increasing, certainly not subsiding, in frequency and intensity; and we witness further weakening of informal controls in the family, neighborhood, and groups. We witness a vast expansion of effort to bring the ordinary citizen into closer rapport with the democratic process, including unprecedented efforts to confer upon the poor the power to make official decisions involving their own fate. Yet at the very same time we witness crisis after crisis in the very institutions in which the new methods of decision-making seemed most appropriate.

It is as though each new program or program expansion were an admission of prior governmental inadequacy or failure without necessarily being a contribution to order and well-being. The War on Poverty programs have become as often as not instruments of social protest. The Watts riots, the movements for police review boards in many cities, the sit-ins and marches even where no specifically evil laws are being enforced against a special race or group, the strikes and protests by civil servants, nurses, doctors, teachers, transport and defense workers, and others in vital occupations—all these events and many others are evidence of increasing impatience with established ways of resolving social conflict and dividing up society's values. Verbal and organizational attacks on that vague being, the "power structure," even in cities with histories of strong reform movements and imaginative social programs, reflect increasing rejection of pluralistic patterns in favor of more direct prosecution of claims against society. Far from insignificant as a sign of the times is the emergence of national party movements on opposite extremes, alike in their opposition to centrist parties, electoral politics, and pre-election compromise. Many of these new patterns and problems may have been generated by racial issues and an unpopular war; but it is clear that these were only precipitants. The ironic fact is that the post-1937 political economy, either because of or in spite of government policies and two wars, had produced unprecedented prosperity, and as the national output increased arithmetically the rate of rising expectation must have gone up geometrically—in a modern expression of the Malthusian Law. Public authority was left to grapple with this alienating gap between expectation and reality.

Prosperity might merely have produced a gigantic race among all to share in its benefits. The expansion of the public sector might have increased the legitimacy of government through redistribution of opportunities to join the prosperity. Instead, the expansion of government that helped produce sustained prosperity also produced a crisis of public authority. Why? Because the old justification for that expansion had so little to say beyond the need for the expansion itself. The class of objects to which a new and appropriate public philosophy should first have been applied, it seems obvious, was to the purposes to which the expanded governmental authority should be dedicated. It should then have been applied to the forms and procedures by which the power could be utilized. In sum, what impact do we want government to have and what consequences can we expect from one kind of approach as opposed to some alternative? What constitutes "due process" in an age of positive government?

Out of the emerging crisis in public authority has developed an ersatz political formula that bears no relation to those questions. The guidance it offers to policy formulation is a set of sentiments that elevate a particular view of the political process above everything else. The ends of government and the justification of one policy or procedure over another are not to be discussed, according to the new view. The *process* of formulation is justification in itself. As observed earlier, it takes the pluralist notion that government is an epiphenomenon of politics and constitutes with that the new ethics of government.

There are several possible names for this contemporary replacement of liberal-conservatism. A strong candidate would be *corporatism,* but its history as a concept gives it several unwanted connotations, such as conservative Catholicism or Italian fascism, that keep it from being quite suitable. Another is *syndicalism,* but among many objections is the connotation of anarchy too far removed from American experience or intentions. However, the new American public philosophy is a variant of those two alien themes.

The most clinically accurate term to describe the American variant is *interest-group liberalism*. It may be called liberalism because it expects to use government in a positive and expansive role, it is motivated by the highest sentiments, and it possesses strong faith that what is good for government is good for the society. It is "interest-group liberalism" because it sees as both necessary and good that the policy agenda and the public interest be defined in terms of the organized interests in society. In brief sketch, the working model of the interest group liberal is a vulgarized version of the pluralist model of modern political science. It assumes: (1) Organized interests are homogeneous and easy to define, sometimes monolithic. Any "duly elected" spokesman for any interest is taken as speaking in close approximation for each and every member.[8] (2) Organized interests pretty much fill up and adequately represent most of the sectors of our lives, so that one organized group can be found effectively answering and checking some other organized group as it seeks to prosecute its claims against society.[9] And (3) the role of government is one of ensuring access particularly to the most effectively organized, and of ratifying the agreements and adjustments worked out among the competing leaders and their claims. This last assumption is supposed to be a statement of how our democracy works and how it ought to work. Taken together, these assumptions constitute the Adam Smith "hidden hand" model applied to groups.[10]

[8] For an excellent inquiry into this assumption and into the realities of the internal life of the interests, see McConnell, *op. cit.;* see also Clark Kerr, *Unions and Union Leaders of Their Own Choosing* (Santa Barbara: Fund for the Republic, 1957); S. M. Lipset *et al., Union Democracy* (New York: Anchor, 1962); and Arthur S. Miller, *Private Governments and the Constitution* (Santa Barbara: Fund for the Republic, 1959).

[9] It is assumed that "countervailing power" usually crops up somehow. Where it does not, government ought to help create it. See John Kenneth Galbraith, *American Capitalism* (Boston: Houghton Mifflin, 1952).

[10] *Cf.* above, Chapter 2.

These assumptions are the basis of the new public philosophy. The policy behavior of old-school liberals and conservatives, of Republicans and Democrats, so inconsistent with liberalism-conservatism criteria, are fully consistent with the criteria drawn from interest-group liberalism: *The most important difference between liberals and conservatives, Republicans and Democrats—however they define themselves—is to be found in the interest groups they identify with. Congressmen are guided in their votes, Presidents in their programs, and administrators in their discretion by whatever organized interests they have taken for themselves as the most legitimate; and that is the measure of the legitimacy of demands.*

It is no coincidence that these assumptions in the interest-group liberal model resemble the working methodology of modern political science, as discussed at length in Chapter 2. But how did all of this become elevated from a hypothesis about political behavior to an ideology about how a democratic polity ought to work, and then ultimately to that ideology most widely shared among contemporary public men?

INTEREST-GROUP LIBERALISM: AN INTELLECTUAL HISTORY [11]

The opening of the national government to positive action on a large scale was inevitably to have an impact upon political justification just as on political technique. However, the inventors of technique were less than inventive in justifying particular policies at particular times. Hansen, for instance, has observed that Keynes was no dedicated social reformer, nor had he any particular commitments to radically new social ends.[12] Keynes helped discover the modern economic system and how to help it maintain itself, but his ideas and techniques could be used, and indeed have been used, to support many points of view. "Collective bargaining, trade unionism, minimum-wage laws, hours legislation, social security, a progressive tax system, slum clearance and housing, urban redevelop-

---

[11] McConnell, *op. cit.*, pp. 62 ff., discerns a similar intellectual history among businessmen. See also Brady, *op. cit.*

[12] Alvin H. Hansen, *The American Economy* (New York: McGraw-Hill, 1957), pp. 152 ff.

ment and planning, education reform," Hansen observed of Keynes, "all these he accepted, but they were not among his preoccupations. In no sense could he be called the father of the welfare state." [13]

Nor was the doctrine of popular government and majority rule, which was so important in the victory of liberalism over conservatism, adequate guidance after the demise of liberalism-conservatism. If one reviews the New Deal period and thereafter one sees how little propensity Americans have had to use the majority-rule justification. The reasons are fairly apparent. Justification of positive government programs on the basis of popular rule required above all a proclamation of the supremacy of Congress. The abdication of Congress in the 1930's in the passage of the fundamental New Deal legislation could never have been justified in the name of popular government. With all due respect to congressmen, they made little discernible effort to do so. Statutory and investigatory infringements on civil liberties during World War II and during the Cold War, plus the popular support of McCarthyism, produced further reluctance to fall back on Congress and majority rule as the fount of public policy wisdom. Many who wished to use this basis anyway sought support in the plebiscitary character of the Presidency. However, "presidential liberals" have had to blind themselves to many complications in the true basis of presidential authority and to the true—the bureaucratic—expression of presidential will.[14]

The very practices that made convincing use of popular-rule doctrine impossible—delegation of power to administrators, interest representation, outright delegation of power to trade associations, and so on—were what made interest-group liberalism so attractive an alternative. And because the larger inter-

---

[13] *Ibid.*, pp. 158–59. Keynes said: ". . . the Class War will find me on the side of the educated bourgeoisie." (*Ibid.*, p. 158.)

[14] No citations are necessary to emphasize the fact that presidential delegation and subdelegation to administrators is just as extensive as congressional. As to the popular basis of presidential authority, see debate between Robert A. Dahl, *Preface to Democratic Theory* (Chicago: University of Chicago Press, 1956); and Willmoore Kendall, "The Two Majorities," *Midwest Journal of Political Science*, 4 (1960), 317–45.

est groups did claim large memberships, they could be taken virtually as popular rule in modern dress. Interest-group liberalism simply corresponded impressively well with the realities of power. Thus, it possessed the approval of science as well as some of the trappings of popular rule. Political scientists, after all, were pioneers in insisting upon recognition of the group, as well as in helping to elevate the pressure-group system from power to virtue. Political scientists had for a long time argued that the group is the necessary variable in political analysis for breaking through the formalisms of government.[15] However, there was inevitably an element of approval in their methodological argument, if only to counteract the kind of recognition of the group that Steffens and other progressives and Muckrakers were more than willing to accord. In 1929, E. Pendleton Herring concluded his inquiry with the argument that:

[The national associations] represent a healthy democratic development. They rose in answer to certain needs. . . . They are part of our representative system. . . . These groups must be welcomed for what they are, and certain precautionary regulations worked out. The groups must be understood and their proper place in government allotted, if not by actual legislation, then by general public realization of their significance.[16]

Following World War II, one easily notes among political scientists the widespread acceptance of the methodology and, more importantly here, the normative position. Among political scientists the best expression of interest-group liberalism was probably that of Wilfred Binkley and Malcolm Moos. The fact that it was so prominent in their American government basic textbook suggests that it tended to reflect conventional

[15] For pioneer expressions, see Arthur F. Bentley, *The Process of Government* (Chicago: University of Chicago Press, 1908); and E. Pendleton Herring, *Group Representation Before Congress* (Baltimore: Johns Hopkins Press, 1929). More recent arguments of the same methodological sort are found in Truman, *op. cit.;* and Earl Latham, *The Group Basis of Politics* (Ithaca: Cornell University Press, 1952); texts and case studies confirming this ideology in the 1960's are too numerous to mention.

[16] Herring, *op. cit.,* p. 268. See Herring's further reflections of 1936, in Chapter 2.

wisdom among political scientists even in 1948. Binkley and
Moos argued that the "basic concept for understanding the dy-
namics of government is the multi-group nature of modern society or the modern state." [17] Political reality can be grasped
scientifically as a "parallelogram of forces" among groups, and
the public interest is "determined and established" through the
free competition of interest groups: "The necessary composing
and compromising of their differences is the practical test of
what constitutes the public interest." [18]

The fact that a doctrine has some support in the realities of
power certainly helps to explain its appeal as a doctrine.[19] But
there were also several strongly positive reasons for the emergence of this particular doctrine. The first, and once perhaps
the only, reason, is that it has helped flank the constitutional
problems of federalism. Manifestations of the corporate state
were once limited primarily to the Extension Service of the
Department of Agriculture, with self-administration by the
land grant colleges and the local farmers and commerce associations. Self-administration by organized groups was an attractive technique precisely because it could be justified as so
decentralized and permissive as to be hardly federal at all.[20]
Here began the ethical and conceptual mingling of the notion
of organized private groups with the notions of "local government" and "self-government." Ultimately, direct interest-group
participation in government became synonymous with self-
government, first for reasons of strategy, then by belief that
the two were indeed synonymous. As a propaganda strategy it

[17] Wilfred Binkley and Malcolm Moos, *A Grammar of American
Politics* (New York: Alfred A. Knopf, 1950), p. 7. Moos became an
important idea man in the Eisenhower administration.

[18] *Ibid.*, pp. 8–9. In order to preserve value-free science, many pluralists ("group theorists") denied public interest altogether, arguing instead
that there is a "totally inclusive interest" and that it is best served by
letting groups interact without knowing what it is. *Cf.* Truman, *op. cit.*,
pp. 50–51.

[19] For discussions of the extent to which group theory is a satisfactory
statement of reality, see my "American Business, Public Policy, Case-
Studies, and Political Theory," *World Politics*, 16 (1964), pp. 677–715,
and the excellent essays cited therein.

[20] For more on the expansion and justification of these practices in
agriculture see below, Chapter 4.

eased acceptance in the courts, then among the locals who still believed the farmer was and should be independent. Success as strategy increased usage; usage helped elevate strategy to doctrine. The users began to believe in their own symbols.

A second positive appeal of interest-group liberalism is strongly related to the first. Interest-group liberalism helps solve a problem for the democratic politician in the modern state where the stakes are so high. This is the problem of enhanced conflict and how to avoid it. The politician's contribution to society is his skill in resolving conflict. However, direct confrontations are sought only by the zealous ideologues and "outsiders." The typical American politician displaces and defers and delegates conflict where possible; he squarely faces conflict only when he must. Interest-group liberalism offers a justification for keeping major combatants apart. It provides a theoretical basis for giving to each according to his claim, the price for which is a reduction of concern for what others are claiming. In other words, it transforms logrolling from necessary evil to greater good. This is the basis for the "consensus" so often claimed these days. It is also the basis for President Kennedy's faith that in our day ideology has given over to administration. It is inconceivable that so sophisticated a person as he could have believed, for example, that his setting of guidelines for wage and price increases was a purely administrative act. Here, in fact, is a policy that could never be "administered" in the ordinary sense of the word. The guidelines provide a basis for direct and regular policy-making between the President (or his agent) and the spokesmen for industry and for labor. This is a new phase of government relations with management and labor, and it is another step consistent with the interest-group liberal criterion of direct access.

The third positive appeal of interest-group liberalism is that it is a direct, even if pathological, response to the crisis of public authority. The practice of dealing only with organized claims in formulating policy, and of dealing exclusively through organized claims in implementing programs, helps create the sense that power need not be power at all, nor control control. If sovereignty is parceled out among the groups,

then who's out anything? As Max Ways of *Fortune* enthusiastically put it, government power, group power, and individual
power may go up simultaneously. *If* the groups to be controlled control the controls, *then* "to administer does not always mean to rule." [21] The inequality of power is always a
gnawing problem in a democratic culture. Rousseau's General
Will stopped at the boundary of a Swiss canton. The myth of
the group and the group will is becoming the answer to Rousseau in the big democracy.

President Eisenhower talked regularly about the desirability
of business-government "partnerships," despite the misgivings
in his farewell address about the "military-industrial complex,"
for he and most other Republicans are interest-group liberals.
However, explicit and systematic expression of interest-group
liberalism is much more the contribution of the Democrats,
and the best formulations can be found among the more articulate Democrats, especially the leading Democratic intellectuals, Professors John Kenneth Galbraith and Arthur Schlesinger,
Jr.[22]

To Professor Galbraith, "Private economic power is held in
check by the countervailing power of those who are subject to
it. The first begets the second." [23] Concentrated economic
power stimulates other business interests (in contrast to the
Smithian consumer), which organize against it. This results in
a natural tendency toward equilibrium. But Galbraith is not
really writing a theoretical alternative to Adam Smith; he is
writing a program of government action. For he admits to the
limited existence of effective countervailing power and pro-
poses that where it is absent or too weak, government policy
should seek out and support or, where necessary, create the

[21] Max Ways, " 'Creative Federalism' and the Great Society," *Fortune,*
January, 1966, p. 122.

[22] A third major intellectual of the Kennedy Administration was
Professor Richard E. Neustadt. That he is a political scientist makes all
the more interesting his exceptional stress upon the necessary independence of the Presidency rather than the desirability of presidential
partnerships and countervailing power. See his *Presidential Power* (New
York: John Wiley and Sons, 1960).

[23] Galbraith, *American Capitalism, op. cit.,* p. 118.

organizations capable of countervailing. Government thereby pursues the public interest and makes itself superfluous at the same time. This is a surefire, nearly scientific guide to interest-group liberalism.

Professor Schlesinger's views are summarized for us in the campaign tract he wrote in 1960. To Schlesinger, the essential difference between the Democratic and Republican parties is that the Democratic party is a truly multi-interest party in the grand tradition extending back to Federalist No. 10. In power, it offers multi-interest administration and therefore ought to be preferred over the Republican party; and:

What is the essence of a multi-essence administration? It is surely that the leading interests in society are all represented in the interior processes of policy formation—which can be done only if members or advocates of these interests are included in key positions of government. . . .[24]

This theme Schlesinger repeated in his more serious and more recent work, *A Thousand Days.* Following his account of the 1962 confrontation of President Kennedy with the steel industry and the later decision to cut taxes and cast off for expansionary rather than stabilizing, fiscal policy, Schlesinger concludes:

The ideological debates of the past began to give way to a new agreement on the practicalities of managing a modern economy. There thus developed in the Kennedy years a national accord on economic policy—a new consensus which gave hope of harnessing government, business, and labor in rational partnership for a steadily expanding American economy.[25]

A significant point in the entire argument is that the Republicans would disagree with Schlesinger on the *facts* but not on the *basis* of his distinction. The Republican rejoinder would be, in effect, "Democratic administrations are *not* more multi-

[24] Arthur Schlesinger, Jr., *Kennedy or Nixon—Does It Make Any Difference?* (New York: Macmillan, 1960), p. 43.
[25] Arthur M. Schlesinger, Jr., *A Thousand Days,* as reprinted in *Chicago Sun-Times,* Jan. 23, 1966, Sec. 2, p. 3.

interest than Republican." And, in my opinion, this would be almost the whole truth.

INTEREST-GROUP LIBERALISM AND PUBLIC POLICIES IN THE 1960's.[26]

This principle has been explicitly applied in the formulation of a large number of policies, especially since the return of the Democrats to power in 1961. That is, policy-makers have in numerous new programs added elements of official group representation and have officially applied "participatory democracy" to the implementation as well as the formulation of law as part of the justification of their action. There are additional policies where evidence of the application of interest-group liberalism is clear even though not as consciously intended or as much a part of the record of self-praise.

President Kennedy provides an especially good starting point because his positions were clear and because justification was especially important to him. No attention need be paid to the elements of liberalism-conservatism in his program [27] but only to the degree to which his actions were consistent with interest-group liberalism. John Kennedy was bred to a politics of well-organized and autonomous units of power. Locally in Boston they were more likely ethnic, religious, and neighborhood organizations, but they had to be reckoned with as pow-

[26] Certain points made here in order to clarify the general argument are repeated at greater length in the more intensive analysis of selected policies in succeeding chapters. Reference will be made where possible.

[27] By proper application of the old-school criteria, Kennedy was, on balance, conservative. Most of his programs belong to the right of center (on Table 3.1, horizontal axis), and he did an amazing number of things that showed a preference for private-sector activity (Table 3.1, vertical axis). Examples include his "actuarially sound" Medicare, his investment tax credit and tax cut proposals, his preference for expansion of housing through investment incentives, his reluctance to ask for new civil rights legislation, his appreciation for governmental contracting and other executive powers to deal with civil rights, his opposition to "Powell Amendments" and parochial school aid in federal education legislation, his concerted effort to make agriculture controls work, his support for very permissive depressed-areas legislation that would bail out needy businesses and industries while reducing needs of or pressures on entrepreneurs to move to some other section of the country.

erful interest groups. The national party he set out to win in 1956 was also a congeries of autonomous factions and blocs; and it has been said that he succeeded by recreating the "New Deal coalition." But there is a vast difference between pluralism inside political parties and legitimized pluralism built into government programs. The one does not necessarily follow from the other, unless leaders believe it is desirable. President Kennedy's proposals and rhetoric mark his belief in that desirability. Many of his most important proposals mark his contribution to the corporatizing of the government-group nexus in the United States.

The agriculture problem, high on the New Frontier agenda, was to be solved somewhat differently from all earlier attempts, and that difference is much to the point. At local levels, federal agriculture programs had always been corporative, with committees of local farm dignitaries applying the state and national standards to local conditions.[28] President Kennedy proposed simply to bring this pattern to the center and to have the farmers, represented by group leaders, *set* the standards as well as apply them. Essentially, this was NRA applied to agriculture.

There was no attempt by Kennedy to reinstitute the NRA pattern in industry, but there were, just the same, moves toward recognition of the organized side of industry in the "interior processes" of government. First, as observed earlier, by direct presidential act guidelines for profits and wages were set up. Notice was thereby served that henceforth "industrial policy" would be made by direct bargaining between the President and each and every leader of an industrial sector. Quite separately, but along parallel industrial lines, this meant the same sort of bargaining between the President and union leaders. It is beside the point to argue whether Kennedy or Johnson has been more lenient in applying the guidelines to the unions. It is even beside the point to argue whether this new technique of control means more government involvement and direction than alternative techniques. The point is that the pat-

[28] See below, Chapter 4.

tern of control and the manner of its impact is basically corporativistic. "Partnership" is the measure of success.

Many other relations of government to industry have tended
toward the same pattern in the 1960's, whether they come this
way full-blown from the President or emerge from Congress
this way only at the end. COMSAT is a 1962 combination out
of 1930's Italy and 1940's France. Like the Italian practice of
"permanent receivership," COMSAT is a combine of kept private companies, sharing in stock and risk with the government.
Like the many French public and mixed corporations, there is
direct interest-group representation on the Board. The "public"
stamp is placed on it by adding to the interest-laden Board
three presidentially appointed members; but one of these is a
representative of Big Labor and one a representative of Big
Industry. By the end of 1966, there was already talk among the
carriers (the communications industries) of forming a combine
within the combine to regularize and stabilize losses suffered
by any of them as a result of obsolescence and competition.

The Trade Expansion Act of 1962, for another example,
was the first American tariff based upon broad categories of
goods rather than single items. From the beginning, categorization of goods paralleled the lines of jurisdiction of the leading trade associations and organized farm commodities
groups.[29] The semi-official role of trade associations was expected to increase and expand through those parts of the new
law providing relief through subsidy for injuries proven to
have been sustained by tariff cuts.

There were, of course, many Kennedy proposals that are
economy-wide in intention, but even some of these have one
peculiarity or another that distinguishes them less from the interest-group policies than first appearances suggest. The investment tax credit, for example, was industry-wide, but it
involved a reduction rather than an enlargement of the governmental sphere. The Appalachia program involved a bold
regional concept overwhelmingly broader than any organized

[29] See Raymond Bauer *et al.*, *American Business and Public Policy*
(New York: Atherton, 1963), pp. 73 ff.

groups; however, the strong veto power given the State governors allows for, and was expected to allow for, maximum return of group representation through the back door. Appalachia is more clearly a case of interest-group liberalism if we
include, as we should, State and local government agencies as
groups to be directly represented in implementation of policies. This becomes an important characteristic of "creative
federalism." In Appalachia the governors in the region commit
Federal funds to development plans formulated by state agencies, local agencies, and private groups.

During the Johnson Administration the doctrines and policies of interest-group liberalism were elevated to new highs of
usage and rationalization. It was coming of age by being provided with new and appropriate halo words. The most important of these is "creative federalism," about which President
Johnson and his Great Society team spoke frequently and
enthusiastically. This and related terms—such as partnership,
maximum feasible participation, and, above all, consensus—
seem to be very sincerely felt by present government leaders.
The sentiments are coming to be shared widely among nongovernment leaders and are at the bottom of the extraordinary
business support Johnson received during his most active
period of legislative creativity. Probably the most accurate and
sympathetic analysis of creative federalism and the role it is
playing in the Great Society has been provided by *Fortune*.
As *Fortune* and many other observers would agree, creative
federalism is not federalism. Federalism divides sovereignty
between duly constituted levels of government. "Creative
federalism" is a parceling of powers between the central government and *all* structures of power, governments and non-
governments. In fact, little distinction is made between what is
government and what is not. It is, according to the enthusiastic
definition of *Fortune* writer Max Ways, "a relation, cooperative
and competitive, between a limited central power and other
powers that are essentially independent of it." The difference
between federalism and "creative federalism" is no mere academic distinction. Creative federalism involves a "new way of
organizing Federal programs . . . [in which simultaneously]

the power of states and local governments will increase; the power of private organizations, including businesses, will increase; the power of individuals will increase." [30]

In line with the new rationale, President Johnson and his administration increased the degree to which private organizations and local authorities become endowed with national sovereignty. Corporativistic programs inherited from the New Deal were strengthened in the degree to which they can share in the new, explicit rationale. This was particularly noticeable in the power and natural resources field, where policies were left to the determination of those participants who know the "local situation" best. It was also at the center of Great Society expansions of existing social programs. President Johnson's articulate Assistant Secretary for Education Francis Keppel described Federal education policy this way: "To speak of 'Federal aid' [to education] simply confuses the issue. It is more appropriate to speak of Federal support to special purposes . . . [as] an investment made by a partner who has clearly in mind the investments of other partners—local, state, and private." [31]

The new Great Society programs bore particularly strong evidence of interest-group liberal thinking. Perhaps the most significant contribution of the Great Society to the growing ratio such corporativistic programs bear to the sum total of federal activity is the War on Poverty, particularly the community action program. To the old progressive the elimination of poverty was a passionate dream, to the socialist a philosophic and historic necessity. To the interest-group liberal, poverty is becoming just another status around which power centers ought to organize. If a group hasn't organized, then organize it. In so organizing it, poverty is not eliminated, but inconsistency in the manner of government's relation to society is reduced. That is to say, organizing the poor, something that

[30] Ways, *op. cit.,* p. 122. *Cf. Wall Street Journal,* March 16, 1966, for a positive report on creative federalism. To the *Journal,* creative federalism was a good thing insofar as it really did keep Federal control of Federal programs minimal.

[31] Quoted in *Congressional Quarterly,* Weekly Report, April 22, 1966, p. 833.

once was done only in *The Threepenny Opera,* helps legitimize the interest-group liberal's preference for dealing only with organized claims. The "Peachum factor" in public affairs is best personified in Sargent Shriver. In getting the War on Poverty under way Shriver was misunderstood in many matters, particularly on any insistence that the poor be represented in some mathematically exact way. But one aspect of the doctrine was clear all the time. This was that certain types of groups should always be involved in some way. As he listed them they are: "governmental groups, philanthropic, religious, business, and labor groups, and the poor." [32] The significance lies primarily in the equality of the listing. "Governmental groups" are simply one more type of participant.

Interest-group liberalism thus seems closer to being the established, operative ideology of the American elite than any other body of doctrine. The United States is far from 100 per cent a corporate state; but each administration, beginning with the New Deal Revolution, has helped reduce the gap.[33] And it is equally significant that few if any programs organized on the basis of direct interest representation or group self-administration have ever been eliminated. To the undoubted power of

[32] Jules Witcover and Erwin Knoll, "Politics and the Poor: Shriver's Second Thoughts," *Reporter,* December 30, 1965, p. 24. See below, Chapter 8.

[33] George La Noue's research suggests that there is no limit to how far the pattern can spread. He reports that in clear contradiction of the First Amendment there is a widely applicable government policy to assist church groups, particularly by assigning them to official tasks. A principal element of the Agency for International Development's *modus operandi* has been "to tie together the government and private programs in the field of foreign relief, and to work with interested agencies and groups." That is the official directive of AID. It has an Advisory Committee on Voluntary Foreign Aid, a 10-member board of lay representatives, whose job it is to approve church and other groups for purposes of official registration. This is a requirement for American groups wishing to participate in our foreign aid programs. The registration is not easily gotten and is most valuable to the groups. As the AID directive puts it, this registration "indicates U.S. government approval of the aims, purposes, and administrative set-up of the agency." This obligation was written into the AID statute in 1961. (La Noue, *The Church-State Relations in the Federal Policy Process,* unpublished doctoral dissertation, Yale University, 1965.)

organized interests has now been added the belief in their virtue. There would always be delegation of sovereignty to interest groups in some proportion of the total body of governmental activities. The new context of justification simply means far more direct delegation than the realities of power, unsupported by legitimacy, would call for.

In sum, modern liberals are ambivalent about government. Government is obviously the most efficacious way of achieving good purposes in our age. But alas, it is efficacious because it is involuntary. To live with their ambivalence, modern policymakers have fallen into believing that public policy involves merely the identification of the problems toward which government ought to be aimed. It pretends, through "pluralism," "countervailing power," "creative federalism," "partnership," and "participatory democracy" that the unsentimental business of coercion need not be involved and that the unsentimental decisions about how to employ coercion need not really be made at all. Stated in the extreme, the policies of interest-group liberalism are end-oriented but ultimately self-defeating. Few standards of implementation, if any, accompany delegations of power to administrators. The requirement of standards has been replaced by the requirement of participation. The requirement of law has been replaced by the requirement of contingency.[34] As a result the ends of interest-group liberalism are mere sentiments, therefore not really ends at all.

THE COSTS OF INTEREST-GROUP LIBERALISM

For all the political advantages interest-group liberals have in their ideology, there are high costs involved. Unfortunately, these costs are not strongly apparent at the time of the creation of a group-based program. As Wallace Sayre has observed, the gains of a change tend to be immediate, the costs tend to be cumulative. However, it takes no long-run patience or the spinning of fine webs to capture and assess the consequences of group-based policy solutions. Three major consequences are

[34] See below, Chapter 5.

suggested and assessed here: (1) the atrophy of institutions of popular control; (2) the maintenance of old and creation of new structures of privilege; and (3) conservatism, in several senses of the world. These consequences will guide later analysis.

(1) In *The Public Philosophy*, Walter Lippmann was rightfully concerned over the "derangement of power" whereby modern democracies tend first toward unchecked elective leadership and then toward drainage of public authority from elective leaders down into their constituencies. However, Lippmann erred if he thought of constituencies only as voting constituencies. Drainage has tended toward "support group constituencies," and with special consequence. Parceling out policy-making power to the most interested parties destroys political responsibility. A program split off with a special imperium to govern itself is not merely an administrative unit. It is a structure of power with impressive capacities to resist central political control.

Besides making conflict-of-interest a principle of government rather than a criminal act, participatory programs shut out the public. To be more precise, programs of this sort tend to cut out all that part of the mass that is not specifically organized around values strongly salient to the goals of the program. They shut out the public, first, at the most creative phase of policy-making—the phase where the problem is first defined. Once problems are defined, alliances form accordingly and the outcome is both a policy and a reflection of superior power. If the definition is laid out by groups along lines of established group organization, there is always great difficulty for an amorphous public to be organized in any other terms.

The public is shut out, secondly, at the phase of accountability. In programs in which group self-administration is legitimate, the administrators are accountable primarily to the groups, only secondarily to the President or Congress as institutions. In brief, to the extent that organized interests legitimately control a program there is functional rather than substantive accountability. This means questions of equity, balance, and equilibrium to the exclusion of questions of overall social policy and questions of whether or not the program should be maintained or discontinued. It also means accountability to experts first and amateurs last; and an expert is a man trained and skilled in the mysteries and technologies of the program. This is the final victory of functional over substantive considerations. These propositions are best illustrated by at least ten separate, self-governing systems in agriculture alone (representing over ten billion dollars per year in spending and lending).[35] There are many other, although perhaps less dramatic, illustrations, as we shall see.

Finally, there is a conspiracy to shut out the public. One of the assumptions underlying direct group representation is that on the boards and in the staff and among the recognized outside consultants there will be regular countervailing, checks, and balances. In Schattschneider's terms, this would be expected to expand the "scope of conflict." But there is nothing inevitable about that, and the safer assumption might well be the converse. One meaningful illustration, precisely because it is an absurd extreme, is found in the French system of interest representation. Maurice Byé reports that as the Communist-controlled union, the CGT, intensified its participation in postwar government it was able to influence representatives of interests other than employee interests. In a desperate effort to insure the separation and counterpoise of interests on the boards, the government issued the decree that "each member of the board must be *independent of the interests he is not representing.*" [36] Review of the politics of agriculture and of five major efforts of postwar Administrations to bring the ten separate self-governing agriculture systems under a minimum of central control suggests that perhaps Byé's case may not be an absurd extreme. It is only the limiting case of a tendency in all similarly organized programs.[37]

(2) Programs following the principles of interest-group liberalism create privilege, and it is a type of privilege particu-

[35] See below, Chapter 4.
[36] Mario Einaudi *et al.*, *Nationalization in France and Italy* (Ithaca: Cornell University Press, 1955), pp. 100–101. (Emphasis added.)
[37] See below, Chapter 4.

larly hard to bear or combat because it is touched with the symbolism of the state. The large national interest groups that walk the terrains of national politics are already fairly tight structures of power. We need no more research to support Michels' iron tendency toward oligarchy in these "private governments." Pluralists ease our problem of abiding the existence of organized interests by characterizing oligarchy as simply a negative name for organization: In combat people want and need to be organized and led. Another, somewhat less assuaging, assertion of pluralism is that the member approves the goals of the group or is free to leave it for another, or can turn his attention to one of his "overlapping memberships" in other groups. But however true this may be in pluralistic *politics*, everything changes when some of the groups are co-opted by the state in pluralistic government. The American Farm Bureau Federation is no "voluntary association" insofar as it is a legitimate functionary in Extension work. Such groups as the NAHB, NAREB, NAACP, or NAM are no ordinary lobbies after they become part of the "interior processes of policy formation." [38]

The more clear and legitimized the representation of a group or its leaders in policy formation, the less voluntary is membership in that group and the more necessary is loyalty to its leadership for people who share the interests in question. And, the more clear the official practice of recognizing only organized interests, the more hierarchy is introduced into the society. It is a well-recognized and widely appreciated function of formal groups in modern societies to provide much of the necessary everyday social control. However, when the very thought processes behind public policy are geared toward those groups they are bound to take on much of the involuntary character of *public* control. The classic example outside agriculture is probably the Rivers and Harbors Congress, a private agency whose decisions in the screening of public works projects have almost the effect of law. And, as David Truman observes, arrangements where "one homogeneous group is di-

[38] See especially the analysis of the War on Poverty in Chapter 8, below.

rectly or indirectly charged with the administration of a function . . . [in a] kind of situation that characterizes the occupational licensing boards and similar 'independent' agencies . . . have become increasingly familiar in regulatory situations in all levels of government." [39]

Even when the purpose of the program is the uplifting of the underprivileged, the administrative arrangement favored by interest-group liberalism tends toward creation of new privilege instead. Urban redevelopment programs based upon federal support of private plans do not necessarily, but do all too easily, become means by which the building industry regularizes itself. A Federal Housing Administration run essentially by the standards of the National Association of Real Estate Boards (NAREB) became a major escape route for the middle class to leave the city for suburbia rather than a means of providing housing for all. Urban redevelopment, operating for nearly two decades on a principle of local government and local developer specification of federal policy, has been used as an effective instrument for Negro removal.[40] Organizing councils for the poverty program have become first and foremost means of elevating individual spokesmen for the poor and of determining which churches and neighborhood organizations shall be the duly recognized channels of legitimate demand. Encouragement of organization among Negroes and the white and nonwhite poor is important. Early recognition of the few among many emerging leaders and organizations as legitimate administrators or policy-makers seriously risks destroying the process itself (more on this directly below).[41]

(3) Government by and through interest groups is in its impact conservative in almost every sense of that term. Part of its conservatism can be seen in another look at the two foregoing objections: Weakening of popular government and

[39] Truman, *op. cit.*, p. 42. For a profound appreciation of the public power of private authorities in occupational licensing, see York Willbern, "Professionalization in State Local Government: Too Little or Too Much?" *Public Administration Review*, Winter, 1954. See also Miller, *op. cit.*

[40] See below, Chapter 9.
[41] See also below, Chapter 8.

support of privilege are, in other words, two aspects of conservatism. It is beside the point to argue that these consequences are not intended. A third dimension of conservatism, stressed here separately, is the simple conservatism of resistance to change. David Truman, who has certainly not been a strong critic of self-government by interest groups, has, all the same, identified a general tendency of established agency-group relationships to be "highly resistant to disturbance." He continues:

New and expanded functions are easily accommodated, provided they develop and operate through existing channels of influence and do not tend to alter the relative importance of those influences. Disturbing changes are those that modify either the content or the relative strength of the component forces operating through an administrative agency. In the face of such changes, or the threat of them, the "old line" agency is highly inflexible.[42]

If this is already a tendency in a pluralistic system, then agency-group relationships must be all the more inflexible to the extent that the relationship is official and legitimate.

The war-on-poverty pattern, even in its early stages, provides a rich testing ground. I observed above that early official co-optation of poverty leaders creates privilege before, and perhaps instead of, alleviating poverty. Another side of this war is the war the established welfare groups are waging against the emergence of the newly organizing social forces. Old and established groups doing good works might naturally look fearfully upon the emergence of competing, perhaps hostile, groups. That is well and good—until their difference is one of "who shall be the government?" Conservatism them becomes necessary as a matter of survival.[43]

The tendency toward the extreme conservatism of sharing legitimate power with private organizations is possibly stronger still in programs more strictly economic. Adams and Gray reviewed figures on assignment of FM ratio broadcasting licenses and found that as of 1955, 90 per cent of the FM sta-

---

[42] Truman, *op. cit.*, pp. 467–68.
[43] *Cf.* Witcover and Knoll, *op. cit.* and below, Chapter 8.

tions were merely "little auxiliaries" of large AM networks. They also note that the same pattern was beginning to repeat itself in FCC licensing of UHF television channels.[44] The mythology may explain this as a case of "interest-group power," but that begs the question. Whatever power was held by the network was based largely on the commitment the FCC implied in the original grants of licenses. Having granted exclusive privileges to private groups in the public domain (in this case the original assignment of frequencies) without laying down practical conditions for perpetual public retention of the domain itself, the FCC had actually given over sovereignty. The companies acquired property rights and legally vested interests in the grant that interfere enormously with later efforts to affect the grant. Thus, any FCC attempt to expand the communications business through FM would deeply affect the positions and "property" of the established AM companies and networks. Issuing FM licenses to new organizations would have required an open assault on property as well as the established market relations. Leaving aside all other judgments of the practice, it is clearly conservative.[45] Granting of licenses and other privileges unconditionally, and limiting sovereignty by allowing the marketing of properties to be influenced by the possession of the privilege, are practices also to be found in oil, in water power, in the newer sources of power, in transportation, in the "parity" programs of agriculture.

Wherever such practices are found there will also be found strong resistance to change. Already the pattern is repeating itself in form and consequences in the policies regarding our newest resource, outer space. As earlier observed, the private members of COMSAT very early in the life of the new corporation made arrangements to protect themselves against the impact of new developments on old facilities. In addition to

[44] Walter S. Adams and Horace Gray, *Monopoly in America* (New York: Macmillan, 1955), pp. 48–50. See also below, Chapter 5.

[45] *Cf.* Adams and Gray, pp. 44–46, and their discussion, from a different point of view, of the "abridgement of sovereignty by grants of privilege." See also Merle Fainsod *et al.*, *Government and the American Economy* (New York: W. W. Norton, 1959), pp. 400–404. They observe the same thing happening in television, and for the same reasons.

that, and more significantly here, the constituents of COMSAT have moved to exclude all other possible entrants and alternative ways of organizing the economics of space communication of the domestic scene. In response to the Ford Foundation's proposal for a separate satellite system for educational television, COMSAT officially moved to cut off any chance of a rival by (1) opposing Ford vigorously, (2) interpreting the statute and charter to be a grant of trust for the entire public interest in the field, (3) seeking a ruling to that effect from the FCC, (4) showing that stockholders in COMSAT and in the carrier members of COMSAT, such as A.T.&T., would be dealt an unfair blow, and (5) producing an alternative plan whereby the Ford system would be created within COMSAT, being underwritten by all the major carriers and "users" (i.e., the telephone and telegraph companies and the commercial networks).[46]

There are social and psychological mechanisms as well as economic and vested interests working against change. As programs are split off and allowed to establish self-governing relations with clientele groups, professional norms usually spring up, governing the proper ways of doing things. These rules-of-the-game heavily weight access and power in favor of the established interests, just as American parliamentary rules-of-the-game have always tended to make Congress a haven for classes in retreat. For example, as public health moved from a regulatory to a welfare concept, local health agencies put up impressive resistance against efforts to reorganize city and county health departments accordingly. Herbert Kaufman chronicles the vain forty-year reorganization effort in New York City.[47] An important psychological mechanism working

[46] See accounts in the *New York Times*, August 2 and August 29, 1966, and *Time* magazine, August 12, 1966, p. 38.

[47] Herbert Kaufman, "The New York City Health Centers," Interuniversity Case Program. Sayre and Kaufman, *op. cit.*, Chapter 19, generalize on this pattern. They visualize "islands of functional power" as the formal power structure of the city. Each island enjoys considerable autonomy, each is a system of administrators and their "satellite groups," each resists interactions with other islands. The big city is possibly in an advanced stage of what is observed here as an important tendency at the national level. Because of the tragic stalemate in the cities, these pro-

against change is one that can be found in criticism of the electoral devices of proportional and occupational representation. Proportional representation tends to rigidify whatever social cleavages first provide the basis for it, because it encourages social interests to organize, then perpetuates them by allowing them to become "constituencies." This is all the more true as interests actually become not merely groups but parties represented by name and bloc in a legislature.[48] Even in less formalized situations, legitimizing a group gives it the advantages of exposure and usage as well as direct power, access, and privilege.

THE NEW REPRESENTATION

Leaders in all democracies probably have at least one common trait: They are ambivalent toward political power. If their lives are dedicated to achieving it, their spirits are tied up with justifying it. American leaders possess this common trait to an uncommon degree. American leaders were, as a consequence, very late to insist upon expansion of the scope of government. That expansion did finally begin to take place, but it only intensified the ambivalence toward power: *With each significant expansion of government in the past century there has been a crisis of public authority.* Social movements, international crises, and varieties of lesser events may trigger off the expansion, but once it occurs in the United States the sense of distress is not ended but simply takes for a while a newer form.

nounced city patterns might serve as a better warning than my illustrations drawn from national practices. See also Herbert Kaufman, *Politics and Policies in State and Local Governments* (Englewood Cliffs: Prentice-Hall, 1963), Chapter 5. *Cf.* below, Chapter 7, on the "New Machines."

[48] *Cf.* Carl Friedrich, *Constitutional Government and Democracy* (Boston: Ginn, 1950), pp. 291–94. See also a classic critique of occupational representations by Paul H. Douglas, "Occupational versus Proportional Representation," *American Journal of Sociology*, Sept. 1932; and Truman, *op. cit.*, pp. 525–26. See also Georges Lavau, "Political Pressures by Interest Groups in France," in *Interest Groups on Four Continents*, ed. H. Ehrmann (Pittsburgh: University of Pittsburgh Press, 1958), pp. 82–84.

For *each such expansion of government and its ensuing crisis of authority has been accompanied by demands for equally significant expansion of representation.* Our ambivalence toward power has thus brought about regular improvements in the mechanisms of representation.[49]

The clearest case in point is the political aftermath of the first big revolution in Federal power, the regulatory revolution that began with the passage of the Interstate Commerce Act of 1887. The political results of the expansion were more immediate and effective than the economic consequences of the statutes themselves. The agrarian movements became the populist movement of the 1890's and the progressive movement of the 1900's. The call went out for congressional reform of rules, direct election of senators, reform in nominating processes, ballot reform, decentralization of House leadership. The results were dramatic: "Reed's Rules," Amendment XVII, the direct primary movement, the Australian ballot, the "Speaker Revolt." This was also the period of initial formation of national pressure groups.

In the Wilson period, progressivist expansion of government and revision of the mechanisms of representation were even more intimately interconnected: Female suffrage (Amendment XIX), the short ballot, initiative, referendum and recall, great extension of direct primaries, the commission form of city government, and the first and early demands for formal interest-representation—leading to formal sponsorship of the formation of the Chamber of Commerce and the farm bureau movement, the establishment of the separate Departments of Labor and Commerce, the first experiments with "self-regulation" during World War I industrial mobilization.

The Roosevelt Revolution involved similar relations between government and the demand for representation. The full expression of the pattern was delayed by World War II, but the immediate expression was profound and lasting. It was the theory and practice of the administrative process.[50] It is at this

[49] *Cf.* Lowi, Introductory Essay in *Legislative Politics U.S.A.* (Boston: Little, Brown, 1965); and Friedrich, *op. cit.,* Chapter 1.
[50] See especially below, Chapter 5.

point, as implied earlier, that political scientists and young
lawyers trained in the new sociological law became the high
priests. The progressive spirit had been replaced. Demands for
representation continued but in these new directions. Administrative law, especially the creation of new agencies, was at first
an expression of demands for representation of the new interests which lacked access in Congress and the courts. Interest-
group liberalism implied a further formalization and generalization of these particular demands for representation, just as
progressivism implied formalization of the earlier types of demands. Obviously the more traditional, progressive demands
did not end. Reapportionment, the slow coming of age of the
Negro politically and economically—beginning with white primary abolition—the politics leading up to the Administrative
Procedure Act, the congressional reforms of 1946 (La Follette-
Monroney Act) are all, in one way or another, traditional progressivist responses to expansion of governmental power. But
these reforms were nonetheless overshadowed by the newer
demands inspired and guided by interest-group liberalism. The
new halo words alone imply the extent to which the new type
of claim now dominates: "interest representation," "cooperation," "partnership," "self-regulation," "delegation of power,"
"local option," "grass roots," "creative federalism," "community
action," "maximum feasible participation," and that odd contribution from the New Left—which seems unable to escape established thought patterns—"participatory democracy."

In whatever form, the function of representation is the
same: to deal with the problem of power—to bring the democratic spirit into some kind of psychological balance with the
harsh reality of the coerciveness of government. But there the
similarity between progressivism and interest-group liberalism
ends. The ultimate consequences of the interest-group liberal
solutions are infinitely inferior to the solutions of progressivism. That proposition is precisely what this chapter attempted
to articulate and what the remainder of the volume is about.

The interest-group liberal solution to the problem of power
provides the system with stability by spreading a sense of representation. But it is the inferior solution because this kind of

representation comes at the probable expense of genuine flexibility, of democratic forms, and of legitimacy. The progressivist solutions built greater instabilities into the system by reducing the time lag between social change and the structure and policy of government. But that was supposedly the purpose of representation, and in the process the procedures of the system and the legitimacy of its policies were clearly more likely to be reinforced. Flexibility and legitimacy are likely to be further reduced by the oligopolistic character of the interest-group liberal's mechanisms of representation, because (1) the number of competitors is deliberately reduced to the most interested and best organized; (2) this tends to eliminate rather than encourage political competition; and (3) this is bound to involve some exchange of legitimacy for the false comfort of stability and the false impression that the problem of power has been solved.[51]

Finally, the interest-group liberal solution to the problem of power is inferior to the progressivist solution because it is basically antagonistic to formalism. All of the foregoing propositions tend to document this in one way or another; put in this general formulation they reveal still further the extent to which some profound requirements of democracy are being weakened.[52] The least evident, yet perhaps the most important, aspect of this is the antagonism of interest-group liberalism to law.[53] Traditional, progressivistic expansions of representation are predicated on the assumption that law is authoritative and that therefore one must seek to expand participation in the making of laws. The "new representation" extends the principle of representation over into administration, since it is predicated on the assumption that lawmaking bodies and conventional procedures cannot and ought not make law. This may be the most debilitative of all the features of interest-group liberalism, for it tends to derange almost all established relations and expectations in the democratic system. It renders formalism impossible. It impairs legitimacy by converting govern-

[51] See below, Chapter 10.
[52] See below, Chapter 10.
[53] See below, Chapters 5 and 10.

ment from a moralistic to a mechanistic institution. It impairs the self-correctiveness of positive law by the very flexibility of its broad policies and by the bargaining, co-optation, and incrementalism of its implementing processes. It impairs the very process of administration itself by delegating to administration alien materials—policies that are not laws. Interest-group liberalism seeks pluralistic government, in which there is no formal specification of means or of ends. In pluralistic government there is therefore no substance. Neither is there procedure. There is only process.

PART II

WHY LIBERAL GOVERNMENTS CANNOT PLAN

"You must first enable the government to control the governed; and in the next place oblige it to control itself."

James Madison

CHAPTER 4

THE ORIGIN AND FIRST CONSEQUENCES OF PLURALISTIC GOVERNMENT

Agriculture, Commerce, Labor

Liberal governments cannot plan. Planning requires the authoritative use of authority. Planning requires law, choice, priorities, moralities. Liberalism replaces planning with bargaining. Yet at bottom power is unacceptable without planning.

Application of pluralist principles in the construction of liberal government has made it possible for government to expand its efforts but not to assemble them. We can invent ingenious devices like the Executive Budget, the Executive Office of the President, Legislative Clearance, Program Budgeting, and Computerized Routines, but we do not use them to overcome the separatist tendencies and self-defeating proclivities of the independent functions. Liberal government seems to be flexible only on the first round of a response to political need. It allows for a certain expansion of functions to take place and then militates against any redistribution of those functions as needs change. New needs therefore result in expansions, never in planning. James Madison could have been writing for 1968 when he observed that government control and government self-control go together. The lack of rationale in our modern government has tended to vitiate its potential for good by sapping the strength and impairing the legitimacy of its authority.

Nowhere are the consequences of pluralist principles better seen than in those agencies in which the principles were first applied. Agriculture policy set the pattern of organizing the government along pluralist lines. Its influence spread far and wide, most notably to the Departments of Commerce and Labor, when these were created. Together the three provide the limiting extremes by which other programs and agencies can be analyzed. With these three departments one can begin to appreciate the extent to which the alienation of public authority has taken place, why it has taken place, and how this is reducing the capacity of modern government to govern responsibly, flexibly, and determinatively.

AGRICULTURE: THE NEW FEUDALISM

Agriculture is that field of American government where the distinction between public and private has come closest to being completely eliminated. This has been accomplished not by public expropriation of private domain—as would be true of the nationalization that Americans fear—but by private expropriation of public authority. That is the feudal pattern: fusion of all statuses and functions and governing through rigid but personalized fealties. In modern dress, that was the corporativistic way, which has been recently revived in a slightly revised form by the French Right. It is also the pluralist way, the way of the so-called Left in the United States. However, the best definition is one which puts the reader in the very presence of the thing.

THE PRESENT ESTATE OF AGRICULTURE

On December 18, 1963, President Johnson summoned a conference of the leaders of major agriculture interests and interest groups. These representatives were asked to formulate a program by which they and their supporters could be served and regulated. The President's call for an agriculture congress was followed on January 31 with a Farm Message. In the message the President proposed the establishment of a bipartisan commission to investigate the concentration of power in the food industry and "how this greatly increased concentration of power is affecting farmers, handlers and consumers. . . ." Such investigations are always popular in farm states in helping spread the blame for high prices despite large subsidies. As one Administration spokesman explained, "We're not making a whipping boy out of anybody, but we're receiving repeated charges that certain retailers are setting market prices and it is clear that some chains do have large concentrations of market power." In the same message the President also called for new legislation to strengthen farmer cooperatives, to encourage their expansion through merger and acquisition, and to provide them with further exemptions from the antitrust laws.

The summoning of an agriculture congress was a call to agriculture to decide for itself what it wants from government. The President's attack in his Farm Message on concentration of market power, coupled with his proposals for expanded and stronger farm cooperatives, was obviously not an attack so much on concentration itself as on the intervention of nonagricultural power into strictly agricultural affairs.

That agricultural affairs should be handled strictly within the agricultural community is a basic political principle established before the turn of the century and maintained since then without serious reexamination. As a result, agriculture has become neither public nor private enterprise. It is a system of self-government in which each leading farm interest controls a segment of agriculture through a delegation of national sovereignty. Agriculture has emerged as a largely self-governing federal estate within the Federal structure of the United States.

President Johnson recognized these facts within three weeks of his accession when he summoned the conference of agricultural leaders. The resulting concession to agriculture's self-government was the wheat-cotton bill of 1964. Because cotton

supports were too high, the cotton interests wrote a bill providing for a subsidy to mills of six to eight cents a pound in order
to keep them competitive with foreign cotton and domestic
rayon without touching the price supports. On the other hand,
wheat supports were too low because wheat farmers in the
1963 referendum had overwhelmingly rejected President Kennedy's plan to provide some Federal regulation along with
supports. The wheat section of the new act called for a program whereby wheat farmers would voluntarily comply with
acreage reduction for subsidies of up to seventy cents a bushel
but without the Federal supply regulations. The press called
this a major legislative victory for Mr. Johnson. But the victory
really belonged to organized cotton and wheat and testified to
the total acceptance by the President, press, and public of the
principle that private agriculture interests alone govern agriculture. It is a sturdy principle; its inheritance by President
Johnson was through a line unbroken by personality or party
in the White House. For example, in one of President Kennedy's earliest major program messages to Congress, on March
16, 1961, he proposed:

> The Soil Conservation and Domestic Allotment Act . . . should
> be amended to provide for the establishment of national farmer
> advisory committees for every commodity or group of related com-
> modities for which a new supply adjustment program is planned
> [as proposed in the same message]. Members of the committees
> would be elected by the producers of the commodities involved or
> their appropriate representatives. In consultation with the Secretary
> of Agriculture, they could be charged with the responsibility for
> considering and recommending individual commodity pro-
> grams. . . .
>
> In order to insure effective farmer participation in the admin-
> istration of farm programs on the local level, the Secretary of Agri-
> culture is directed to revitalize the county and local farmer com-
> mittee system and to recommend such amendments as may be
> necessary to safeguard such farmer participation.

ORIGINS IN ECONOMICS AND TACTICS

The reasons for agricultural self-government are deep-
rooted, and the lessons to be drawn from it are vital. For a

century agriculture has been out of joint with American economic development. Occasional fat years have only created unreal expectations, making the more typical lean years less bearable. As industries concentrated, discovered the economies of scale and how to control their markets, agriculture remained decentralized and subject to the market. As industries showed increasing capacity to absorb technology and to use it to increase profit, agriculture took on technology only with net debt. Profit from increased productivity was either neutralized with lower prices or absorbed by the processing, distributing, and transporting industries interposed between agriculture and its markets. After the Civil War America's largest and most basic industry was never for long out of trouble. At the beginning of World War I, for example, net farm income was $3.6 billion. By 1919, it was $9.3 billion; but two years later it was back down to $3.7 billion. It rose slowly to $6.1 billion in 1920–30 and had fallen off to $1.9 billion by 1932. At a higher level, these fluctuations have beset agriculture since World War II as well. The only things stable about agriculture have been (1) its declining relative importance in the census and in the economy, (2) the reverence it enjoys in the American mythology, and (3) the political power it possesses despite (1) and largely because of (2).

Organized agriculture was early to discover the value of political power as a counterweight to industrial wealth. The land grant and homesteading acts were followed by governmental services in research, quarantine, and education. But continuing distress despite governmental support led to bolder demands. First the movement was for a redistribution of wealth and power toward agriculture. As a debtor class, farmers saw inflation as the solution; William Jennings Bryan was one of many spokesmen for cheaper money and easier credit. Farmers also sought government regulation of those economic forces they had identified as the causes of their problems. The monopolies, the railroads, the grain merchants and other processors, the banks, and the brokers were to be deprived of market power by dissolution or by severe restraints upon the use of that power. Finally farmers sought solutions by emulating the business system: almost simultaneously they hit upon the cooperative to restrain domestic trade, and international dumping over high tariff walls to restrain international trade.

All these mechanisms failed the farmers. The blunderbuss—inflation of the whole economy—failed both for want of enough legislation and because more and more of the national debt was held by the industrial rich. Regulation of industry failed for want of will and power to administer it; a governing elite opposed to inflating the business system could not be expected to dismantle it. International dumping never was given the test; Coolidge and Hoover vetoed the Smoot-Hawley tariff bills that would "make the tariff work for agriculture." The cooperative movement did not fail; it simply did not succeed on a large enough scale.

By a process of elimination, organized agriculture turned then to another way: *the regulation of itself*. In the Democratic party of 1930 and the Democratic party philosophy, to be called the New Deal, agriculture found an eager handmaiden. And in the modest government assistance programs of the pre-New Deal period the appropriate instrumentalities and precedents were found. After the 1932 election all that remained was to ratify in legislation the agreements already reached. The system created then has remained with only a few marginal additions and alterations. Bitter political conflicts within the agriculture community have been fought out over the margins, but on the system itself there is almost total consensus among the knowledgeable minority and total apathy and ignorance among the nonagricultural majority.

The principle of self-regulation might have taken several forms, the most likely one being a national system of farm representation within a farmer's type of NRA. Instead, a more elaborate and complicated system of "cooperation" or local self-government developed largely for constitutional reasons. There was already experience with local districts in the Extension Service that had become a proven way for the Federal government to get around the special constitutional problem of regulating agriculture. Agriculture was the most "local" of the manufactures the government was attempting to reach. The appearance if not the reality of decentralizing federal programs through local, farmer-elected committees helped to avoid straining the interstate commerce clause and to escape the political charge of regimentation.

Eventually, many separate programs were created within the government-agriculture complex. Each constituted a system in and of itself. The programs were independently administered and often had conflicting results. But underneath all the complexity of parity, forestry, conservation, electrification, education, extension, and credit there was a simple principle: it amounted to the loan of governmental sovereignty to the leadership of a private sector to accomplish what other sectors could accomplish privately. Agriculture was so decentralized and dispersed that private, voluntary agreements to manipulate markets were obviously too difficult to reach and impossible to sustain. Therefore it was not going to be possible to emulate business. So, in a travesty of the Declaration of Independence, to secure these rights governments were instituted among farmers. Administrative agencies were created to facilitate agreements, and, once reached, public authority was expected to be employed where necessary to sustain them.

THE SYSTEM: BUILDING ON LOCAL COMMITTEES [1]

The prototype, the Federal Extension Service, is "cooperative" in the sense that it shares the expense of farm improvement with the States, the land-grant colleges, the county governments, and the local associations of farmers. The county agent is actually employed by the local associations, which are required by law. In the formative years, the aid of local cham-

---

[1] The following studies were invaluable in locating the several separate agriculture systems, although none of the authors necessarily shares my treatment of the cases or the conclusions I have drawn: Grant McConnell, *The Decline of Agrarian Democracy* (Berkeley: University of California Press, 1953); M. R. Benedict, *Farm Policies of the United States, 1790–1950* (New York: Twentieth Century Fund, 1953); Charles Hardin, *The Politics of Agriculture* (Glencoe: The Free Press, 1952). However, the most important source was the U.S. Code. The secret of agriculture success, as well as the significance of interest-group liberalism, lies in the extent to which pluralism is written into the statutes. No specific citations are made in the chapter because each system was pieced together from elements of all of the above sources.

bers of commerce was enlisted; the local association was the "farm bureau" of the chamber. In order to coordinate local activities and to make more effective claims for additional outside assistance, these farm bureaus were organized into State farm bureau federations. The American Farm Bureau Federation, formed at the Agriculture College of Cornell University in 1919, was the offshoot. A filial relationship between farm bureau, land-grant college, and the Extension Service continues to this day. This transformation of an administrative arrangement into a political system has been repeated in almost all agriculture programs since that time. The Extension Service exercises few sanctions over the States and colleges, which in turn leave the localities alone. All are quick to scream "Federal encroachment!" at the mere suggestion that the Department of Agriculture should increase supervision or investigation, or that it should attempt to coordinate Extension programs with other Federal activities.

As other agriculture programs came along, most were similarly organized. Any inconsistency of purpose or impact among programs has been treated as nonexistent or beyond the jurisdiction of any one agency. The Soil Conservation Service operates through its soil conservation districts, of which there were 2,936 in 1963, involving 96 per cent of the nation's farms. These districts are actually considered units of local government, and each is in fact controlled by its own farmer-elected committee, which is not to be confused with other farmer associations or committees. Agreements between the farmer and the Service for acre-by-acre soil surveys, for assistance in instituting soil-conserving practices, and for improving productivity are actually made between the farmer and the district committee. Enforcement of the agreements is handled also by the district committee.

Additional aid to the farmer channels through the cooperatives, which are in turn controlled by farmer-elected boards. Four out of five farmers belong to at least one co-op. The Farmer Cooperative Service touches the farmer only through the boards of directors of the cooperatives as the boards see fit.

When the stakes get larger the pattern of local self-government remains the same. Price support, the "parity program," is run by the thousands of farmer-elected county committees of farmers, which function alongside but quite independent of the other local committees. Acreage allotments to bring supply down and prices up are apportioned among the States by the Agricultural Stabilization and Conservation Service. (The ASCS is the lineal descendant, thrice removed, of the AAA.) State committees of farmers apportion the allotment among the counties. The farmer-elected county Stabilization and Conservation Committees receive the county allotment. The county committees made the original acreage allotments among individual farmers back in the 1930's, and they now make new allotments, bring about any adjustments and review complaints regarding allotments, determine whether quotas have been complied with, inspect and approve storage facilities, and act as the court of original jurisdiction on violations of price support rules and on eligibility for parity payments. The committees are also vitally important in campaigning for the two-thirds-vote acceptance of high price support referenda. Congress determines the general level of support, and the Secretary of Agriculture proclaims the national acreage quotas for adjusting supply to guaranteed price. But the locally elected committees stand between the farmer and the Congress, the Secretary, the ASCS, and the Commodity Credit Corporation.

In agriculture credit, local self-government is found in even greater complexity. The Farmers Home Administration (FHA, but not to be confused with Federal Housing Administration) and the Farm Credit Administration are, in essence, banks; and as banks they are unique. Credit extended by the FHA is almost entirely controlled by local FHA farmer committees. There is one per county, and again these are not to be confused with the other committees. The much larger Farm Credit Administration, an independent agency since 1953, was within the Department of Agriculture from 1938 until 1953 and was autonomous before that. But its departmental status is irrelevant, because it also operates through local farmer control.

There is not one but three "bodies politic" within the FCA. (1) Membership in the mortgage loan "body politic" requires the purchase of stock in a local land bank association. Broad participation is so strongly desired that it has been made mandatory. The farmer borrower must purchase an amount of voting stock equal to 5 per cent of his loan in one of the 750 land bank associations. (2) In the short-term loan "body politic," 487 separate production credit associations own virtually all the stock, and the farmer-owners or their representatives pass upon all requests for loans within their respective districts. It is a point of pride in the FCA that ownership and control of these banks has passed from government to local, private hands. (3) The third "body politic" within the FCA is the cooperative system, controlled by elected farmer-directors and operated by credit available from the FCA's Central Bank for Cooperatives and its 12 district Banks for Cooperatives.

THE TEN SYSTEMS AND POLITICS

Taking all the agriculture programs within or closely associated with the Department of Agriculture, there are at least ten separate, autonomous, local self-governing systems. These account for the overwhelming proportion of government activities, expenditures and capital transactions in the field of agriculture. In fiscal 1962, $5.6 billion of the total $6.7 billion Department of Agriculture expenditures were administered through one or another of these self-governing systems. In calendar 1962, an additional $5.8 billion in loans were handled similarly. This $11.4 billion constitutes a rather large proportion of the total of federal activity in the domestic economy, and the local and district farmer committees constitute the vital element in the administration of the $11.4 billion. To the individual farmer, the local outpost of each of these systems is the Department of Agriculture, perhaps the government itself. Loyalty is always most likely to focus upon the spot where authoritative decisions are made.

Due to the special intimacy between federal agriculture programs and private agriculture, each administrative organization becomes a potent political instrumentality. Each of the self-governing local units becomes one important point in a definable political system which both administers a program and maintains the autonomy of that program in face of all other political forces emanating from other agriculture systems, from antagonistic farm and non-farm interests, from Congress, from the Secretary, and from the President.

The politics of each of these self-governing programs is comprised of a triangular trading pattern, with each point complementing and supporting the other two. The three points are: the central agency, a congressional committee or subcommittee, and the local or district farmer committees. The latter are also usually the grass roots element of a national interest group.

The classic case is Extension. The Extension Service at the center of this system is supported in Congress by the long-tenure "Farm Bureau" members of the agriculture committees, particularly in the Senate. The grass roots segment is composed of the Farm Bureau Federation and the local extension committees around which the Farm Bureau was originally organized and to which the Bureau continues to contribute assistance. Further interest group support comes from two intimately related organizations, the Association of Land-Grant Colleges and Universities and its tributary, the National Association of County Agricultural Agents.

Another such triangle unites the Soil Conservation Service with Congress primarily through the Subcommittee on Agriculture of the House Committee on Appropriations, through which SCS managed to double its appropriations between 1940 and the early postwar years while severely limiting the related activities of the FHA and the old AAA and its successors. The third point is the local soil conservation districts, which speak individually to the local congressman and nationally to Congress and the President through the very energetic National Association of Soil Conservation Districts. The SCS draws further support from the Soil Conservation Society of America (mainly professionals) and the Izaak Walton League of America (formerly Friends of the Land, mainly urban well-wishers).

Similar but much more complex forms characterize the price-support system. The Agriculture Stabilization and Conservation Service ties into Congress through the eight (formerly ten) commodity subcommittees of the House Agriculture Committee and the dozens of separately organized interest groups representing each of the single commodities. (Examples: National Cotton Council, American Wool Growers Association, American Cranberry Growers Association.) These in turn draw from the local price-support committees.

As in geometry and engineering, so in politics the triangle seems to be the most stable type of structure. There is an immense capacity in each agriculture system, once created, to maintain itself and to resist any type of representation except its own. These self-governing agriculture systems have such institutional legitimacy that they have become practically insulated from the three central sources of democratic political responsibility: (1) Within the Executive, they are autonomous. Secretaries of Agriculture have tried and failed to consolidate or even to coordinate related programs. (2) Within Congress, they are sufficiently powerful within their own domain to be able to exercise an effective veto or to create stalemate. (3) Agriculture activities and agencies are almost totally removed from the view of the general public. Upon becoming the exclusive province of those who are most directly interested in them, programs are first split off from general elective political responsibility. (Throughout the 1950's, for example, Victor Anfuso of Brooklyn was the only member of the House Committee on Agriculture from a non-farm constituency.) After specialization there is total submersion.

THE CORPORATE STATE

Important cases illustrate the consequences. In fact, in even a casual reading of the history of agriculture policy such cases are impossible to avoid.

Case 1. In 1947, Secretary of Agriculture Clinton P. Anderson proposed a consolidation of all soil conservation, price-support, and FHA programs into one committee system with a direct line from the committees to the Secretary. Bills were prepared providing for consolidation within the price-support committees. Contrary bills were produced providing for consolidation under soil conservation districts. Stalemate, 1947. In 1948, a leading farm senator proposed consolidation of the whole effort under the local associations of the Extension Service. Immediately a House farm leader introduced a bill diametrically opposed. The result, continuing stalemate.

Case 2. In Waco, Texas, on October 14, 1952, presidential candidate Eisenhower said, "I would like to see in every county all Federal farm agencies under the same roof." Pursuant to this promise, Secretary of Agriculture Ezra Taft Benson issued a series of orders during early 1953 attempting to bring about consolidation of local units as well as unification at the top, mainly by appointing some professional agriculture employees to membership in local committees. Finally, amid cries of "sneak attack" and "agricrat," Benson proclaimed that "any work on the further consolidation of county and state offices . . . shall be suspended."

Case 3. From the very beginning, Secretary Benson sought to abandon rigid price supports and bring actual supports closer to market prices. In 1954, as he was beginning to succeed, Congress enacted a "commodity set-aside" by which $2.5 billion of surplus commodities already held by the government were declared to be a "frozen reserve" for national defense. Since the Secretary's power to cut price supports depends heavily upon the amount of government-owned surplus carried over from previous years, the commodity set-aside was a way of freezing parity as well as reserves. Benson eventually succeeded in reducing supports on the few commodities over which he had authority. But thanks to the set-aside, Congress, between fiscal 1952 and 1957, helped increase the value of commodities held by the government from $1.1 billion to $5.3 billion. What appeared, therefore, to be a real Republican policy shift amounted to no more than giving back with one hand what had been taken away by the other.

Case 4. President Eisenhower's first budget sought to abolish farm home-building and improvement loans by eliminating the budgetary request and by further requesting that the 1949 authorization law be allowed to expire. Congress overrode his request in 1953 and each succeeding year, and the President answered Congress with a year-by-year refusal to implement the farm housing program. In 1956, when the President asked again explicitly for elimination of the program, he was rebuffed. The Subcommittee on Housing of the House Banking and Currency Committee added to the President's omnibus housing bill a renewal of the farm housing program, plus an authorization for $500 million in loans over a five-year period, and the bill passed with a Congressional mandate to use the funds. They were used thereafter at a rate of about $75 million a year.

Case 5. On March 16, 1961, President Kennedy produced a "radically different" farm program in a special message to Congress. For the first time in the history of price supports, the bill called for surplus control through quotas placed on bushels, tons, or other units, rather than on acreage. An acreage allotment allows the farmer to produce as much as he can on the reduced acreage in cultivation. For example, in the first ten years or so of acreage control, acreage under cultivation dropped by about 4 per cent, while actual production rose by 15 per cent. The Kennedy proposal called for national committees of farmers to be elected to work out the actual program. This more stringent type of control was eliminated from the omnibus bill in the Agriculture Committees of both chambers and there were no attempts to restore them during floor debate. Last-minute efforts by Secretary Orville L. Freeman to up the ante, offering to raise wheat supports from $1.79 to $2.00, were useless. Persistence by the Administration led eventually to rejection by wheat farmers in 1963 of all high price supports and acreage controls.

The politics of this rejected referendum is of general significance. Despite all the blandishments and inducements of the Administration the farmer had his way. The local price-support committees usually campaign in these referenda for the Department of Agriculture, but this time they did not. And thousands of small farmers, eligible to vote for the first time, joined with the local leadership to help defeat the referendum.

It is not so odd that wheat farmers would reject a proposal that aimed to regulate them more strictly than before. What is odd is that only wheat farmers are allowed to decide the matter. It seems that in agriculture, as in many other fields, the regulators are powerless without the consent of the regulated.

ECONOMIC POLICY FOR INDUSTRIAL SOCIETY: THE EMPTY HOUSES

The Departments of Commerce and Labor, along with Agriculture, are very special units of government. From the very beginning, these departments were founded upon their dependence, not their independence. Widely known as "clientele departments," they are organized around an identifiable sector of the economy and are *legally* obliged to develop and maintain an orientation toward the interests that comprise this sector. While there are other governmental agencies of the same type, these are the only three of Cabinet status and scope. All other departments of Cabinet rank are organized around some governmental process or function rather than around a set of persons legally identified as desirable.

As clientele agencies the Departments of Commerce and Labor are not meant to be governing agencies except in some marginal way. They are and were meant to be agencies of representation. They were, in other words, set up not to govern but to be governed. In a manner not unlike the early German and Italian Councils of Corporations, these departments provide "functional representation," to be contrasted to the geographical representation provided for in Congress under the Constitution. With Agriculture, these departments are three Economic Parliaments; they constitute a true Fourth Estate in our governing order. Since Agriculture possesses many powers along with its representation function, largely because it represents the class in retreat, Commerce and Labor are left as the pure cases of functional representation.

The Departments of Commerce and Labor were founded simultaneously in 1903 as a single Department of Commerce and Labor "to foster, promote, and develop the foreign and domestic commerce, the mining, manufacturing, shipping, and fishing industries, and the transportation facilities of the United States." But this arrangement was not at all satisfactory to the newly organizing AFL, which rightly saw itself as the poor relative in the family. Labor had been seeking representation in a Cabinet department for many years. They had taken only minor satisfaction in the Bureau of Labor, established in the Department of Interior in 1884; and no improvement was seen in making that Bureau an independent but non-Cabinet agency in 1888.

Labor was not to get its full representation until 1913, when the separate Department of Labor was created to "foster, promote, and develop the welfare of the wage earners of the United States, to improve their working conditions, and to advance their opportunities for profitable employment."

Merged or separate, however, the entire history of Commerce and Labor attests to their special character and function in the governmental scheme. From the beginning they were both "feedback" agencies. Both were charged with any and all research and statistical work necessary to make certain that the problems and needs of their "clients" were known at every turn. The original Bureau of Labor, a research agency, was the core of the new Department, and long after Cabinet elevation references were frequently made to the "Department of Labor Statistics." Commerce always housed our census, geographical surveys, weights and measures, domestic and international business surveys, and other research activities essential to commercial enterprise.

While the pattern of development has not been exactly the same in the two departments, neither has departed from its original responsibility for being an official collectivity of unofficial economic interests.

As the national government grew in size and power, these two departments grew also, but consistently in a way reflecting their special legal and political character: they grew through expansion of services and promotional activities. Neither department took on more than one or two of the functions involved in the new relationships between government and the economy. The revolution of the modern state bypassed them almost completely.[2]

COMMERCE: GOVERNMENT ITALIAN STYLE

Functional representation in the Department of Commerce quickly expanded after 1903 in response to business needs. To its research activities was very early added the mission of encouraging business representation in government through one of the most significant of business institutions, the trade association. Trade associations, which were just beginning to form in significant numbers after 1903, are essentially, as observed earlier, legalized restraints of trade. Each serves its members and helps "regularize" relations among competitors by sharing information, eliminating "cutthroat competition," standardizing products, pooling advertising, and so on.

The Department of Commerce fostered the trade associations where they already existed and helped organize them where they did not yet exist. Thus the Department took the initiative in founding the U.S. Chamber of Commerce. Without official endorsement in 1912, the fusion of local chambers into one national business association would more than likely never have taken place. Most of the negotiating sessions among local leaders, the National Association of Manufacturers, and others were arranged by, and took place in, the office of the Secretary of Commerce and Labor. The final organization charter was written there.

The practice of official recognition and representation of trade associations in the inner processes of policy formulation was established, very much in a manner to anticipate NRA, during the war years of the Wilson Administration. This was fostered and given doctrinal support in the 1920's, primarily by Secretary of Commerce Herbert Hoover. In 1924, Secretary Hoover observed:

[2] See, for example, Chapter 5, below.

Legislative action is always clumsy—it is incapable of adjustment to shifting needs. . . . Three years of study and intimate contact with associations of economic groups convince me that there lies within them a great moving impulse toward betterment.[3]

Even then the vision was one of codes of business practice formulated by trade association processes and promulgated by the Department of Commerce. This Hoover saw as "the strong beginning of a new force in the business world." [4]

These relationships were further formalized early in the New Deal when Roosevelt's first Secretary of Commerce organized the Business Advisory Council to guide the Department on "matters affecting the relations of the Department and business." This group, under the Kennedy name of Business Council, remains central to the *modus operandi* in the Department. During the 1950's a new agency, the Business and Defense Services Administration (BDSA), was set up around a vast network of specialized business advisory committees to determine cold war industrial policies.

LABOR: LITTLE SIR ECHO

Although growth in the Department of Labor produced a different pattern, it fulfilled the same purpose of bringing private interests into the interior processes of government. Here it did not take the form of fostering a trade association movement because, ironically, labor was more laissez faire than business. Labor unions lacked status, but they had their "magna carta" in the Clayton Act and were, following Gompers, officially opposed to government intervention in the affairs of collective bargaining.

As a consequence, the Department remained quite small, and the primary addition to statistics in its functional representation was the evolution of the office of the Secretary itself. During the first 20 years, that Cabinet post was filled with people taken directly from the leadership ranks of organized labor. The appointment of Frances Perkins, Louis Schwellenbach, and Maurice Tobin during the New Deal-Fair Deal period did

[3] Quoted in McConnell, *op. cit.*, p. 66.
[4] *Loc. cit.*

not really constitute a change from this tradition since labor representation continued to be lodged in the office of the Secretary. And the recent role of the Secretary in intervening in disputes, settling strikes, and helping with guidelines is a natural result of the Department's evolution.

COMMERCE, LABOR, AND THE MAINSTREAM

The histories of these two Departments present a stunning contrast to the history of American government. The twentieth-century political revolution has erected an enormous apparatus for public control of economic life, and the end is apparently not in sight. Yet, the Departments of Commerce and Labor have been bypassed almost altogether. As clientele agencies they are simply not to be entrusted by anyone with significant direct powers over persons and property. The existence of functional representation meant that the growth of new functions of government would almost have to take place outside the Cabinet and, therefore, in a piecemeal and uncoordinated fashion.

The original Department of Commerce and Labor included a Bureau of Corporations, armed with power to make the Sherman Antitrust Act more effective. Within a decade this had become the core of an independent Federal Trade Commission, and its removal took from Commerce the only significant regulatory and planning powers it was ever to have. One by one, and with increasing frequency, new powers and agencies of public power over business were created outside the Department and outside the Cabinet. Regulation of railroads in the ICC predated Commerce by 16 years. However, positive planning for a national railway system, a function not necessarily consistent with rate regulation, also passed to ICC when the rails were returned to private ownership after 1920. For 46 years this anomalous situation continued, until the new Transportation Department was created—outside Commerce, independent of and equal to Commerce, larger than Commerce, too late to influence the shape of transportation.

Radio communication, from the beginning a part of commerce near the very center of public domain, was also from the beginning made the responsibility of a new agency—outside and independent of Commerce. Commerce got a small piece of civil aeronautics control under the 1934 Act, but by 1938 even this had been lost to the semiautonomous Civil Aeronautics Administration and then to the fully autonomous Federal Aviation Agency. The entire realm of securities, credit, banking, and currency are outside Commerce. The power industry, including civilian atomic development, developed its own, non-Cabinet agencies.

True, Commerce did get the Maritime Administration in 1950, but this is a semiautonomous subsidizing agency with an altogether independent tradition and constituency. The Bureau of Public Roads is Commerce's only significant traditional exercise of commerce power, and it is clear that the Secretary's authority over the Bureau is almost nonexistent. For example, the April 8, 1967 release of $1.1 billion in highway construction funds was authorized by the President and the Budget Director without any reference whatsoever to the Secretary of Commerce.

Governmental responses to the civil rights revolution have also bypassed Commerce, despite the deep involvement of civil rights laws in business decisions. The only part of the historic 1964 Civil Rights Act going to Commerce was the Community Relations Service, which is essentially a center for communications, conciliation, and conference holding. The only part of the New Frontier-Great Society in which Commerce has participated has been the Area Redevelopment Administration, an important but relatively declining feature of the new social legislation which, by 1965, as the Economic Development Administration, had become essentially a public works program. The Appalachia Program was developed in Commerce but immediately became the property of the Appalachian states. In sum, almost every significant commerce power of the Federal government is lodged somewhere other than in Commerce.

The Department of Labor is a pint-sized version of the same story. On the eve of the Roosevelt Revolution, Labor was a microscopic Cabinet department whose only significant governing activity was the Immigration and Naturalization Service. (This unusual responsibility for controlling the noncitizen competitors for jobs comprised 80% of the Department's budget.) During the 1930's government expanded its relation to the laboring man in many ways, but little of this involved the laboring man's department. On the contrary, the Department declined relative to virtually every other sector of public activity.

Over the protest of Frances Perkins, almost all New Deal labor programs escaped her department. The 1934 railway labor legislation came early in her incumbency and set the tone for what was to follow. A board was set up with 36 representatives, outside Labor, to deal with railway labor disputes in a gray area somewhere between private arbitration and public adjudication. The National Labor Relations Board became an independent commission. All but one of the social security programs, the least important one, were organized outside the Department of Labor. The National Bituminous Coal Commission, with its many labor responsibilities, escaped both Labor and Commerce.

The only major governmental responsibilities entrusted to Labor by Roosevelt were the regulatory programs under the Walsh-Healy and Fair Labor Standards Acts, now administered by the one Wages and Hours and Public Contracts Division. But while Labor was gaining those tasks, it was losing still more. Of its four original core jurisdictions—labor statistics, immigration, conciliation, and children—Labor lost as follows: immigration went to Justice in 1940; the Children's Bureau went to the Federal Security Agency (now HEW) in 1946; the Federal Mediation and Conciliation Service was converted by the Taft-Hartley Act into an independent agency. Labor even lost the Bureau of Employment Security in 1939, regaining it in 1950 only after a long struggle.

In general, Labor has participated almost as little as Commerce in the social revolution of the past decade. This includes almost all the most significant features of the New Frontier-Great Society programs. OEO, VISTA, and the antidiscrimination provisions of the civil rights and antipoverty legislation are in the labor field but not in the Labor Department. About half of the manpower training program of 1962 comprises all of Labor's share of the government explosion of the 1960's.

PLURALISTIC POWER AND PLURALISTIC GOVERNMENT

In 1967 the President made a serious but vain proposal to merge once again the Departments of Commerce and Labor, just over half a century after their original union was dissolved. Some types of merger can be significant. Merger of the National Guard with the Reserve would be significant. Merger of Nassau County with New York City would be significant. The very insignificance of the proposed Commerce-Labor merger raises all sorts of fundamental questions about the politics and administration of economic policy in the national government of the United States.

Nothing possible could have been changed by making a duplex out of the House of Labor and the House of Commerce. Nothing would have been subtracted except one voice from Cabinet meetings. Nothing would have been added except frustrated expectations. No additional order, coordination, purpose, or policy could have come out of the merger *because the really important controls over economic life would not have been involved.*

This only barely suggests the state of things. The insignificance of the Commerce and Labor Departments is a monument to the overwhelming innocence of the liberal spirit in America, which has justified the tangle of government controls as necessary for maximum flexibility, maximum expertise, and maximum insurance for keeping control "out of politics." The real economic powers of government are nonpolitical if Humpty-Dumpty is your lexicographer. They seem flexible only because they are numerous. They seem rational only because they are specialized. Control over the American economic system is split up among the Treasury, the Budget Bureau, the Council of Economic Advisers through the President, the Joint Committee on Internal Revenue Taxation, the Federal Reserve Board, the Social Security System, the ten or more agriculture systems, the many specialized regulatory agencies, the Office of the Secretary of Defense—and others. All of them exist separately and independently. There is hardly a scintilla of central control, because no such control could ever be entrusted to any one of them. No governing institution possesses central control, because in the liberal state a virtue is made of its absence.

Commerce and Labor are on the periphery still further because they were captured by too narrow a range of interests. As a consequence their very existence works a positive harm. They have done little more than help prevent expansion of the Cabinet toward an attempt at central control. And the two departments not only helped prevent development of an integrated and rational economic policy establishment; the harm goes further. The processes of functional representation in Labor and Commerce have helped to blind national leadership to the need for integration by creating and reporting "business consensus" and "labor solidarity" when the only consensus was that among the very special interests established therein. Merger of Commerce and Labor would have created false hopes and expectations. A bold approach to economic policy can be begun only with their *abolition*.

There will also be little rationality to national economic policy until somehow agriculture is integrated, and this is an even more difficult problem, because the Department of Agriculture administers real government programs and therefore cannot simply be abolished. Political responsibility and the prospect of planning were destroyed when agriculture policy-making was parceled out to the most interested parties. No progress toward correcting that situation can be made until it is fully realized that over $10 billion of government-agriculture intimacy per year is too much agriculture policy to be entrusted to agriculturalists.

Reversing the situation in agriculture is made still more difficult by the fact that the autonomy of agriculture is grounded in the still more legitimated local committees. To attack them is to chip away at idols. This legitimacy reinforces the very considerable political power of agriculture interests, the source of which is often misunderstood. The problem of "rural versus urban political power" was never really one of simply poor legislative apportionment. Rural interests hold sway because of the specialization of their concerns and the homogeneity of interests within each agriculture system. Rural congressmen and state assemblymen, for example, are recruited by and owe their elections to the same forces that operate the quasi-public committees, and each level of activity reinforces the other. Mere legislative reapportionment is not likely to change this as long as there is no direct confrontation between agriculture interests and non-agriculture interests.

This confrontation will not take place until some other public values replace interest-group liberal values. The cases of Agriculture, Commerce, and Labor suggest that weakened national efficacy and impaired political responsibility—the incapacity to plan—are not recent developments. Blame must be cast in numerous directions. However, special responsibility rests with the Eisenhower, Kennedy, and Johnson Administrations. Pluralistic solutions may have been thrust upon the New Deal due to the seriously weakened state of public confidence and public finance. The weakened state of the Presidency and the Democratic party under Truman made fresh departures in domestic affairs close to impossible.[5] But after 1952 there was peace, confidence, and efficacy. In Europe and the United States in the 1930's pluralist solutions were turned to out of weakness. The state was forced to share its sovereignty in return for support. *In the 1960's pluralist solutions have not been forced upon national leaders but are voluntarily pursued as the highest expression of their ideology.* This must change before the pattern will change.

[5] Despite this weakness, the Fair Deal was considerably less pluralistic than the programs of Eisenhower, Kennedy, and Johnson.

CHAPTER 5

LIBERAL JURISPRUDENCE
Policy Without Law

Liberal jurisprudence is a contradiction in terms. Liberalism is hostile to law. No matter that it is motivated by the highest social sentiments; no matter that it favors the positive state only because the positive state is the presumptive instrument for achieving social good. The new public philosophy is hostile to law.

In a country with a strong rule-of-law tradition, those who are hostile to law are doomed to silence. Thus perhaps the most damning evidence of the liberal position on law is that there will be disagreement over the mere discription of its jurisprudence as well as disagreement over its meaning and consequences.

Interest-group liberalism has little place for law because laws interfere with the political process. The political process is stymied by abrupt changes in the rules of the game. The political process is not perfectly self-correcting if it is not allowed to correct itself. Laws change the rules of the game. Laws make government an institution apart; a government of laws is not a simple expression of the political process. A good clear statute puts the government on one side as opposed to other sides, it redistributes advantages and disadvantages, it slants and redefines the terms of bargaining. It can even eliminate bargaining, as this term is currently defined. Laws set priorities. Laws deliberately set some goals and values above others.

In brief, law, in the liberal view, is too authoritative a use of authority. Authority has to be tentative and accessible to be acceptable. If authority is too be accommodated to the liberal myth that it is "not power at all," it must emerge out of individual bargains.

The legal expression of the new liberal ideology can be summed up in a single, conventional legal term: *delegation of power*. Delegation of power refers technically to actions whereby a legislature confers upon an administrative agency certain tasks and powers the legislature would and could itself exercise if that were not impracticable. Delegations can be narrow or broad, but the practice under the liberal state has most generally and consistently been broad. As Professor Davis puts it, Congress in effect says, "Here is the problem: deal with it." [1] Delegation of power provides the legal basis for rendering a statute tentative enough to keep the political process in good working order all the way down from Congress to the hearing examiner, the meat inspector, the community action superviser, and the individual clients with which they deal. Everyone can feel that he is part of one big policy-making family.

Delegation of power enjoys strong standing in the courts. The broadest applications of the doctrine have been accepted by the Supreme Court for over 30 years. The last major statute invalidated for involving too broad a delegation to either public agencies or private associations was the "sick chicken case" of 1935.[2] The 1935 decision has never been reversed, but the Supreme Court has not seen fit to apply it since that time. Policy without law is what a broad delegation of power is. Policy

---

[1] See below, Chapter 10.

[2] *A.L.A. Schechter Poultry Corporation v. United States*, 295 U.S. 495. The Court held that the National Industrial Recovery Act, in giving the President the authority to promulgate codes of fair competition, had gone too far in delegating lawmaking power which was "unconfined and vagrant . . . not canalized within banks to keep it from overflowing." The ruling was confirmed in a major case in 1936 but not seriously applied thereafter.

without law is clearly constitutional, according to present judicial practice.

The doctrine of delegation of power also meets with strong support among academic political scientists and historians. Too much law would obviously be intolerable to scientific pluralist theory. In a vitally important sense, *value-free political science is logically committed to the norm of delegation of power because delegation of power is the self-fulfilling mechanism of prediction in modern political science.* Clear statutes that reduce pluralistic bargaining also reduce drastically the possibility of scientific treatment of government as simply part of the bundle of bargaining processes and multiple power structures. A good law eliminates the political process at certain points. A law made at the center of government focuses politics there and reduces interest elsewhere. The center means Congress, the President, and the courts. To make law at a central point is to centralize the political process. If this is too authoritative for interest-group liberalism it is too formal for modern political science.

Hostility to law, expressed in the principle of broad and unguided delegation of power, is the weakest timber in the shaky structure of the new public philosophy. This, more than any other single feature of interest-group liberalism, has wrapped public policies in shrouds of illegitimacy and ineffectiveness. This, more than any other feature, has turned liberal vitality into governmental and social pathology.

It is of course impossible to imagine a modern state in which central authorities do not delegate functions, responsibilities, and powers to administrators. Thus the practice of delegation itself can hardly be criticized. The practice becomes pathological, and criticizable, at the point where it comes to be considered a good thing in itself, flowing to administrators without guides, checks, safeguards. Historically, delegation had a rather technical meaning that emerged as the price to be paid in order to reap the advantages of administration. Delegation today represents a bastardization of earlier realities, and it is the bastardization that is at issue.

EVOLUTION OF PUBLIC CONTROLS IN THE UNITED
STATES: THE DELEGATION OF POWERS AND
ITS FALLACIES

Delegation of power did not become a widespread practice or
a constitutional problem until government began to take on
regulatory functions. The first century was one of government
dominated by Congress and virtually self-executing laws. Congressional Government, as Woodrow Wilson could view it in
the 1880's, was possible for two reasons: Either its activity was
insignificant, or it sought only to husband private action. Between 1795 and 1887, the key Federal policies were tariffs, internal improvements, land sales and land grants, development
of a merchant fleet and coastal shipping, the post offices, patents and copyrights, and research on how the private sector
was doing. Thus, after a short Hamiltonian period when the
Economic Constitution was written—including assumption
and funding of debts, the taxation system, currency and banking structure, establishing the power to subsidize—the Federal
government literally spent one century in the business of subsi-
dization. It was due to this quite special and restricted use of
government that Congress could both pass laws and see to
their execution. There must have been considerable corruption
in this method, but it did build a nation, and it did, after a century, make possible the following characterization by Lord
Bryce, on the very eve of the revolution in public control and
in congressional government:

It is a great merit of American government that it relies very little
on officials [i.e., administrators] and arms them with little power
of arbitrary interference. The reader who has followed the descrip-
tion of Federal authorities, state authorities, county and city or
township authorities, may think there is a great deal of administration; but the reason why these descriptions are necessarily so
minute is because the powers of each authority are so carefully and
closely restricted. It is natural to fancy that a government of the
people and by the people will be led to undertake many and vari-

ous functions for the people, and in the confidence of its strength will constitute itself a general philanthropic agency for their social and economic benefit. There has doubtless been of late years a tendency in this direction. . . . But it has taken the direction of acting through the law rather than through the officials. That is to say, when it prescribes to the citizen a particular course of action it has relied upon the ordinary legal sanctions, instead of investing the administrative officers with inquisitorial duties or powers that might prove oppressive. . . .[3]

DELEGATION DEFINED

The American system Bryce was describing was one whose regulations were few, whose resources were many, and whose central government was unobtrusive.[4] It was a system ideally suited for congressional government. When this system was revolutionized, beginning in 1887, it was one no longer susceptible to direct rule by legislature. Means had to be found to insure that even with the decline of the legislature there would be no equivalent decline in law. This would be no minor achievement, if it were at all possible. Involved was no less than reducing the hallowed role of the legislature and revising the even more hallowed separation of powers, while yet maintaining a sense that we were a government of laws and not of men.

The first move, so strongly feared, was made only in response to terrifying agrarian agitation and a Supreme Court decision which abolished all State efforts to deal with the problem.[5] This move, the Interstate Commerce Act of 1887, reflects

[3] James Bryce, *The American Commonwealth* (1888), from the chapter "The Strength of American Democracy."

[4] The prescribing to which Bryce refers was almost all state and local practice. Therefore, the problem of delegation to an administrative process began earlier in the States. Unfortunately, coverage of these developments would overly complicate the presentation here. For a short treatment, yet one of the best, see Robert E. Cushman, *The Independent Regulatory Commissions* (New York: Oxford University Press, 1941), Chapter 2.

[5] *Wabash, St. L. & P.R. v. Illinois,* 118 U.S. 551 (1886). The Supreme Court in this case made railroads an interstate problem, whether Congress liked it or not, by declaring that the states could not regulate interstate railroad traffic within their own borders even in the absence of

all of the problems and all of the concerns that have plagued government regulation ever since. In this famous Act, Congress (1) delegated its own power to regulate an aspect of interstate commerce (2) to an administrative agency (3) designed especially for the purpose. However, as will be emphasized strongly below, debate over the problem of delegation and how to delegate began before the passage of the Act and continued until the question of delegation became a dead issue with interest-group liberalism.

Congressmen were intensely concerned with constitutional issues during this first step toward a new venture in federal government. They were obviously aware that the Interstate Commerce Commission was an innovation, even if they did not altogether appreciate its significance as a model for the future. Fifty years later Landis best captured its significance in two passages of his classic essay:

> In terms of political theory, the administrative process springs from the inadequacy of a simple tripartite form of government to deal with modern problems. . . . (P. 1.)
>
> [I]t is obvious that the resort to the administrative process is not, as some suppose, simply an extension of executive power. Confused observers have sought to liken this development to a pervasive use of executive power. But the administrative differs not only in regard to the scope of its powers [a special sector or industry defined by statute]; it differs most radically in regard to the responsibility it possesses for their exercise. In the grant to it of that full ambit of authority necessary for it in order to plan, to promote, and to police, it presents an assemblage of rights normally exercisable by government as a whole. . . . (P. 16.) [6]

Constitutional concerns of the sort implied in Landis' definition of the administrative process were addressed in the Interstate Commerce Act in two ways. First, there was a fairly clear specification of standards regarding jurisdiction of the Commission and regarding the behavior of the railroad deemed un-

congressional action. This was indeed the categorical imperative for the commitment of the Federal government at long last to an interventionist role. *Cf.* Cushman, p. 38.

[6] James M. Landis, *The Administrative Process* (New Haven: Yale University Press, 1938).

lawful. There was no rigid codification, but conduct central to railroad abuses was specified quite sufficiently. These included such practices as rate discriminations, rebating, pooling, long-versus-short-haul adjustments. The Commission's power to enjoin railroad rates that were "undue or unreasonable" was guided, therefore, by standards in the Act. Second, however, the Act itself was the culmination of a long history of public efforts vis-à-vis rail service and rates, efforts in State law and in the common law. In effect, congressional language, even where vague, had been "freighted with meaning" by history.[7] As a consequence, it was possible for Judge Friendly in 1962 to view the original 1887 Act as a paragon of delegation. The fact that the Commission was hobbled for over a decade by a hostile Supreme Court may only attest to the need for administrative tribunals to overcome anachronistic courts in the industrial age. The Act was good law, because standards concerned with goals, clientele, and methods of implementation were clear, and it bred good legal behavior in the Commission by keeping pressure on for further and further exegesis of explicit rules and definitions by the Commissioners.[8] As we will see shortly, the Commission became "old" and was captured by its railroad clientele only after it was given new and entirely different responsibilities in 1920.

To summarize: In the Interstate Commerce Act, there was delegation of the "full ambit of authority"—executive, legislative, and judicial—in a single administrative body. It was given the power to be flexible, but it was relatively well shackled by clear standards of public policy, as stated in the statute and as understood in common law. From the beginning, the whole notion of vesting great authority in administrative tribunals was never separated from the expectation that standards of law would accompany the delegation. Much fun has been made of the myth the courts tried to create, that agencies were merely "filling in the details" of Acts of Congress. But neither the myth nor the mirth can hide the fact that when a

[7] Quoted in Henry J. Friendly, *The Federal Administrative Agencies* (Cambridge: Harvard University Press, 1962), p. 13.
[8] *Cf.* Friendly, p. 29 ff.

delegation was broad positive rules of law attached themselves to it.

It has even been suggested that restriction on delegation was never intended, because prior to the Panama and Schechter cases in 1935 the Supreme Court had never declared a delegation unconstitutional and after 1936 no further delegations were invalidated. Jaffe has even asked, perhaps Socratically, "whether Schechter is only of historical significance." [9] However, the question is badly put. The question of proper standards can be posed, and was indeed posed, without necessarily involving constitutionality. Obeying its own rule of restraint on constitutional issues, the Court merely filled in the congressional and presidential void with specifications of its own—or so construed the statute as to render the agency powerless. Jaffe himself provides the best example. The Federal Trade Commission Act of 1914 so poorly defined the key term, "unfair method of competition," that the Supreme Court invalidated order after order issued by the FTC through most of the first 20 years of its life.[10] The question of accompanying delegations with proper standards of law did not become a dead issue—in the courts or in congressional debate—until the 1930's and 1940's.

DELEGATION TO THE ADMINISTRATIVE PROCESS: A DEVELOPMENTAL ANALYSIS

Throughout the formative period of Federal control of economic life delegation was considered a problem. It had to be encountered because an administrative component had to be added to government, and delegation was the only way to accomplish it. Delegation was nonetheless the central problem, and it was faced with various partial solutions. However, a curious thing happened in the history of public control after 1887: As public control extended to wider and more novel realms, delegation became a virtue rather than a problem. *The*

[9] Louis L. Jaffe, *Administrative Law* (Englewood Cliffs: Prentice-Hall, 1959), p. 49.

[10] *Ibid.*, pp. 60–61; *cf.* Cushman, *op. cit.*, p. 412, and esp. *Federal Trade Commission v. Gratz*, 253 U.S. 421 (1920).

question of standards disappeared as the need for them increased. To pursue this proposition it is necessary first to pursue the actual developments in the practice of delegation itself.

The diagrammatic summary, Table 5.1, attempts to capture developments in the logic and practice of public control. From top to bottom the diagram is roughly but not exclusively chronological. There is an underlying logical progression among public controls, but Congress moved within this order in something slightly less than an orderly fashion, inventing techniques once in a while somewhat "before their time." For example, the granting of overall market powers to the ICC in the Transportation Act of 1920 anticipated a certain type of control by over a decade. However, it will be clear that the order is chronological in terms of the frequency and effectiveness in the use of each type of control.

At the Federal level, modern public control—*administered* public control—began with the ICC and was followed up quickly by the Sherman Antitrust Act (1890). These early instances were not any less regulative than anything that came later. They added the stick of direct coercion to the carrot of subsidies. The peculiarity to be emphasized for purposes of later comparison is this: In both these early instances, the objects to be regulated were known entities easy to designate. In the case of ICC jurisdiction, the objects were quite clearly the railroads. Similar legislation in the states extended to grain elevators and public conveyances and services of various sorts, suggesting that the general category, insofar as we can say there is a category at all, is "utilities." These are the so-called natural monopolies, which must be regulated because it was felt they could not and ought not be subject to normal competition.

In the second case, antitrust, another concrete category was involved, not really any more abstract and in need of definition than the first. "Trusts" referred to all large companies and company combinations, but the actual category in practice was comprised of a numerous but namable collection of companies and identifiable conducts. (Therefore, *The* trusts.) The category was further specified by the fact that it fit into an established legal-governmental tradition, as did the concepts of rails and utilities. That is to say, two factors helped solve the problem of how to guide delegations with standards. The statute could easily identify scope and jurisdiction for the administrator because these were so close to real quantities. Second, the

TABLE 5.1

THE DEVELOPMENT OF PUBLIC CONTROLS IN THE U.S.

An Analytic Summary

SCOPE OF CONTROL	OBJECTS OF CONTROL	DEVELOPMENTAL CHARACTERISTICS
A. The railroads in Interstate Commerce (1887–) *	The railroads	concrete specific traditional rule-bound proscriptive
B. The Trusts (1890–)	Oil trust, sugar trust, liquor trust, cottonseed oil trust, etc.	concrete general † traditional rule-bound proscriptive
C. Goods (1906–)	Qualities of things. Substandard foods, impure drugs, immoral women, obscene literature, etc.	abstract specific traditional rule-bound proscriptive
D. Commerce (1914–)	Relationships. Competition, fair and unfair. Qualities of commerce.	abstract general traditional discretionary prescriptive

* Dates given may often disregard some antecedent, but these are provided only to suggest when a particular phase seems to have begun in earnest.

† The major innovation of each phase is underlined.

TABLE 5.1 (*continued*)

SCOPE OF CONTROL	OBJECTS OF CONTROL	DEVELOPMENTAL CHARACTERISTICS
E. Factors (1933–)	Qualities of commodities behind commerce. Qualities of land, capital, labor and relations relevant to them.	abstract general novel <u>discretionary</u> proscriptive
F. Exchange (1933–)	Qualities of relationships. Open-ended.	abstract <u>universal</u> novel discretionary prescriptive
G. Markets (1934–)	Structures of relationships. Open-ended.	abstract universal novel discretionary <u>categoric</u>
H. System (1946–)	The environment of conduct.	concrete universal traditional redistributive ‡ categoric

‡ See my "American Business," *op. cit.* This issue is beyond the scope of the present inquiry.

task of definition was eased still further by the fact that history had "freighted them with meaning." [11]

The third stage of development (C. on the diagram) constitutes a new twist relative to the first two, although at first

[11] For an extended and balanced treatment, see Donald Dewey, *Monopoly in Economics and Law* (Chicago: Rand-McNally, 1959), Chapters 9–11. Dewey shows that the sanctions at common law were much too confused to have constituted a sufficient approach to enforcement without aid of positive, statutory law. But his review of concepts and cases shows that the contracts and practices that were considered part of the category, restraint of trade, were unmistakably clear.

glance nothing seems special. Here the objects of regulation were goods in commerce. The now time-honored techniques were regulatory taxation,[12] inspection, publicity, and outright prohibition and seizure of goods that were of low quality [13] or were considered to be immoral [14] or harmful to health.[15] The new twist was that for the first time scope and/or jurisdiction were to be defined not by mere designation of known companies and behaviors but by *abstract categorization*.

Rather than by actual designation the effort was to identify the objects of regulation through definition of a quality or characteristic that inheres in all of a defined or designated class of objects. Following that, flexible but effective guides could be set down for the administrator's decision on how to designate the actual objects below the cutoff point of *sub*standard, *im*moral, *un*healthy. Obviously the ability of Congress to guide and control the administrator is far more limited at this point, for definition by abstraction and categorization involves philosophic and philological as well as technological and empirical and just plain unpredictable dimensions. At what point of smell or bacteriological content is meat spoiled or are apples rotten? What kinds of actions define the point at which a woman's movement across State lines becomes immoral?

The difference between regulation of goods and that of railroads and trusts may seem slight as a matter of degree, but it is great in principle. The step may not have appeared so great at the time, as indeed it might not today, because control of certain goods was an old State and local practice, and had traditions which, again, "freighted with meaning" these early congressional efforts. Appreciation of the difference and its signifi-

[12] For example, we once dealt with liquor by prohibiting its manufacture and sale. We now control its use by setting upon it a tax so high that presumably people will be led to use it in moderation. Some regulatory taxes constitute an actual prohibition whenever the article has an elastic demand curve (e.g., oleomargarine, goods made by child labor) rather than an inelastic one (liquor).

[13] Examples range from rotten apples to sick chickens.

[14] There are, fortunately, few examples of such goods, the most famous being immoral women, kidnapped children, sawed-off shotguns, narcotics, and liquor.

[15] The best-known examples are drugs, cosmetics, and cigarettes.

cance increases in light of later developments. The move from concreteness to abstractness in the definition of public policy was probably the most important single change in the entire history of public control in the United States. Certainly it is the most important step to those concerned for rule by law.

The very next phase in the development of government controls underscores the significance of the effort made in regulating goods, and also represents significant changes in its own right. The very definiteness of the Sherman Antitrust Act was beginning to cause strains on the Court and Congress. The language, tradition, and plain meaning of the Act seemed clearly to forbid *all* conspiracies to restrain trade. Yet, the burgeoning of multi-million-dollar firms through patents, through growth, and through consolidation at that very time gave the Court and many others second thoughts.[16] As the Court retreated one step after another by drawing distinctions among reasonable and unreasonable restraints, the trust category became more and more muddied. In 1914, Congress made a stab at systematically defining what it had only had to point at in 1890. The Clayton Act and the Federal Trade Commission Act constitute valiant but vain efforts of Congress to define competition and to enumerate the actions that were to constitute restraints upon it.[17] The Clayton Act did manage to list three specific evils,[18] but all told these Acts contributed a new and grievous characteristic to government control. Although regulation of goods (C.) was based upon abstractions, the standards governing implementation were quite specific. Congress had tried to be specific in Clayton, but ultimately failed. The language of Clayton and FTC was abstract *and* general. Taking these two attributes of law together, the result was inevi-

[16] Compare the radically purist position of the Court in 1897 in *U.S. versus Trans-Missouri Freight Association* (166 U.S. 290), one of the first test cases, with *Standard Oil Co. v. U.S.* (221 U.S. 1) and *U.S. v. American Tobacco Co.* (221 U.S. 106), in 1911.

[17] *Cf.* Richard W. Taylor, "Government and Business," in Jack W. Peltason and James M. Burns, eds., *Functions and Policies of American Government* (Englewood Cliffs: Prentice-Hall, 1967), p. 230; and Cushman, *op. cit.*, pp. 186–87.

[18] These were price discrimination, exclusionary agreements, and interlocking directorates or ownership of stock in competing firms.

tably an enormous grant of discretion to the new Commission. This was new, this unguided discretion involved in the grant of power to enforce the law against "unfair methods of competition . . . and unfair or deceptive acts or practices." Note that the language creates an abstract category of behavior (commerce), decrees an abstract characteristic which is to adhere to all such behavior (competition), and provides an abstract standard to guide decisions (fairness). This may sound identical to the abstract category "goods" and the characteristics "standard-substandard" or "healthy-unhealthy," but obviously there is a difference. In the regulation of goods, both the categories (beef, apples, morphine) and the qualities (this was even true of the notion of morality applied to transporting women, i.e., prostitution) possessed both a plain meaning and some capacity for measurement. Laws governing "competition" could have very little of either (although some tradition still adhered at that time). Therefore, the need was for greater and greater definition in the Act, and, clearly, definition was not being provided.

Almost identical actions were taken regarding the new grant of powers to the ICC by the Transportation Act of 1920. Briefly, the Act added the power over minimum rates to the ICC's existing power over maximum rates.[19] Perhaps it is true that Congress did not appreciate what it was doing, but it is no less true that the change in ICC power at that time, when the railroads were passed back to private ownership, totally altered the Commission. Power over *maximum* rates was specified fairly clearly by the lists in the 1887 Act, by the 1906 Hepburn Amendment, and in common law. This was particularly true of the core of the ICC's jurisdiction—discrimination, exclusiveness, intimidation, and such matters as attended monopoly power. Power to raise *minimum* rates was granted with no such specification. The 1920 Act was a grant to the agency to find out the meaning of the Act itself, because the ICC was instructed only to act on what was "just and reasonable." In effect this meant case-by-case bargaining (called "on the

[19] For a detailed treatment, with which this section is fully in accord, see Friendly, *op. cit.*, Chapter 4.

merits"), the results putting the Commission on every side of every issue. As we shall see, this totally altered the meaning of the ICC.

Much as the courts fought the FTC,[20] the 1914 and 1920 Acts changed the entire practice and concept of regulation in ways from which there were to be no later departures. The next phase involved the move to include the factors of production that lay behind interstate commerce. While some of these factors might themselves have been in interstate commerce (currency), most were not so but rather were known to bear some intimate relation to the national—interstate—economy. Thus the big change here was not in the logical structure of the statute but in substantive expansion of the scope of Federal authority. This turn of events got far more attention than either the FTC Acts or the Transportation Act of 1920, but it involved no more important an innovation in government. It emphasizes once again an earlier observation, that there are two meanings to the term "limited government," and that Americans were concerned about only one of them. So, the only question was whether the Federal government had the "power" to reach such things as forest lands, child labor, working conditions, wages, and so on.[21] The issue of whether power existed required years to settle and involved some of the finest constitutional minds. Few except a Court of old men gave notice to the *other* dimension of limited government— how the power was to be exercised—and they were eagerly replaced.

Regulation of a few factors of production had been trifled with during the Wilson Administration. But conservation legislation and child labor legislation were minor precursors of attempts to regulate factors of production during the Roosevelt Administration. The invalidation of child labor legislation twice by the Supreme Court and the reaffirmation of that atti-

[20] As, for example, in the *Gratz* case reported above, in which the courts intervened to prevent the FTC from defining the scope and nature of its own powers and thus inhibited FTC development for 20 years.

[21] Currency management involves no such problems because power to create a Federal Reserve is explicitly granted by the Constitution via *McColloch v. Maryland.*

tude during twelve Republican years in the White House slackened the pace of development. Therefore the most serious Federal legislation in this area came almost simultaneously with the next step in the process of development—regulation of commercial exchange. This is a more advanced stage of development because it is a more abstract characterization of commerce. It is no further back along the flow of commerce, but that is a small part of the complexity of government's relation to economic life. Abstraction requires definition, and that is precisely what is absent from these more contemporary forms of regulation. Furthermore, this phase seems to carry to greater conclusiveness another feature that had been expressed only as a tendency before—the more positive or prescriptive character of the regulation. The regulation in question included the exercise of power over stock and grain exchanges, holding companies, agriculture land-use, and key aspects of marketing of both agricultural and processed commodities. All of this legislation emanated from virtually universal, not merely general, categories of jurisdiction, as well as, typically, the most abstract of indications, if any, of the characteristics of the objects to be included.[22] They moved away from the more restricted realm of activities already on the verge of hurting trade (1) into the sum total of all transactions and (2) toward certain qualities of all actions and transactions that may be deemed hurtful. The Robinson-Patman addition to the FTC constituted a significant expansion of FTC jurisdiction toward the hypothetical realm of all pricing, by defining the jurisdiction as price discrimination "between purchasers of like grade and quality . . . ," with differentials permitted for "due allowance for difference in cost of manufacture, sale, or delivery." [23] Under this legislation the FTC need only find "reasonable pos-

[22] This I have tried to indicate on the diagram with the term "open-ended." That is, a category of scope of jurisdiction is indicated but its limits are not defined. "Factors affecting competition," for example, is part of a long causal chain. Attempts are made to reduce universality with provisos, "due allowance for . . . ," etc., but great abstractions are too powerful to be easily limited by small abstractions.

[23] Section 2 of the Clayton Act as amended by the Robinson-Patman Act.

sibility of injury" from what it identifies as a price discrimination. This compounds and confounds abstraction by piling one hypothetical universe upon another. Similarly, regulation of securities extended to the complete universe of exchange, and certain qualities thereof, in that particular sector. Regulation of marketing, pricing, and acreage in the price-support field constitutes a less abstract definition of scope but one no less universal in intention. Its concept of the total structure of agriculture links up this phase of regulation with the last regulatory phases on the diagram. Price-support regulation also stands as the best example, although far from the earliest, of prescriptive control. Predicating quota and marketing controls upon a referendum does not alter the fact that the powers of the old AAA (see Chapter 4) include "thou shalts" as well as "thou shalt nots." There is also prescription of varying degrees and types in securities, holding company, and fair-trade regulation.

Finally, the most advanced development in administrative process is the effort to reach the structure and/or composition of markets themselves. Licensing and franchising are old and established instruments of local regulation. However, while cities and States usually stipulate some conditions prior to granting the license, the market concept involved at the Federal level has been significantly different.[24] The essence of the difference is that Federal regulation is based on an abstract concept of the whole market—i.e., what practices ought to constitute it and which and how many participants ought to be involved. The practices and numbers are not specified, but the concept implies them; certification according to "convenience and necessity" implies them. The Transportation Act of 1920 was obviously searching for a concept of a whole transportation market,[25] but the real examples began with radio, then

[24] State occupational licensing comes closest to being an antecedent. Licensing of doctors, barbers, and the like is both a means of securing quality and of keeping control of the number who can participate. The local utility is another analogue, except that here the market is usually filled up by one entrant.

[25] This act came closest to the concept described here in the granting of power to the ICC to forbid abandonment or construction of lines on the basis of "present or future public convenience and necessity," but the rail market was virtually stabilized by then anyway.

communications, where chaos over the airwaves dictated a whole-system concept with absolute control over entry, prescription of certain behavior "in the public interest," and meticulous prescription of territory and range through control of frequencies and transmission strength. The whole-market approach was then applied to airways, maritime traffic, motor carrier traffic (after 1935), domestic atomic energy, and satellite communication. This type of regulation went beyond the abstract, universal, nontraditional (novel), prescriptive character of the earlier phase by bringing entry and ownership—the very condition of livelihood—into the public domain. The term *categoric* seems appropriate, although it is not supposed to suggest that these agencies quit proscribing and prescribing conduct.[26]

There is still another step on the diagram, but this is actually a quantum step into another type of public control altogether. Approach to the whole economic system is not regulation or administrative process in any ordinary sense, in that it does not seek to specify conduct directly. Conduct is indeed influenced, but the influence is exerted through the environment of conduct rather than conduct itself. This final step is included on the diagram only to define the limits of the development of public control through regulation. No developmental characteristic is identified as novel simply because this phase constitutes a return (with a vengeance) to the Hamiltonian or constitutional period briefly identified earlier in this chapter. The Federal government was expected all along to create and maintain the whole system or environment of conduct. The real difference here is that by the time we returned to such tasks two new developments had taken place: (1) The system had become so integrated that considerable manipulation (as distinct from mere maintenance) was now possible. And (2) economic science had developed new insights and manipulatory techniques. Social security (Chapter 8) is an early and

[26] It is also not supposed to suggest a new extreme in coercion, but only a new method of delegation of broad administrative discretion. While the potential for heavy public control is there, in practice, as we have already seen in agriculture, the permissive statute has allowed for private expropriation of public domain, not the reverse.

rudimentary case of a system concept, but it was formalized first in the Employment Act of 1946. The central techniques of this phase—fiscal and monetary policies—are not dealt with except in Chapter 10.

SUMMARY: THE RISE OF DELEGATION, THE DECLINE OF LAW

Empirically, the stages of development in the administrative process can be summarized as follows:

(1) There is an expansion of the scope of Federal control in the sense of the number and types of objects touched by directly coercive Federal specification of conduct. This is what has been meant traditionally by the "expansion of government."

(2) There has also been an expansion of the scope of power in the more philosophical sense of expansion to the whole universe of objects or qualities of objects in a predefined category. This expansion proceeds as categories grow larger, eventually to include certain characteristics (e.g., trade) which any and all persons in the country might at one time or another possess. (On the diagram this is indicated by the move from General to Universal.)

(3) Implied in (2) and necessary to it is the development from the concrete to the abstract. This development was observed at two levels. First, the jurisdictional categories became more and more abstract. Second, the standards by which actual qualities are designated moved rather quickly from the specific to the general.

(4) The development also involved changes in sanctions. The movement seemed to be from the negative to the positive, the proscriptive to the prescriptive. The latter did not replace the former but only supplemented them.

Taking these few dimensions together, other realities emerge from slightly below the surface to show how much the relation between citizens and public control actually changed even though such labels as "regulation" and "administrative process" remained the same and implied a false sense of continuity throughout the entire century. As regulation moved from the denotation to the connotation of what is subject to public policy, discretion inevitably increased; and the process unavoidably centered on administration. This factor seems far more important in the rise of administrative power than the usual cry of how complex and technological a new field is. Thus, the same citizen might receive the same injunction under phase E as under phase B, but the problems involved in his relation to the injunction would not be the same. The command under B is issued to him for an act he committed against a law dealing with that act. Under E, or even D, he receives the command not because of who he is or what he does but because abstractly he belongs to a type, or his behavior is of a type, that comes within public policy. "Get off the grass" under A or B is an order a policeman issues to an elephant because an elephant hurts the grass. More and more, as we move down the diagram, the "get off the grass" order becomes derived from a definition of the "grassness" of the behavior. Establish grass as part of a category of public policy, then state grassness (without quite defining it) as a quality adhering or not adhering to acts, and you have the essence of modern regulation.

Obviously *modern law has become a series of instructions to administrators rather than a series of commands to citizens*. If at the same time (1) public control has become more positive, issuing imperatives along with setting limits, and if at the same time (2) application of laws and sanctions has become more discretionary, by virtue of having become more indirect as well as more abstract, why should we assume we are talking about the same governmental phenomena in 1968 as in 1938 or 1908? The citizen has become an *administré*, and the question now is how to be certain he remains a citizen.

As has been said already, and as will be reiterated thematically, delegation has been elevated to the highest of virtues, and standards have been relegated to the wastebasket of history because that is the logic of interest-group liberalism. Bargaining—or, as Schlesinger might call it, participation in the "interior processes of policy-making"—must be preferred over authority at every level and phase of government. The

idea that the universal application of bargaining solves the
problem of power was just appealing enough to win out over
alternative doctrines that appeared so conservative in light of
the desperation of the 1930's. Victory can be measured by the
almost universal application of the principle of broad delegation in regulatory policies and the meekness of the otherwise
activist Supreme Court. The conversion of delegation from
necessity to virtue also led to the spread of the practice to non-
regulatory programs—in the name of partnership, creative
federalism, and the like.

As late as 1938 Dean Landis could still express ambivalence.
On the one hand he could exclaim that when government seeks
to regulate business it "vests the necessary powers with the administrative authority it creates, not too greatly concerned with
the extent to which such action does violence to the traditional
tripartite theory of governmental organization. . . . The administrative process is, in essence, our generation's answer to
the inadequacy of the judicial and the legislative processes.
. . ." [27] On the other hand he agonized over the need and the
problem of accompanying delegation with standards. Although
he insisted that a general principle applicable to standards for
any delegation could not be enunciated, he went on to give a
horrible example of a situation where no standards existed.
The House version of the Public Utility Holding Company Act
of 1935 would have granted the SEC power to exempt holding
companies from the "death sentence" if such exemption were
found to be in the public interest. Such a delegation, turning
over "the whole burning issue . . . to the Commission . . .
was an impossible responsibility. It meant nothing less than
that the Commission, rather than Congress, would become the
focal point for all the pressures and counter-pressures that had
kept the Congress and the press at a white heat for months.
Instead of the controversy being concluded, it would have
been protracted interminably. . . ." [28]

By 1968, perhaps even by 1958 or 1948, none of this reserve

[27] Landis, *op. cit.*, pp. 12, 46.
[28] Landis, pp. 55–56.

was left. There was only untarnished exuberance for a system built upon unregulated regulation.[29]

LAW VERSUS LIBERALISM

A close review of developments in the administration of public controls turns present conventional wisdom on its head. It is widely assumed that the "administrative process" is an emergent phenomenon all of a single piece. It is also assumed that after three quarters of a century of experience and after the development of still greater complexity of social organization it is no longer possible to require that broad delegations of power be accompanied by clear legislative standards. It is further assumed that standards are not desirable anyway. But the truth seems to lie almost completely the other way around. In our day it is possible to enunciate effective standards precisely because businessmen, economists, and government officials have had three quarters of a century's experience with the problems of modern industrial practice. Standards are both necessary and desirable today except for those who wish to see the power of the democratic state drained away. The drainage would not be, as Lippmann feared, down into electoral constituencies. It would not be, as congressmen hope, back into Congress—for legislative oversight and review are forms of committee privilege, not law-making. And it would not be a drainage, as interest-group liberals expect, into a benign equilibrium. At its best the system is a hell of administrative boredom. At its worst, it is a tightly woven fabric of legitimized privilege.

[29] For an important example, see Murray Edelman, "Interest Representation and Policy Choice in Labor Law Administration," *Labor Law Journal*, March, 1958. Edelman provides excellent cases of labor laws without standards. However, he errs grievously in his assessment of the consequences of such laws. He claims that laws with hard standards are no more predictable in implementation, yet his only proof is that one particular law involved a more positive judicial intervention (p. 225). How this proves lack of predictability is a mystery. It mainly proves that a pluralistic view, even in the hands of so excellent an analyst as Edelman, leads to hostility to courts as well as to law itself.

Nonetheless many express concern lest the revival of law destroy bargaining. Bargaining, they say, is one of the great virtues of democracy. It maintains flexibility, and this is supposedly the way to avoid turning citizen into *administré*. But this concern only reveals the extent to which an interest-group liberal view disorders meanings and narrows vision. An attack on delegation is an attack not on bargaining but on one type of bargaining—logrolling. The attack is on a confusion of the two meanings of bargaining and the consequent misapplication of the whole idea. First, there can be bargaining over the decision on a particular case. This type of bargaining over the stakes is logrolling. It has to do with whether certain facts are to be defined as identical to some earlier set of facts. It has to do with whether the case will be prosecuted at all, and with how much vigor. It has to do with whether monetary sanctions apply, if so, how much, whether contrition plus compliance in the future are sufficient. Second, and worlds apart, there can be bargaining on the rule or rules applicable to the decision. This can take the form of simple insistence that the authority state some rule. It can be a quibble over the definition of a concept or a profound analysis of what Congress could possibly have intended. It could be a process of defining the agency's jurisdiction.

Once this distinction between two kinds of bargaining is stated it is impossible to imagine how they could possibly become fused or confused. The differences in their consequences ought to be clear. In any libertarian, unmobilized society, some logrolling is likely to occur on every decision at every stage in the governmental process. However, if by broad and undefined delegation you build your system in order to ensure the logrolling type of bargain on the decision, you are very likely never to reach bargaining on the rule at all. If, on the other hand, you build the system by stricter delegation to insure bargaining on the rule, *you will inevitably get logrolling on the decision as well.*

These propositions are not true merely because the morality of the general rule is weaker than the stakes of the individual case. Bargaining on the rule is especially perishable because

broad delegation simply puts at two great disadvantages any
client who wishes to bargain for a general rule rather than
merely to logroll his case. Here is what he faces: First, the
broad delegation enables the agency to co-opt the client—i.e.,
to make him a little less unhappy the louder he complains. On
top of that, the broad delegation reverses the burden of initiative and creativity, the burden of proof that a rule is needed.
If the client insists on "making a federal case" out of his minor
scrape, he must be prepared to provide the counsel and the
energy to start a rule-making process himself. This means that
the individual must stop his private endeavors and for a while
become a creative political actor. Most behavioral research
agrees that this is an unlikely exchange of roles.

Case 1 is an only slightly fictionalized dialogue. It is the first
of four cases of the consequences of policy without law.

Wages and Hours Regional: Mr. Employer, we find that you owe
your ten employees a total of $10,000 in back wages, plus fines,
for having them take telephone messages while having lunch on the
premises.
Employer: I object. You interrogated my employees without my
knowledge, and did not interrogate me at all. And, besides, where
do you get off saying my boys were "on call" because they heard
the phone ring? Talk to my lawyer.
Regional: How about $5,000 in back pay and no fines?
Employer: Good God, now I'm really disgusted. I want in writing
your official interpretation governing such a case. And aren't there
rules about notice and hearings?
Regional: How about $2,500 in back pay?
Employer: Well, hell, I . . .
Regional: How about an exchange of memoranda indicating future
compliance?
Employer: Mmm . . . [aside: Lawyers' fees . . . trips to testify
. . . obligations to that damned congressman of ours . . .]
Official memo from Regional, weeks later: You are hereby directed
to cease . . .
Posted in employees' toilet: You are hereby directed to eat lunch
off the premises.

This drama could have taken place in one long-distance call or
in half a dozen letters strung out over many weeks. However,

the demoralizing part is not what one might expect. It isn't "bureaucracy." The parable depends little on red tape and the like. It was hardly even a question of being caught. The employer is not a sweatshop operator. Perhaps he even agrees with the purpose and spirit behind Regional's case, and he in any event demurred on the facts. Disgust, disappointment, and distrust would arise in such a case because the agency appears "gutless." Its effort to avoid enunciating a rule may be rationalized as flexibility, but to most intelligent people directly involved in such a problem it can end in reduced respect—for the agency and for government. And meanwhile, no rule.

Case 2 is a real case on a much higher level. It involves the history of the Interstate Commerce Commission from 1920, when it received general power over minimum rates, first over the railroads and later over motor transport as well.[30] From that moment on the ICC fell into a bargaining relation to rail and trucking companies that produced most of the deleterious effects now regularly identified by ICC critics. It was after 1920 that the ICC developed the only principle to which it has held consistently, and that is the principle of bargaining on each decision; each case involving reasonable rates had to be decided "on its own merits in light of the facts of record in the case." With principle operating in the context of a vague enabling statute, it was impossible for the ICC to avoid developing what later came to be called "congenital schizophrenia." [31] The Commission has been on all sides of its own rules and rationalizations. Often, for example, it has operated as though its governing rule were maximization of profits for the transportation system as a whole. However, it may be fortunate that this was never fully articulated, because the ICC has often (but not consistently, of course) denied rate reductions below what was necessary for a carrier to gain or maintain a "fair share," despite the fact that a still lower rate would still have been remunerative to the carrier without disrupting the market. "Fair share" itself sounds like a rule too, and the above instance sounds at first like the application of this rule to a group of truckers to keep the railroads happy. But it rarely works

[30] Reported in detail in Friendly, *op. cit.*, Chapter 6.
[31] *Ibid.*, p. 129.

that way simply because much of the traffic deserting the rail-roads is due rather to Commission-imposed, carrier-approved, artificially high rail rates, which if lowered would have resulted in increases of shares all around.[32]

On the other hand, *any* assumed rule relating to fair profits or fair shares violates another rule long assumed, at least in Congress, yet never clearly enunciated by anyone; it has been applied, but never consistently. This is the original notion that through power over maximum *and* minimum rates the ICC could plan an intergrated transportation system. Obviously this goal would require occasional deliberate reductions of rates and fair shares in order to achieve a balance of factors. But a closer look at the ICC reveals the impossibility of applying such a principle, even if the Commission espoused it. The ICC staff is not in any way equipped to assess the real value and functions of the carriers and carrier systems. It acquires little data completely independently. Often it appears as though a regional ICC official calls a carrier representative and asks, "By the way, what are you worth today?" Worse, the ICC has no data, is equipped to get no data, and seems to feel no need to acquire data, on transportation investments, costs, or expenses below the level of total companies. It would thus be impossible for the ICC to assess "fair shares" or "fair profits" to help work out a balanced transportation system in a given metropolitan region. It is obvious, as most specialized observers have concluded, that decisions are bargained out between the ICC and each individual contender, and then "the Commission selects whatever theory appears best to fit the case at hand." [33]

This sort of situation is not flexible, only loose. It is not stable, only static. The phenomena are the same, but the significance is far different. The absence of bargaining at the level of rule and principle has destroyed the capacity of the government to grow in this particular area of control. Decision-oriented bargaining, i.e., logrolling, deprived the Commission's history of any experience by which Congress, or even the ICC

[32] *Ibid.*, p. 130, especially the case and study cited in note 12.
[33] Quoted in *ibid.*, p. 139. See also *ibid.*, note 98, quoting results of still another scholarly review.

commissioners themselves, might have been pushed into the formulation of improved rules or statutory standards. To state the case as generally as possible, Congress is less likely to be able or willing to work by "successive approximations" toward decent statutory treatment of complex modern problems to the extent that problems of rule-formulation are successfully avoided in administrative bargaining.[34] Thus, after 20 years of presumed experience, Congress in the Transportation Act of 1940 "created as many contradictions as were dissipated"; and, following still another 18 years in which the Commission made decisions "without reference to any . . . general objective," Congress in the Transportation Act of 1958 gave back to the Commission with one hand the ambiguities it had tried to remove with the other.[35] *Decision-oriented bargaining is non-cumulative experience.* Since 1920 in the transportation industry this has meant that Congress benefits not from 50 years' experience but from one year's experience 50 times.

Case 3 reveals the same tendency in other fields by comparing the histories of the Federal Trade Commission and the National Labor Relations Board. The immense grant of undefined discretion in the two organic Acts of the FTC—the Federal Trade Commission Act of 1914 and the Clayton Act of 1914—dictated immediate involvement of the new Commission with each client in decision-oriented bargaining. The FTC was given "power" to make lists of unfair practices, which it proceeded to do in regular consultation with industries in industrial conferences. Thus from the very beginning the FTC developed an intimacy with trade associations and their codes of fair competition that was to become the practice and precedent for NRA corporatism during the New Deal, as well as the apple of Herbert Hoover's eye.[36]

The weakness of FTC law and practice in the antitrust field led to the rise of the still more undefined and corporativistic

[34] See below, Chapter 10, especially the discussion of the work of Kenneth C. Davis.

[35] Friendly, *op. cit.*, p. 140. See especially Friendly's sources, in notes 86–101.

[36] *Cf.* Hoover's opinions quoted in Chapters 3 and 4, below, and at greater length in McConnell, *op. cit.*

"consent decree" method in the Department of Justice Antitrust Division. The "consent decree" is the name given to individual bargains on monopoly and restraint-of-trade issues; it is made on promise that no prosecution on the same alleged infractions will take place at a later time.[37] In the FTC itself, discretion led to weakness, and weakness led to the adoption of, essentially, a "policy of no policy."

As a consequence, Congress has had neither experience nor doctrine to guide it. Congress' first FTC action after 1914 came 24 years later, with the Robinson-Patman Act of 1938. But two things are most peculiar about it. First, it was merely an amendment to Section 2 of the Clayton Act and did not touch other aspects of the organic law at all. Second, the Robinson-Patman Law, both in letter and in spirit, tended to forbid competitive practices rather than restraints on trade.[38] It is fantastic that nothing in the 24-year history of FTC cast any particularly inconsistent light upon what Messrs. Robinson and Patman were trying to do in 1938. Moreover, since 1938 there has still been nothing remotely resembling a full-scale reconsideration of FTC legislation, despite barrages of criticism from all sides. An important antimerger amendment to Section 7, plus a vain effort to change basing-points practices in 1948–50, constitute the sum total of congressional effort.[39]

[37] *Cf.* Jaffe, *op. cit.*, pp. 59 ff., and citations. Incentive to enter consent decree bargaining is sweetened by court-backed protection against triple damage suits by injured parties. The "consent decree amounts to an innoculation against a number of legal difficulties." *Cf.* William D. Rogers, "Is It Trust Busting or Window Dressing?" *Reporter* (Nov. 1, 1956), 21.

[38] *Cf.* Robert Bork and Ward S. Bowman, "The Crisis in Antitrust," reprinted in Randall B. Ripley, ed., *Public Policies and Their Politics* (New York: W. W. Norton, 1965), pp. 90 ff. Even the more positive Corwin Edwards cannot deny that under Robinson-Patman a very large proportion of FTC prosecutions involves small firms and that in general the Act has had "no uniform effect of raising or lowering prices." *The Price Discrimination Law* (Washington: The Brookings Institution, 1959), Chapter 4.

[39] To push the point still further, basing-points policy got a full airing during that period precisely because FTC doctrine against the practice was known and rather consistently applied. For another example see Bork and Bowman, *op. cit.*, pp. 91–93, where they compare conse-

Law in the National Labor Relations Board has had quite a different history. From the beginning of collective bargaining–fair labor practices legislation in Section 7 of the National Industrial Recovery Act of 1933, through the National Labor Relations Act to Taft-Hartley and Landrum-Griffin, labor law has contained clearer standards of implementation. Although the NLRB was explicitly set up as an adjudicatory body to deal with the merits of individual cases—and although NLRB must certainly be guilty of its share of abuses—labor law has always been more heavily weighted toward rule-oriented bargaining. Its history is as a consequence superior to that of the FTC or ICC. There has been far more omnibus legislation and review in 30 years of the NLRB than in the entire 55-year history of the FTC or 47-year history of the ICC under its minimum rate-making powers. And the end is not in sight.

Case 4 is of a different order. It has to do with the important hypothesis in the literature on the political process that there is a natural, secular decline in concern for law among administrative agencies and that, parallel to this, agencies ultimately become captured by their clienteles.[40] The analysis here suggests that age and nature have almost nothing to do with the decay of legal integrity, or, as the pluralist might put it, with the development of "whirlpools" or "communities of interest" or "equilibrium." To Bernstein the maturity, i.e., the onset of decline, of the ICC dates from 1920; [41] but that happens to be the year when the legal integrity of the agency was all but destroyed in a single stroke by the grant of minimum rate-making powers, a factor Bernstein does not even mention. Rather, he pictures ICC decline as a long and natural process

quences of one antitrust provision with legal integrity to the more typical laws on price fixing and mergers, which have no legal integrity.

[40] *Cf.* Marver Bernstein, *Regulating Business by Independent Commission* (Princeton: Princeton University Press, 1955), Chapter 3; and Samuel P. Huntington, "The Marasmus of the ICC: The Commission, the Railroads, and the Public Interest," *Yale Law Journal,* April 1952. *Cf.* also Harmon Ziegler, *Interest Groups in American Society* (Englewood Cliffs: Prentice-Hall, 1964), pp. 119–20, for an example of standard textbook treatment of this hypothesis.

[41] Bernstein, *op. cit.,* p. 90.

in which original support groups run out of steam, hostile groups make their peace, and the agency makes all this possible by learning how to espouse the business interest in the interest of peace, friendship, and equilibrium. In an earlier study Huntington speaks of "gradual withering away" and "marasmus" as though regulatory agencies were animal organisms. But in truth the agency is an agency operating under a statute. Again it is as though the statute is not a relevant political datum. The cases above, as is true of the entire argument of this book, militate against such notions of natural political tendency. Jaffe's critique of the pluralist thesis seems much more supportable, and provides a suitable summary: "Much of what the agencies do is the expectable consequence of their broad and ill-defined regulatory power." [42]

These cases and histories involving the presence or absence of standards in legislative delegations and rules in administrative practice overwhelmingly support the simple proposition that *law begets law*. Agencies that begin in a context of statutes that associate guidance with power are agencies that begin with legal integrity and have histories of greater legal integrity. Agencies that begin with little or no legal integrity are very unlikely to develop any along the way.

An attack on the practice of delegation turns out actually to be a hopeful view. If the rise of delegation and the decline of law were the mere result of technical complexity it would be an irreversible process because technical complexity is the law of modernity. However, this review suggests that the real problem is one of abstraction rather than one of complexity.[43] It is from abstraction that uncontrolled discretion flows. Abstraction is reversible, with the increase of knowledge, *but only if*

[42] Louis Jaffe, "The Effective Limits of the Administrative Process: A Reevaluation," *Harvard Law Review*, May, 1959, p. 1134.

[43] Not only do the cases of the ICC and FTC themselves oppose the idea that complexity is the problem. Much of labor-management law (as already suggested), social security law (see below, Chapter 8), civil rights law (Chapters 7 and 9), and drug control law, to name but a few, deal with extremely complex situations; yet, there is a great deal of legal integrity to be found in these areas, and there is strong rule-oriented bargaining in between frequent legislative phases.

the leadership desires to reverse it. This is why a change of public values is so essential.

The decline of Congress, the decline of democracy, the decline of independence among regulatory agencies, the general decline of law as an instrument of control are all due far more than anything else to changes in the philosophy of law and prevailing attitude toward laws. Admittedly the complexity of modern life forces Congress into vagueness and generality in drafting its statutes. Admittedly the political pressure of social unrest forces Congress and the President into premature formulations that make delegation of power inevitable. But to take these causes and effects as natural and good, and then to build the system around them, is to doom the system to remaining always locked into the original causes and effects.

No present-day liberal is prepared to propose that a government of laws is impossible or undesirable, just as no politician would propose that we do without the Constitution. But the system the present-day liberal would build is predicated upon just such propositions. Statutes without standards, policy without law, will yield pluralism and bargaining throughout the system—just as political science predicts and liberalism prescribes. Overlooked and neglected is the converse proposition, which is also axiomatic; yet peculiarly enough the converse proposition does not yield opposite results: Policies that are real laws do not destroy pluralism but merely reduce its scope to those points in the system where decisions on rules can be made or reformed.

If this proposition is true, then it obviously follows that its application could revitalize Congress and sever agency-clientele relations. The effort to regulate, especially when it comes as late as in the United States federal system, immediately attaches a morality to government. When that morality is a criterion for the regulatory act, it is bound to have a characteristic influence of some sort on the political process. When the regulation is done permissively and in the deliberate absence of the morality implied in the very use of coercive language, the result can only be expected to be demoralizing, to the agency, the law itself, and the clientele. The group process is dynamic and cumulative when groups have an institutional structure against which to compete. Without that formal structure the group process is not truly pluralistic at all. It is merely co-optive. And it is ineffective. Worse, it converts mere ineffectiveness into illegitimacy.

Liberal sentiments remain, and indeed they may be the best sentiments. But the interest-group liberal method is as inappropriate for our time and for those sentiments as was the laissez-faire liberal method for 1929. The interest-group method was an ideal means of achieving a bit of equity. Its day is done, for equity is no longer enough. It has proven itself unequal to the tasks of planning and achieving justice. A grant of broad powers to administration is not a grant of power at all. It is an imposition of impotence.

CHAPTER 6

MAKING DEMOCRACY
SAFE FOR THE WORLD

*On Fighting
the Next War*

Modern liberals cannot plan in domestic affairs because of their opposition to stating real goals in clear and authoritative language. They cannot plan in foreign affairs for almost the opposite reason, for here they seem to set enormously high store upon having rules—or at least programmatic rhetoric. However, the two apparently opposite tendencies have a common base. In both domestic and foreign politics interest-group liberals display too little trust in the formal institutions of democracy.

Put in its most elementary textbook fashion, democracies are supposed to operate between frequent elections through formally constituted institutions which are supposed to possess all the power necessary to carry out their responsibilities. Modern liberalism has so defined the problem that Congress now does its duty only when it seeks to alienate the power it truly possesses and to retain power which inherently it does not and cannot possess. In both cases there is only one guarantee, which is that power will not be very effectively used at all.

Vietnam is simply one, albeit a classic, illustration. Academically it has little significance beyond any of the cases to be dealt with here in detail. The war has contributed to the liberal crisis in the United States. But most assuredly liberal attitudes have been instrumental in the escalation of the war to the crisis level. Liberals are not saber rattlers. In their revulsion against mere self-interest, many have in fact turned to a form of pseudo-isolationist withdrawal. The liberal contribution to the war has been rather its support of a system of politics that is almost completely inappropriate for foreign policy formulation by a major power. During the period of America's emergence to world leadership the public philosophy interfered with the emergence of appropriately mature structures of foreign-policy-making and implementation.

At the end of World War II Americans were properly impressed with two facts. We had been "opened up," having become an international power despite ourselves. And we had prosecuted the war with incredible efficiency and impressively rational integration of strategy, production, and diplomacy. The most pressing problem toward the end of the war and afterwards was somehow to perpetuate the organizational successes of the war in order to use our power properly to prosecute the peace. Harnessing an eighteenth-century constitution and institutions that were perfectly geared to peacetime irresponsibility into a force for consistency, continuity, restraint, and understanding—in short, for planning on an international scale—involved nearly the reverse of Woodrow Wilson's goal for World War I. We had somehow to make democracy safe for the world.

Success has thus eluded America twice, for making democracy safe for the world has not proven altogether possible. Our peacetime efforts have lacked the one condition that made our wartime efforts successful. In the peace there is no longer the crisis of the war itself. In the United States this made a difficult task impossible. Crisis constitutes a very special condition in the workings of American foreign policy. Crises are fortunately not everyday occurrences; however, a crisis does tend to bring out the very best in Americans. Postwar examples of exemplary behavior in crisis include Greek-Turkish Aid and the Truman Doctrine, the Berlin Airlift, the response to the Korean invasion, the 1956 Arab-Israeli intervention, the Cuban missile crisis of 1962, Dienbienphu in 1954.[1] Due to our poorer record in foreign affairs when there are no crises our capacities to deal with crises are consistently underestimated by potential enemies. This is a major reason why guerilla warfare is such an effective anti-American weapon.

Crisis situations are special because they combine intensity of conflict with shortage of time. Politically this means a very narrow scope of participation and an extremely limited range for bargaining. The public and public-serving institutions are far removed. Decisions are made by an elite and are usually highly legitimate—if we may measure by the largely cere- monial and affirmative responses crisis decisions tend to re- ceive.

At first glance these patterns seem to confirm C. Wright Mills's idea that the United States is run by a "power elite" when it comes to making the key decisions for the country: "Within the higher circles of the power elite, factions do exist. But more powerful than these divisions are the internal disci- pline and the community of interests that bind the power elite together. . . ." [2] On further inspection of crisis decisions it would seem that Mills did not go far enough. As is well known, Mills defined his power elite to include all holders of the top institutional positions in the military, the executive branch of the national government, and industry. Inspection of crisis de- cisions suggests that the real participants comprise an even smaller elite than the so-called power elite. Even when the crisis offers a small grace period, such as was true of Dienbien- phu in 1954 and the British withdrawal from Greece in 1947, rarely has more than a small segment of the standard power elite been directly involved before the fact. Moreover, it was a

[1] I will frequently make these value judgments in this chapter. In all instances they will be grounded upon the following assumptions: (1) The United States has some vital and legitimate interests abroad. (2) The United States is acting rationally when it pursues these interests, especially if the results do not too palpably disturb international equilib- rium. (3) Rational foreign policy is good foreign policy and irrational foreign policy is bad foreign policy.

[2] C. Wright Mills, *The Power Elite* (New York: Oxford University Press, 1959), p. 283.

very special segment whose reality is inconsistent with both the pluralist and the Mills model of the distribution of power. *Crisis decisions in foreign policy are made by an elite of formal officeholders.*

Rarely is there time to go further. Rarely is there need to go further unless the aftermath of the crisis is a longstanding commitment that itself becomes unpopular.

There is an obvious corollary to this first proposition, which is that in times of crisis the people who make the decisions are those who were elected and appointed to make those decisions. That is to say, *under crisis conditions our government has operated pretty much as it was supposed to operate,* all theories of the informal distribution of power to the contrary notwithstanding.

There is also a normative corollary. Since our record of response to crisis is good, then the men in official positions have been acting and are able to act rationally. If, when there is no crisis, officials and their policies appear to be less rational, then we must conclude that something is wrong with the structures and institutions within which they operate.

After World War II the effort of the U.S. to face the peace as a world leader took the form of great expansion of the instruments of foreign policy formulation and implementation. New agencies were established, and old ones were greatly expanded. However, while there was so vast an expansion of the units there was no creation of a foreign policy establishment, or as Europeans would call it, a foreign ministry. As in domestic government, each new foreign policy commitment was set up in a new instrumentality, each was given separate but inevitably overlapping functions, and each was given a grant of legal independence from the others. Whether instinctively or according to the dictates of ideology, the founders of our international posture in peace were groping their way toward the maximization of rule by bargaining. From this fact emanates most of the foreign policy problems we face today.

The cases analyzed below were chosen because they involve the basic instruments and commitments for dealing with noncrisis foreign policy. They have a double value to the analyst.

First, each is a history of decision-making through which we can assess the behavior of individuals and the values they apply to decisions. That is, each is a study in the "political process." Second, each of these basic decisions led to the creation of a program or instrument which contributed, for better or worse, to the political process of all later decisions.

Each case tells about the same political story with about the same moral. When there is time for planning there is time for disagreement. Since there is nothing in American culture to limit the course of disagreement, disagreement spreads. It spreads among all individuals who have the interest and the resources. It ultimately becomes public and involves all of the engines and motives of public politics, as well as all of the unpredictability of publicly made decisions. This natural tendency in American politics was, during the postwar years, exaggerated to dangerous extremes, with consequences dangerous to world order, by men who believed in its goodness and proceeded to construct the foreign policy system around it.

INSTITUTIONS: IN SEARCH OF AN ESTABLISHMENT

MARSHALL PLAN: HOW TO AVOID AN ESTABLISHMENT
IN FOREIGN ECONOMIC POLICY

The story of the "opening of America" is the story of the Economic Cooperation Act (ECA), or Marshall Plan (European Recovery Plan). Its reputation as a proud moment in American history will not be attacked here because its economic timeliness and its accomplishments in Europe are not at issue.[3] Reassessment is necessary in order to identify the kind of politics it reflects and, after passage, contributed to.

Almost everything about the structure and operation of ECA reflected the effort to impose a bargaining frame of reference upon it. But the most compelling evidence can be found

---

[3] For a detailed but quite readable account, see Joseph Jones, *The Fifteen Weeks* (New York: Viking, 1955).

in the placement of the agency itself, for the price of our peacetime involvement in world affairs was the creation of a second State Department in the ECA. Everything else about it seems to follow from that fact.

The State Department draft of the European Recovery Plan called for an administrator "whose every function, especially those involving foreign policy, would be performed 'subject to direction and control of the Secretary of State.'" [4] Ultimate State Department control was something President Truman and General Marshall had insisted upon. But Senator Vandenberg, with Congress behind him, was dissatisfied, even though he had earlier been aware of the problem of having dual responsibilities in foreign affairs.[5]

Bipartisanship, invented as a harness for Senator Vandenberg, became instead a whip by which Congress might influence the Executive and the overly liberal State Department. In the Act, the Administrator was given a fully independent agency and the authority and status of Cabinet rank. Since it would be bad form to have two Secretaries of State, there would just have to be "successful liaison" [6] between the Administrator and the Secretary of State. Optimistically, Section 105(b) of the Economic Cooperation Act provided that the Administrator and Secretary were to keep each other "fully and currently informed on matters, including prospective action . . . pertinent to the duties of the other." Somewhat more realistically and very much in point is Section 105(b)(3), which provided that ". . . if differences of view are not adjusted by consultation [between Administrator and Secretary], the matter shall be referred to the President for final decision."

If there had been any doubts about the likelihood of such an

[4] Arthur H. Vandenberg, Jr., *The Private Papers of Senator Vandenberg* (Boston: Houghton-Mifflin, 1952), p. 388. See also President Truman's message to Congress, December 19, 1947: "The Administrator must be subject to the direction of the Secretary of State on decisions and actions affecting our foreign policy." *State Department Bulletin* (December 28, 1947), p. 1243.

[5] On Marshall, see H. B. Price, *The Marshall Plan and Its Meaning* (Ithaca: Cornell University Press, 1955), p. 69; on Vandenberg, see *Papers,* p. 388.

[6] Vandenberg, p. 393.

arrangement becoming a second State Department, all actions
following passage should have dispelled them. Marshall's
choice for Administrator was his Undersecretary of State Will
Clayton. Vandenberg successfully opposed Clayton on the
grounds that the "overriding Congressional desire [was] that
the ERP Administrator come from the outside business world
with strong industrial credentials and *not* via the State Department. . . . [T]his job as ERP Administrator stands out by
itself—as demonstrated in all of the Congressional debates—as
requiring particularly persuasive economic credentials unrelated to diplomacy." [7] On similar grounds, President Truman's
initial proposal of Dean Acheson was also vetoed. Paul Hoffman suited the requirement of business experience to a T.

Hoffman's operational code for ECA was based upon a profoundly political decision to be nonpolitical: "I believed that in
fighting communism in Europe, we would lose all our moor-
ings if we adopted the Machiavellian philosophy that the ends
justify the means. Therefore I insisted on confining ourselves to
the recovery field. . . . I had a strong belief that no pattern
imposed by a group of planners in Washington could possibly
be effective. . . . Coming into this with a business back-
ground, I thought that if we in the ECA adopted a new role—
as a kind of investment banker—that would be the right
approach." [8]

The statute also provided for a Special Representative to
Europe, with rank of Ambassador Extraordinary and Pleni-
potentiary (Section 108). The Special Representative was to
direct the special ECA missions, which were to be established
in each country *independent from the regular diplomatic mission* (Section 109). In any disputes with diplomatic missions,
the chief of the ECA mission and the Ambassador in each
country were considered equal parties in consultation that
could be carried up to the Administrator and Secretary of State
(Section 105(b)(3)).

The staffing of ECA made it in reality the second State Department. Averell Harriman, appointed Special Representa-

[7] *Ibid.*, p. 393. (Emphasis in original.)
[8] Quoted in Price, *op. cit.*, pp. 73–74.

tive, had been Truman's Secretary of Commerce. He had served as an ambassador, but in his experience in foreign affairs he was more accustomed to dealing directly with the President. William C. Foster, named Deputy Special Representative, had been Undersecretary of Commerce. The Deputy Administrator was Howard Bruce, a Baltimore industrialist-financier and formerly Director of Materiel, Army Service Forces. Others in offices close to Hoffman included: three professors of specialties important to ECA; two New York Attorneys, one of whom was also president of Time, Inc.; a onetime president of the Export-Import Bank; the chief of Foreign Agricultural Relations in the Department of Agriculture; and a couple of professional administrators. There was some experience in foreign affairs among them, *but there was not a single professional from the State Department in the entire company* (unless Harriman's very special experience is counted). The list contains several important departures from Hoffman's principle of business experience, but no departures from an unspoken rule of independence from the "other" State Department. Among the first chiefs of ECA missions were: Thomas K. Finletter, executive, attorney, air expert sent to the United Kingdom; David Bruce, Assistant Secretary of Commerce, 1947–48, sent to France; J. D. Zellerbach, San Francisco businessman, sent to Italy; and Roger Lapham, former Mayor of San Francisco, sent to China. Only David Bruce had had State Department experience prior to his appointment to ECA, and that was as a vice consul in Rome, 1926–28.

The initial expectation was that ECA would be a small agency whose staff would be essentially a few experts in agriculture, industry and procurement.[9] But once in operation, ECA began to grow, not merely in obedience to some Parkin-

[9] Price, *op. cit.*, p. 75; see also Truman's ECA message, *op. cit.*, p. 1242: ". . . I expect that the Economic Cooperation Administration will need only a small staff. No vast new agency or corporation is needed to perform functions for which government facilities now exist." The facts in this section are taken largely from Price, Vandenberg, and Robert Asher's *Grants, Loans and Local Currencies* (Washington: The Brookings Institution, 1961); however, none of these authors would necessarily agree with my interpretations.

son's law of bureaucracy, but in a politically significant manner. The staff turned immediately to analysis of economic conditions in order to have independent means of assessing the plans of the Organization for European Economic Coordination (OEEC). Although the autonomy of OEEC and the independence of the program were stressed from the very beginning (see Hoffman's attitude above, for example), it is impossible to believe that the framers of the aid agency were naive enough to think they could make the whole process self-executing and nonpolitical. If ECA was not going to accept OEEC plans as final, it was going to have to make value judgments. That is the implication of their "analyses of economic conditions." If only to that extent, ECA had to become a second State Department.

A second aspect of this expansion of the political character of ECA was early growth and elaboration of the Special Representative's Office in Paris, despite the fact that it was expected to be a staff merely for the Representative himself: "Never before had an overseas regional office been set up to play so large a part in a peacetime operation of the United States government." [10] This separated still further our economic aid from our central political arms, while at the same time it further guaranteed that political considerations would be involved in ECA's "economic" decisions. With complete lack of concern for the political dimension, the Administrator also set up an Office of Labor Advisors for propagandizing European unions on the commitment of American labor to the democratic point of view.

ECA was a partial decision. In effect, Congress said, "You can have the money but you cannot use money as a means of realizing our interests abroad and you cannot use money as a means of unifying our far-flung foreign operations." Congress was not altogether at fault, but its compulsion for access fed upon general confusions as to how a democratic foreign policy operation should operate. Frequently domestic policy is so partial that it is nugatory (e.g., the Employment Act of 1946). Sometimes it can be so partial as to be confusing beyond words

[10] Price, *op. cit.*, p. 76.

(e.g., three or four different ways granted the President to control strikes). Policies can be so partial that they are self-destructive (as when one program is dedicated to getting people off farms while another serves to keep them on). This is called "slack in the system," and through such means we buy time, displace conflict, avoid the costs of planning. Obviously this is expensive, and perhaps a rich country can afford partial decisions. We cannot, however, afford them in the international realm; but they occur, as in the Marshall Plan. When they occur here, they are evidence of a bargaining pattern and logrolling values.

The objection to the original presidential plan was not so much to the lodging of such additional international power in the State Department. Perhaps that sentiment could be found among many left-over isolationists, but not among the new or the old internationalists. The stronger objection was to lodging so much power in a State Department *to regulate the domestic economy* for purposes of manipulating international patterns. The isolationists disliked power because they did not want to shape the world. The new liberals did not want the power because they did not really want to shape the United States. Placed outside the State Department, pure economic aid could be seen as merely an expansion of trading domain, but that approach robbed the program of much of its value as an instrument of foreign affairs. However well ECA may have served Europe, its independence deprived the United States of a major opportunity to regulate and coordinate its own resources. Formulation of ECA, far from being a case of elite or of presidential power, is a reflection of the inability of officialdom during the postwar period to formulate effective policies. It was also one of their contributions to the decentralized and bargaining system of foreign policy that continues to formulate undependable policies.

BUILDING A NONESTABLISHMENT IN DEFENSE

Following World War II, everyone seemed to desire unification, and it seemed not only possible but necessary. Success of that new invention, the Joint Chiefs of Staff, proved the possibility. Bipolarity proved the necessity by constantly pushing marginal issues toward high policy. Occupation policy and collective security proved the necessity because of their whole-country view of obligations and resources. Development and control of atomic power obviously proved the necessity. Yet, we did not get unification in 1947, and no very serious effort has been made since that time to make up the difference. The malefactors in the first instance were Congress, in cooperation with military jealousies. The interest-group liberal approach to foreign policy can best be seen in how liberal leaders rationalized these patterns and then coped with this system in the later years.

The core of the new Defense Establishment was the National Security Council (NSC), which was set up in the statute as an ex officio body with very little in the way of arms and legs. It was a committee of the Cabinet with all the representativeness of a committee and none of the coherence of a working organization. Moreover, it came to mean the existence of a second Cabinet for defense by which disputants were given their choice of forum.[11] Except for the Central Intelligence Agency (CIA), the statute contemplated no organizational reality for NSC at all, for there was not even the mention of a Department of Defense. There was to be a small Office of the Secretary of Defense.[12]

Everything below was confederation. There was even a "Tenth Amendment." Section 202 provided the Secretary with some general powers but further provided that each of the respective military services "shall be administered as individual executive departments . . . and all powers and duties relating to such departments not specifically conferred upon the Secretary of Defense by this Act shall be retained by each of their respective Secretaries." The powers left to the Secretary of De-

[11] *Cf.* Paul Hammond, "The National Security Council as a Device for Interdepartmental Co-ordination," reprinted in *Readings in the Making of American Foreign Policy*, ed. Andrew Scott and Raymond H. Dawson (New York: Macmillan, 1965), p. 360.

[12] The 1947 Statute provided for only a "National Military Establishment, and the Secretary of Defense shall be head thereof." (Section 201a.)

fense were largely fiscal and, despite some change after 1958, remain the same today. The fact that so many Secretaries have been out of Big Finance or Big Business seems more a reflection of the true function of the job than of the "power eliteness" of the incumbents. The narrowness of the Secretary's powers is most clearly evidenced by the rights of the military branches, too well-known to belabor here. Not only did the Act totally brush aside the civilian Secretaries of each service department, it went so far as to provide for no chairman of the Joint Chiefs but rather allowed them to "take rank among themselves according to their relative dates of appointment. . . ." (Section 208b). The scheme favored by the President, the Collins Plan, called for a single chief of staff of the Armed Forces responsible to the Secretary of Defense.[13] In Millis' judgment ten years later, this decentralization rendered the Joint Chiefs "almost constitutionally incapable of resolving the major problems which the National Security Act had confided to them . . ."; but since no other unit in the establishment had power to do better, "there was something to be said for leaving them to an agency which, rather than resolve them wrongly, would not resolve them at all." [14]

At about the time of Millis' observations the Eisenhower Administration made some attempt to strengthen the center of the Defense Establishment. However, the opinions of students of the Act suggest that the statutory effort was meek and unhelpful. While enlarging the Office of the Secretary and adding an under-secretary and some assistant secretaries to the Department of Defense created in 1949, the 1958 Act continued to forbid the Secretary to encroach upon the "combatant functions assigned to the military services" while also making it quite explicit that the new assistant secretaries "should not be in the direct line of administrative authority between [the Secretary] and the three military departments. . . ." [15]

[13] Paul Y. Hammond, *Organizing for Defense* (Princeton: Princeton University Press, 1961), pp. 213 ff.
[14] Walter Millis and Harvey Mansfield, *Arms and the State* (New York: Twentieth Century Fund, 1958), p. 183.
[15] Gene M. Lyons, "The New Civil-Military Relations," in Scott and Dawson, *op. cit.*, pp. 414–15.

If the position of the Secretary of Defense has been strengthened in the 1960's it is not due to conscious plans of the policy-making elite but rather to the chance and unpredictable factors of technology and personality.[16] As to the first, it is clear that new weapons and the expansion of research and development gave the center a stronger hand, because the assignment of new missions and functions is a powerful source of influence when used with the desire for influence clearly in mind. The second factor is strong personality and intellect—that is, Robert McNamara. Personal rationality coupled with special techniques of program budgeting and cost-benefit analysis gave the Secretary and the Office of the Secretary an unusually strong hand. During the late 1950's and 1960's, as a consequence, the civilian service secretaries lost reputation and then power to the Defense undersecretaries and assistant secretaries, and that meant the decline of an office that had become a source of special pleaders. During the same period it seems clear that the Joint Chiefs also lost relative to the Secretary. Their inability to centralize around a real Chief and their consequent inability to reach and hold agreements gave McNamara and his predecessors some of their opportunities to exert influence.[17]

However, if one looks closely at these recent developments one cannot find any strong evidence that fundamental change has taken place. The modern Secretary is a more powerful figure, but his enhanced power rests upon the subterfuges of budgetary controls—the allocation of moneys and missions. That suggests that real cohesion around the Secretary and the President has not been institutionalized. Any greater accountability in recent years is due to bargaining advantages and must be treated as possibly ephemeral. Secretary McNamara's very strength could be the undoing of his successors. His initial assignments of roles have used up many of the options of future Secretaries. (Perhaps it is indicative that the Navy an-

[16] In all of this I am indebted to Hammond, to Lyons, and to Millis and Mansfield; however, they would not necessarily agree with the interpretations I have put upon their research.

[17] In Lyons' opinion this is the most important explanation for the increase of civilian authority. (*Op. cit.*, p. 415.)

nounced its decision not to use the F-111 shortly after McNamara's retirement.)

Much more could and should be said of the internal life of the Pentagon. But there is more to be learned by looking briefly outside the Department to the relations between it and the other working parts of our total defense activity. Of those parts the most fascinating is the Atomic Energy Commission. No one any longer questions the proposition that the AEC is very loosely connected to central political controls. Relations here are so loose as to make foreign governments wonder whether the United States has any national interests at all.

The Atomic Energy Commission's powers within its vast domain exceed "those of any department of the government ever before established. The Commission has, in effect, a plenary charter to do anything in the field of atomic energy that will promote the public safety and welfare." [18] Section 4 of the Act of 1946, for instance, turns over all ownership of fissionable materials and control of all production facilities. Decisions on fissionable material to be released for research or as irrelevant to bomb production are left to the Commission. The Commission was set up deliberately and legally as a monopoly.

There was probably never any issue over whether atomic energy and its production would or would not be a government monopoly. The issues, rightfully in my opinion, revolved around how the monopoly would relate to the rest of the government. But the significant thing here is the alternative control features debated. In high-sounding tones the fate of atomic energy was defined as passing to "civilian control" or to "military control." This simplified things for purposes of debate in Congress and in the press; and, better, this definition of the problem gave everyone a point of reference by fitting the perplexing atom into established (prewar) liberal-conservative alignments.[19] But obviously it had very little to do with the real problems of how to make the atom serve national inter-

[18] James R. Newman and Byron S. Miller, *The Control of Atomic Energy* (New York: Whittlesey House, 1948), p. 27.

[19] *Cf.* Byron S. Miller, "The Atomic Energy Act of 1946," in *Legislative Politics U.S.A.*, ed. Theodore J. Lowi (Boston: Little, Brown, 1962, 1965), p. 267.

ests. To the combatants, "civilian control" meant ease of access to atomic information and materials by universities and businesses, and "military control" meant access and control by the separate military services. It is clear from the debates that few on either side sought to vest control in *neither* of these sides. Almost none of the interested parties expected that control should rest in the hands of the political executives who would run the Defense Establishment. Dahl and Brown are left to ask five years later whether the Commission should or should not be placed within the Department of Defense. Since the overwhelming proportion of its work has been in military and strategic uses, why should the program be anything more than one part of the arms program? [20] The question should emphasize the fact that the separation of the AEC from the executive was almost a foregone conclusion, and that with its founding the decentralized and bargaining system of foreign policy has been institutionalized still further.

Thus, the AEC became its own boss. It was made independent, and apparently continues to be just as independent, of State and of Defense, and, therefore, of the Presidency. In security affairs, the AEC is a coequal partner of Defense. AEC-Defense disputes, like ECA-State disputes, have been settled, according to the Act, by the President. At first this arrangement may appear to be a sound principle of insuring presidential involvement, but that would be mere rationalization of the inevitable. During the formative years, through 1951, only one dispute—over the custody of atomic weapons—was taken to the President, and that one would have gone up to him regardless of AEC location. More important is the fact that the President decided this one in favor of the AEC and that, given the spirit of the Act, that was really the only decision possible.[21] So long as the AEC possesses a monopoly of the secrets [22] along

[20] *Cf.* Robert A. Dahl and Ralph S. Brown, *Domestic Control of Atomic Energy* (New York: Social Science Research Council, 1951), pp. 25–26.

[21] *Cf.* Dahl and Brown, p. 24.

[22] Section 10, in which the Commission was given power to "control the dissemination of restricted data" and also to decide what were "restricted data." (Sec. 10[b][1] defined "restricted data" as *all* data

with its monopoly of the materials, it will also possess most of the advantages in bargaining with the President. There is paraphernalia inside the AEC for military representation and joint consultation, but that was put in largely to guarantee access for the separate services, not particularly for the highest echelons, as part of the fight among the services for operational control of the bomb.

This left (and leaves) the Secretary of Defense as simply the biggest customer of the AEC but with no statutory rights of direction. In stark contrast, Congress gave to itself an extremely strong statutory right to participate in, with the distinct possibility of controlling, AEC decisions. This means that all the arguments about the novelty and the unique significance and the international security importance of atomic energy are largely empty rhetoric. The setup is essentially like every other independent agency created since the ICC. H. L. Nieburg, in an excellent paper on the AEC, has detected several spiritual ages in the life of the Commission, roughly paralleling the tenure of each AEC chairman.[23] But were these really distinct ages? Even during the period of strongest executive orientation Nieburg saw the AEC as an "independent commission," by which we must assume he meant that it was a question not of the AEC's loyalty to the President but of its being free to try to play the President off against Congress and against other agencies to maintain its own integrity as a separate executive agency. If that is the case, then the history of the AEC can be taken, without doing any injustice to Nieburg's findings, as a case of variations on this single theme. Nieburg himself goes so far as to characterize atomic policy during all of Eisenhower's last years as "not congressional predominance in its simplest form," but rather an alliance between the AEC and the Joint Atomic Energy Committee [24]

having to do in any way with fissionable material for bombs or power, and then it left it to the Commission to decide what data could be published.)

[23] H. L. Nieburg, "The Eisenhower AEC and Congress," *Midwest Journal of Political Science* (May 1962), pp. 116–117.

[24] *Ibid.*, p. 116.

against President, Treasury, Budget, and State. The change of administration and the restoration of common party majorities in both branches did not change this pattern very much. In a later publication Nieburg observed that AEC Chairman Seaborg has "not yielded to congressional direction, but through the graceful maneuvers of politics, his boss the President [Kennedy] has." [25] Only the rhetoric seems to be different.

The AEC is another partial decision, wrought out of the same conflict and compromise that seem inevitably to characterize traditional American political decision-making. In accommodation to industry and military service interests the AEC was made "independent." As a result, however, atomic energy, atomic weaponry, and information regarding them are not a direct part of the resources of diplomacy or of strategy. In war, of course, AEC separatism, like all agency and group particularism, might disappear. But that is in war. When fragmentation and conflict are perpetuated in separate agencies, each with statutory integrity, none enjoying many rights to intervene against others, policy decisions are inevitably shaped by the momentary requirements of getting agreement, not the ultimate fact of realizing foreign objectives. [26] Creating an unassailable AEC, a sacred separation among the Services, an independent NASA, a subterranean CIA, and so forth must seriously impair efforts to put any of these instruments to the service of political strategies. More academically, their separate existence should destroy any claim that foreign policy formulation is a fundamentally different kind of system, or that it is in any considerable way insulated from domestic political forces. [27] These instruments are all partial decisions in themselves and their existence produces partial decisions in the

[25] H. L. Nieburg, *Nuclear Secrecy and Foreign Policy* (Washington: Public Affairs, 1964), p. 36.

[26] *Cf.* Samuel P. Huntington, "Strategy Planning and the Political Process," *Foreign Affairs*, XXXVIII (Jan., 1960), 291.

[27] These patterns are not ancient errors unlikely to be committed again. For examples one need only look at the international aspects of COMSAT, the modern CIA, the cooperation of AID with missionary groups.

everyday activities of the central political leaders. Let us look directly at how these central leaders respond to the diffuse system created for them.[28]

POLICIES: OVERSELL, NOT OVERKILL

The liberal state that prizes agency independence, bargaining, letting-all-the-people-in, and general unpredictability has succeeded beyond its hopes in the foreign policy field even as it was failing in the domestic field. International liberals got the country committed to the international system, but the liberal system of organization has interfered with fashioning these commitments into a self-serving force. These patterns have left the President and his foreign policy elite a hopeless task of making a ministry out of what can at best be a coalition. Despite the frequency with which this system is praised, and despite the valiant efforts in 20 years to make do with it, the real behavior of the President and his elite reflects the real problems and the pathologies. Their behavior since World War II can be summarized as "oversell": They have been forced to oversell every remedy for world ailments and to oversell each problem for which the remedy might be appropriate.

OVERSELLING THE REMEDY

Support for the United Nations was a policy the United States as determined to fashion after World War II, if only as repayment for having helped destroy the League of Nations. Enormous care was taken to insure passage of the United Nations Charter as a treaty in the Senate—passage without crippling amendment or embarrassing debate. So well

[28] Kenneth Waltz has insisted that fragmentation exists in Britain and the USSR and that it does not constitute a special American problem of disunity. True, most advanced states are highly differentiated (fragmentation being reserved for differentiation one does not like). However, this becomes a special problem in the United States because it lacks the centripetal institutions possessed by the other countries. *Cf.* Waltz's *Foreign Policy and Democratic Politics* (Boston: Little, Brown, 1967).

was the UN sold that when the Charter came before the Senate for advice and consent, almost no opposition remained. As Bertram Gross recorded it: "Since little defense of the Charter was needed, few senators planned to speak on its behalf and there was genuine danger that an impression of disinterest would be created. As a last-minute measure . . . Senator Connally . . . was seen walking around the floor with a pad of paper in one hand and a pencil in the other, button-holing one senator after another and beseeching them to speak on behalf of the United Nations." [29]

What seemed politically appropriate and successful for the occasion, however, proved to have been almost too heavy a price to pay, for many of the most attentive members of the public had become convinced that the UN would be a real instrument of our foreign policy. Thus, when the critical emergency of aid to Greece and Turkey arose, the possibility of a timely response by the United States ran into serious difficulty from unexpected sources. Once the news of direct United States action in Greece and Turkey became known, "the overwhelming attachment of the American public to the United Nations made itself felt in no uncertain terms, and many of the staunchest supporters of the President's policy, who were at the same time backers of the United Nations—including Walter Lippmann, Marquis Childs, Barnet Nover, and Anne O'Hare McCormick—were deploring the failure of the President to notify the United Nations and to adopt other procedures that would have brought his proposed action 'within the spirit of the United Nations.'" [30]

Hands were burned but apparently no lessons were learned, for Administration leaders treated Greek-Turkish aid and the larger ideas created to package this aid as though it would be the last time Congress and the public would ever have to be faced. These programs were "proposed and accepted with panacean overtones" [31] for the quickie rebuilding of Europe,

[29] Bertram Gross, *The Legislative Struggle* (New York: McGraw-Hill, 1953), p. 368.

[30] Jones, *op. cit.*, p. 181.

[31] Gabriel Almond, *The American People and Foreign Policy* (New York: Harcourt, Brace, 1950), p. 88.

righting the wrongs in underdeveloped lands, and containing the Communists once and for all. So, the original Policy Planning Staff memorandum prior to Marshall's Harvard speech stressed that "the program must contain reasonable assurance that if we support it, this will be the last such program we shall be asked to support in the foreseeable future." [32] President Truman stressed this "get it over with" theme in his December, 1947, special message on aid.

Two years later when the pressures for expansion of economic and military involvement were so great—note NSC 68 alone [33]—the Korean outbreak must have come as a considerable relief to those who had to face Congress, for without the war the totalism of the Marshall Plan would have made any reassessment look like badly broken pledges. One other important aspect of oversell in the aid programs was the stress the public was allowed to put upon the doctrines of (1) self-help and (2) anticommunism. Soon after passage, the Administration got into hot water over the glaring inconsistencies of opposition to helping Spain (anti-Communist and ready to help herself) and eagerness to help Yugoslavia (Communist).

Examples of oversell can just as easily be found in noneconomic policies, and they serve even better as indices to the politics of the foreign policy establishment. The most interesting is the case of the Administration's perjury on American troop commitments under the NATO treaty. At the time of the treaty ratification, there was intense opposition in Congress to the degree of entanglement implied in NATO. To the treaty unanimously reported by the Foreign Relations Committee, Senator Wherry, for himself, Taft, and Watkins attempted to attach the reservation that none of the parties was committed "morally or legally to furnish or supply arms. . . ." [34] Due to unequivocal assurances made publicly and privately at that

[32] Quoted in Jones, *op. cit.*, p. 250.

[33] Millis and Mansfield, *op. cit.*, p. 256. NSC 68 was a major policy paper dealing with the escalation of the cold war toward a period of "maximum danger" in 1952.

[34] Quoted in Bradford Westerfield, *Foreign Policy and Party Politics* (New Haven, Yale University Press, 1955), p. 332. See also *Hearings*, cited below, pp. 119–20.

time, the reservation was withdrawn and the treaty was allowed to pass unamended. A year later, when we did become committed to stationing troops aboard, these early assurances hurt.

In April, 1949, Senator Hickenlooper asked Secretary Acheson: "Are we going to be expected to send substantial numbers of troops over there as a more or less permanent contribution to the development of these countries' capacity to resist?" Acheson's 1949 reply was: "The answer to that question, Senator, is a clear and absolute 'No.'" [35] In the 1951 hearings, Acheson, when reminded of 1949, attempted to get out of his embarrassment with labored definitions. He explained that if the "expected to" in the 1949 question meant that under the treaty we had undertaken a commitment, the answer was "No"; however, that did not mean an absolute "No" to a question whether we "intended to" send them.[36] His testimony was accompanied by an elaborate brief showing that the President, in his role as commander-in-chief, needed no congressional authorization for sending the troops, and that the treaty had not affected this power one way or the other.[37] No one questioned this, but many felt that such a brief would have been more appropriate in 1949.[38]

What is significant is that such misrepresentation was necessary. What is significant is that there could be no proper conspiracy among leaders in the pursuit of the national interests of the United States. Misrepresentation by the Administration in the presentation of the package to Congress is a strong example of oversell. Moreover, it was the sense of misrepresentation felt by Congress that had brought forth the 1951 Wherry Resolution in the first place. The Wherry Resolution declared that

[35] Committee on Foreign Relations, *Hearings on the Assignment of Ground Forces of the United States to Duty in the European Area* (Washington, 1951), p. 111. For further reference to "absolute assurance," see p. 120. These extraordinary hearings were held pursuant to the Wherry Resolution discussed below.

[36] *Ibid.*, p. 112.

[37] *Ibid.*, pp. 88 ff., 110. This contrasts with the Administration's 1949 assurance that the treaty would be resubmitted if troops were contemplated (p. 120).

[38] *Ibid.*, p. 120.

no troops would be stationed in Europe under NATO "pending the adoption of a policy with respect thereto by the Congress." [39] This incredible expression would have forcibly pried open the foreign policy establishment. The hearings pursuant to the Wherry Resolution achieved the following, according to Senator Russell: "It is the first time, I suppose, in such a critical international situation that any great power has laid all of its cards on top of the table not only to be seen by our allies but by our potential enemies." [40] This is the reaction of a consumer who discovers he has been oversold.

Overselling of package doctrines has been repeated over and over again in the years since the postwar period. Eisenhower's personal diplomacy ("I shall go to Korea," "spirit of Camp David"), Dulles' brinkmanship, and Charles E. Wilson's "bigger bang" were necessary parts of the task of selling the New Look—which in turn was marketing language for making the absolutely necessary downward budgetary adjustments in the post-Korean period. Since so much foreign policy between Korea and Sputnik involved implementation and amendment of basic instruments already in existence, naturally much of the process in these years landed in the fiscal area. Consequently, Congress enacted fiscal versions of the Wherry Resolution as a means of dispelling for itself the fog of oversell. In 1951, Congress enacted a requirement that military departments must "come into agreement" with the Armed Services Committees on virtually all transactions involving real estate for military installations.[41] Eight years later it was repealed through constitutional (Attorney General) construction, and only after that by Congress. But it was immediately replaced by another "fiscal Wherry Resolution," the Russell Amendment. This stated: "No funds may be appropriated after December 31, 1960, to or for the use of any armed force of the United States

[39] *Ibid.*, pp. 38–39.

[40] *Ibid.*, p. 87.

[41] See Raymond H. Dawson, "Innovation and Intervention in Defense Policy," in Robert L. Peabody and Nelson W. Polsby, eds., *New Perspectives on the House of Representatives* (Chicago: Rand-McNally, 1963), p. 283. This amendment was vetoed by Truman and then passed as a rider to another bill.

for the procurement of aircraft, missiles, or naval vessels unless the appropriation of such funds *has been authorized by legislation enacted after such date.*[42]

It seems then that one special development in foreign policy since the formative years has been the institutionalization of second thoughts in Congress. This is the mentality of "Stop the world, we want to get on" that has arisen out of the failure of leaders to find means of dealing with each other frankly yet confidentially. And the Kennedy and Johnson Administrations have given no signs of change. The Common Market was so far oversold to Congress as to imperil the 1962 Trade Act. The Alliance for Progress was packaged to sound like an attempt to revolutionize the hemisphere. The lack of coherence that makes oversell necessary caught Presidents Eisenhower and Johnson in outright lies on the U-2 incident and the Pueblo affair. It caught the more sophisticated Kennedy in one of the most disastrous adventures in the history of national prestige. The Bay of Pigs is the classic case of the partial decision: "You may go to war in Cuba but you may not have the support necessary to succeed." No wonder the President must propagandize his colleagues and the country if he is to avoid the partial decision.

No policy has escaped injury to itself and to national interests and international stability in the years since American statesmen have felt the need to oversell policies in order to avoid coming up with a partial decision. The current war in Vietnam has been just another instance of the point. The fighting in the South was not of our making. The crisis was. The escalation was. The involvement in Vietnam was sold by American image-makers as a case of unambiguous aggression and therefore of the need for military victory. Perhaps it was both of these things, but to sell it on the front pages that way in order to insure support at home left world diplomats, including our own, with almost no options. Under increasing popular pressure, magnified by congressmen who might rightly feel that they have not been properly informed, the extremes of oversell are exceeded over and over again. From domino theo-

[42] *Ibid.,* p. 273. (Emphasis added.)

rics we got the Rusk Doctrine of the total involvement of the credibility of the United States. From that we got the almost total commitment to the Ky regime, whose weaknesses almost brought down all of our shaky justifications. There was the invention of the myth of viable democracy to replace the Ky regime and then the myth of eminent military victory to support everything else. It may take years to de-escalate meanings and deflate myths about Vietnam.

When experiments must be sold as sure things and specialized sure things must be sold as cure-alls, frustration and failure are inevitable. An experiment may be partially successful; but after oversell partial success must be accepted as failure. Failure leads to distrust and frustration, which lead to more oversell and to further verbal excesses, as superlatives become ordinary through use. Since international politics is special in the amount of risk involved, these responses become especially intense. All of which leads to the worst possible abuse of oversell, the rhetoric of victory. While it has been resisted, with exceptions, up to now, the rhetoric of victory is constantly on the verge of gaining ascendancy. It is the last stage before the end of politics.

OVERSELLING THE THREAT

The second type of oversell is essentially the attempt to create the moral equivalent of war. It is the conversion of interactions into incidents, incidents into challenges, challenges into threats and threats into crises for the purpose of imposing temporary and artificial cohesion upon the members of the foreign policy establishment. It is the escalation of meanings. When peace is in peril, all Presidents have found it necessary to create that sense of self-restraint, self-sacrifice, and devotion to higher causes that seems to come about so naturally in war. For modern Presidents, this tactic has become necessary, compelling, and regular whether there is a true crisis or not.

Typically, a Briton provided us with our most important concepts. In the vocabulary of oversell no doctrines have been as important as "cold war" and "iron curtain." (Also typically, the British proceeded to take it all less seriously than we.)

There were, of course, varying amounts of truth underlying both terms. Perhaps there is a total but unseen war. Perhaps there has been a Communist devil who will "get you if you don't watch out." But the analytic value of the terms was lost to their hortatory value: We might get some cohesion in the policy-making elite if we can only attribute to our enemies a singleness of purpose and a perfection of rational means to achieve it. These two Churchillian themes proved to fill basic psychological and political needs in our system, and they have been used to help oversell crises ever since.

"Containment," first seized upon to help provide a package for Greek-Turkish aid, was also found to be generally valuable. It became a significant American contribution to the more pervasive themes of cold war and iron curtain. It helped show that all local wars, guerilla actions, and *coups d'état* were interrelated and cumulative.[43]

Along with these pervasive themes are the more specialized, *ad hoc* emotions. President Eisenhower had an important oversell mechanism in McCarthyism. Functionally, McCarthyism was the internal equivalent of containment, and it helped bring the 20-year Democratic, tea-sipping, and Soviet-friendly State Department into line as well as to silence much independent opposition. Late in his Administration, Eisenhower found overselling of foreign crises increasingly valuable as his per-

[43] *Cf.* Lippmann: "All the postwar Presidents have taken it for granted that they had to create the majority they needed [for unpopular foreign policies], and that, while some . . . might respond to argument, the others had to be scared into joining up. . . . As a result, it has become part of the established procedure of American foreign policy to invoke the threat of Communist takeover whenever American opinion is divided. As the practice has grown, the formula has been generalized. Now we are accepting the unique burden of resisting the advance of Communism everywhere. . . ." Lippmann refers to this as the "all-purpose myth" despite the "essential fact" about disorders like Vietnam and the Dominican Republic that "they are at bottom indigenous to the countries where the social order is broken down, not originally, not essentially, conspiracies engineered from the centers of Communist power" (*Newsweek*, May 4, 1965, p. 23). He goes on to argue that the myth will be used to "reassure our people that Mr. Johnson is not going to take part in an unending series of wars," because we can teach the "masterminds of a universal conspiracy" a lesson in only one or two encounters.

sonal prestige declined. Dulles became famous for such talk as the "brink of war" and "massive retaliation." The latter phrase was particularly effective because it helped oversell the positive value of atomic over conventional arms, and at the same time helped create the sense of the seriousness and immediacy of the threat that made nuclear retaliation necessary. Dulles opposed containment as "negative, futile, and immoral" and implied its replacement with rhetoric that (especially for Europe) verged on preventive war. But he continued to sell all outbreaks the world over as interrelated and cumulative. Finally there was the use of Sputnik for a variety of issues in the arms race during the "Sputnik age."

Much of the activity in Kennedy's short term was of the same nature. In fact, Kennedy spent more of his earlier months on creating a moral equivalent of war than on just about anything else. The "ask not" passage of his inaugural address appeared to be a suitable method of national mobilization. The idea of man-on-the-moon-by-1970 had all sorts of value besides the increasing of space appropriations. A race always implies a threat to virility. The Bay of Pigs, once survived, became an excellent means for creating a sense of unity, then some real unity, on a host of defense-related items. (It is hard to forget the Kennedy-MacArthur, Kennedy-Hoover, Kennedy-Truman, and so forth, unity pictures.) During the Dominican conflict, President Johnson added another major variant to the threat of Communist encirclement. His approach was almost like a parody of Southern racial fears: a thirty-secondth fraction of Communist blood makes a local movement part of the "world Communist conspiracy."

Techniques of overselling the nature of a crisis are not as specific and selective as those of overselling remedies. This is why themes have been stressed. But they are no less a reflection of the pathologies of the system. Facing real political stress, and committed to real goals about which there is usually a great deal of consensus, the President must employ domestic strategies that may give him the means of realizing the goals without having a partial decision on his hands. He turns public because his major resources are public. He oversells because that is what one must do to sway a large public. There is always hope, as we must judge from his actions, that he can reverse the aphorism, "He who mobilizes the elite mobilizes the public." What has become important to the President is the possibility that "he who can mobilize the public may mobilize the elite."

The special relationship of the President to the public makes this an attractive recourse. In international affairs, presidential acts or events unambiguously associated with the President tend to increase public support for the President no matter what the act or event was. Such acts or events can even reverse a long-range slump in presidential prestige. This pattern is borne out in the public opinion polls with uncommon consistency. On Table 6.1. are the results of questions asked a national sample concerning how they felt in general about the way the President was doing his job. This question is asked on each poll once every three weeks or every month. The poll is not timed according to national or international events and does not seek to get a referendum on any particular action. In each case shown here, a poll was chosen that had been taken immediately before the event and as soon as possible after the event. The results are extremely suggestive. A disaster, like the Bay of Pigs, tended to rally the people to the President regardless of their attitude toward the event itself. Even a low-pressure event like President Johnson's 1966 visit with former Premier Ky in the Pacific bolstered the President's faltering popularity. Of even greater interest are the 1962 data. Here one can see how clearly the public discriminates between a domestic and an international action. Immediately following the dispatching of Federal troops to the University of Mississippi campus, President Kennedy's standing dropped. At the time of the next poll the Cuban missile crisis had occurred and President Kennedy's standing had gone up significantly.

The logic of the situation is clear. If the President can revive his major resource, his public following, with almost any international act with which he can clearly associate himself, then he must always be under some pressure to prefer such actions. Yet such unambiguous acts are the worst enemy of interna-

TABLE 6.1

THE PRESIDENT'S RELATION TO HIS PUBLIC *

"Do you approve of the way the
President is handling his job?"

		% YES
June, 1950	Before Korean outbreak	37
July, 1950	After U.S. entry	46
August, 1956	Before Israeli, British, French attack on Suez	67
December, 1956	After U.S. opposition to the attack	75
July, 1958	Before Lebanon	52
August, 1958	After U.S. marine landing	58
May, 1960	Before U-2 incident	62
June, 1960	U-2 debacle; collapse of Summit	68
March, 1961	Before Bay of Pigs	73
April, 1961	After Bay of Pigs	83
September, 1962	Before troops to Mississippi	67
October, 1962	After troops, eve of Cuban missile crisis	61
December, 1962	After Cuban missile crisis	74
October, 1966	Before tour of Pacific	44
November, 1966	After tour of Pacific	48
June, 1967	Before Glassboro conference	44
June, 1967	After Glassboro conference	52

* Source: Press releases of the American Institute of Public Opinion (AIPO). *Cf.* Nelson W. Polsby, *Congress and the Presidency* (Englewood Cliffs: Prentice-Hall, 1964), p. 26; and Waltz, *op. cit.*, Chapter 10.

tional diplomacy. Inevitably an unambiguous act encourages other unambiguous acts, military rhetoric tends to displace political rhetoric, and eventually military functions replace diplomatic functions.

The special, direct relationship our President has with his public becomes still more dangerous because after twenty years of international involvement that public has not been matured in its international conscience. It possesses insufficient

tolerance for ambiguity. The public did not become interna-
tionalist, it became neo-isolationist. It seems satisfied only if
the world is put to rights. As Denis Brogan observed during
the McCarthy period, there is an "illusion of omnipotence"
such that our power to put the world to rights is thought by us
to be limited only by stupidity or treason in high places. Sixteen years later one looks at the polls and wonders whether
progress has been made: In November of 1967 the polls
showed that 23 per cent of the people approved and 53 per
cent rejected President Johnson's handling of the Vietnam war,
but 63 per cent were for stepping up rather than reducing the
military effort. The intimacy between the President and his
public is intensified and is rendered more militaristic by large-
scale peacetime conscription. Large-scale jeopardy, uncertain
futures, special kinds of deferments, and eventual service in
foreign involvements require continual attention to and continuous provision of sufficient reason for sacrifice. There is also a
certain rigidity in all of this that perhaps a plebescitary Presidency cannot escape—except by becoming less plebescitary.

There is further danger in overselling threats because the
technique is so nonspecific. Even if the sense of crisis may provide the proper setting for putting an important policy across,
it can create expectations of war that falsely affect allies and
adversaries. More gravely still, the President's own flexibility is
further reduced at a later point when he would like the crisis
to "be over." He might, in other words, wish it on at will, but
he cannot so easily wish it off.

Given the regular use of oversell despite such obvious dan-
gers, the need for it must be enormous. This is all the more
true considering that it continues largely to be unsuccessful.
The President continues to manufacture an occasional crisis
out of a minor challenge, but he still gets partial decisions that
require still more oversell. He must still mortgage a large part
of the value of trade control as a political weapon in order to
get any trade act at all. He must still expect to be forced into
an occasional war, to be forced to fight it one-handed, and
then be expected to win military victory. In diplomacy, the
only thing worse than unambiguous defeat is unconditional

victory. This is the Scylla and Charybdis of presidential power in the politics of survival.

THE FEDERATIVE POWER: BEGINNING OF MATURITY

Democracy is not safe for the world so long as it is not organized for consistently rational action. Without a capacity for real planning, allies cannot trust the system and enemies can too easily miscalculate.

The villain of the piece is not the public, the foreign affairs agencies, Congress, its committees or leaders, the President, or peace agitators. The villain is the outmoded system itself and the outmoded beliefs that support it. It is the system itself that has so often made our international relations so inimical to our own best interests. Interest-group liberalism did not, of course, create this system, but interest-group liberalism perpetuates it by worshipping its virtues. The liberal system today is an anachronism in foreign affairs. Their liberal Presidency is a hopeless burden for the man and a dangerous responsibility for the country.

The Vietnam war is the most recent case in point. Even though most liberals ultimately came to oppose it, their system will ultimately produce another. The expectation that Everyman carries Vietnam data and true understanding in his briefcase, the assumption that every senator and even every member of the House has rights of access to the international machinery, the belief that the press could carry on its own international relations, the expectation that military men are independent factors rather than creatures of politics, the pressure of all of these on the President to respond in logical and justifiable propositions—all these took the issue of a dirty little misadventure on behalf of a hopelessly illegitimate regime and, between 1963 and 1966, almost elevated it into a holy war involving the totality of America's past, present, and future. The escalation of meanings preceded and in great part caused the escalation of conflict. Even in 1966 it was already too late to denounce the peace marchers. They were only availing themselves of rights accorded them by the behavior of the leaders in the irresponsible ways they went about creating consensus and justification for their actions.

After twenty years of world leadership we must ask whether a pluralistic democracy can adjust to the requirements of its world role. The interest-group liberal, quasi-egalitarian requirement will never be conducive to modern foreign-policy-making. The autonomy of international agencies, the direct and intimate relationship of our plebescitary President to his public, and the opportunities each has to influence the other, are as frightful for foreign policy as they would be attractive for domestic policy.

Adjustment will obviously not be easy, even if possible. A step in the proper direction might be taken, however, by appreciating the fact that democracy does have its problems. We could take the most productive step beyond that if we find, next war, some means of imposing the most severe requirements of self-restraint upon our leaders, in their relations with each other and with the public at large. Ultimately the solution will be found in restoring respect for formal institutions and for the roles assigned to them before the outbreak of war. This involves returning to John Locke's Second Treatise and reading all of it. If we wish to salvage our eighteenth-century system we will have to take as an essential part of the Separation of Powers the separation of the "federative power," by which Locke meant, "what is to be done in reference to foreigners."

At first these proposals may seem to constitute an elitist view of a cure. But it is elitist only in the sense that democracy does have special elitist tendencies. The elite in a democracy is comprised of those persons directly responsible to the largest electorates. This elite was expected to have great powers— allowable because the elite could be peacefully cashiered—but great powers nonetheless.

This is actually a *formalistic* rather than an elitist view. And that returns us to a central concern of this book. Legitimacy is bound to suffer if the real veers too far away from the formal. Since there is bound to be great natural divergence, why make a virtue of it? Democracy is a very formalistic system. Everything about it is an attempt to commit power to a regular and understandable exercise. Americans in particular have always been committed to these forms as though they had some bearing on realities. Even the greatest of informalisms, political parties, are subject to hundreds of pages and thousands of titles and sections of State laws. Voluntary associations operate by an iron law of formalism whereby after the first meeting they give themselves a name and elect officers, and after the second meeting write themselves a constitution.

Until recent years these preferences were called due process, and too much informality was called arbitrariness. In our times, stress on formalities is pejoratively called formalism, and informality is called flexibility, participatory democracy, creative federalism, or even due process. This is why the new liberal state suffers from illegitimacy despite its generosity. That is why it is weak at planning, domestic or foreign. That is also why the liberal state cannot achieve justice, an oft-repeated proposition which must now be tackled head-on.

PART III

WHY LIBERAL GOVERNMENTS CANNOT ACHIEVE JUSTICE

". . . we find ourselves on wide, filthy, hostile Fifth Avenue, facing that project which hangs over the avenue like a monument to the folly and the cowardice of good intentions. . . . The projects in Harlem are hated. They are hated almost as much as policemen, and this is saying a great deal. And they are hated for the same reason: both reveal, unbearably, the real attitude of the white world, no matter how many liberal speeches are made. . . ."

James Baldwin

CHAPTER 7

CITIES

The American Tragedy

The United States has been an urban nation for several decades. Why is it only now, when resources are sufficient to meet all basic needs, that most cities are in a state of real or impending disorder?

This will prove to be the most crucial domestic question of our time. Already, on at least three occasions, presidential inquiries have asked the question in one way or another. They came up with useless answers because each was rigidly committed to established, therefore outmoded, thought patterns. The first of these, the so-called Moynihan Report, blamed the problems in the cities on the dissolution of the Negro family and Negro social structure. This conveniently proved that the struggle would be long and would ultimately rest more on general improvement within the Negro community than upon formal redress at law. The second inquiry, following the Los Angeles riots in the Watts area, took a straight deterministic view and laid the blame on economic deprivation. This conveniently proved that the War on Poverty was the best of all possible urban and civil rights policies. The third inquiry, completed at the very time of Martin Luther King's assassination, took the even more brutally frank position that the blame lies with white bigotry. This conveniently proved that the burden of revolution should fall on the white lower classes.[1]

There seems to be no longer any doubt that the Negro's response to the ghetto has been inferior to the responses of the white lower classes preceding the Negroes in the ghetto. The Negro masses seem to be running on a track from personal to social anarchy. However, two flaws in the presidential inquiries explain why they failed to reach the real problem and also why, despite their undoubted sympathy for Negroes, they failed to enjoy the enthusiastic acceptance of Negro leaders. The first is a flaw of strong implication. The reports cannot and do not prove that ghetto conditions are different in the extreme from ghetto conditions of earlier times, yet the reports show that the Negro response has been more extreme. If one takes a socially deterministic explanation for conduct, as almost all applied social scientists do, then one is led unavoidably to the conclusion the the Negro is after all an inferior person.[2] The second flaw in these reports is a sin of omission rather than of implication. At no point is there the charge, or even speculation, that the constitutional structure, governmental activity (including the commissions themselves) or national and local leadership, or the basic laws of the liberal state might be the malefactors.

Such will be the contention of this and the two succeeding chapters: Life is on the decline in our cities because govern-

[1] For the first, see *Daedalus,* Fall, 1965, pp. 745–70. For the second, see "A Time to Listen . . . A Time to Act" (Washington: U.S. Commission on Civil Rights), Nov., 1967; this volume includes an exhaustive bibliography of related government and private studies. For the third, see *Report of the Presidential Commission on Civil Disorders* (New York: Bantam, 1968).

[2] The best the Civil Rights Commission could come up with was a plea for recognition of "black power" as bona fide and a plea for expansion of real participation in society. These are interest-group liberal sentiments predicated on the notion that poor participation and organization structure directly produced the "Negro problem." Meanwhile, recent studies are bringing into question the comfortable myths about Negro family structure and the low level of indigenous organization. *Cf.* the important but obscure study of the National Health and Welfare Council (sponsored by the National Institute of Mental Health), reported in the New York *Times,* February 20, 1966.

mental structure and policy have become incapable of dealing
with modern social problems. Chapters 8 and 9 deal with the
social policies of the liberal state and why they can never succeed. This chapter deals with only the structures of those governments that will have most to do with implementing any
social policies. It will be guided by three propositions: (1) Liberal ideology supports and fosters a division of powers such
that the real sources of the crisis of our time fall in a no-man's-
land among duly constituted but politically impoverished governments inside the metropolitan region. (2) Liberal ideology
in the guise of local government reform has so structured the
central city governments that they are increasingly incapable
of using in a socially significant way the vast powers that do remain in their hands. (3) The metropolitan region, the city, and
the State have failed to get socially meaningful support from
Washington because the Presidency in the liberal state is incapable of dealing in a direct and discretionary way with
urban life.

Old Shame and New

Close observers should have known for years a fact about
urban life that nowadays almost everyone is being forced to
recognize: Cities are well run but badly governed. Modern local governments are generally honest, impressively efficient,
and decently humanitarian. Nonetheless the city is badly governed, and the racial strife that reflects the city's failure may
yet render the city ungovernable. Two general suppositions in
the prevailing ideology have tended to exonerate the political
structure. The first, reflected in the presidential inquiries, is
that there is something socially very new going on in the cities.
A socially deterministic approach requires that we sift all the
social facts and that until the mystery is uncovered the "metropolitan problem" must be allowed to go through a long period
of pluralistic bargaining and experimentation. The second sup-
position is that reform of large city governments toward tech-
nologically meaningful, efficiently bureaucratized political

power is an appropriate form of governmental structure for all the problems the cities will ever face, and that any departures could only result in less efficiency and, therefore, in a reduction of the public interest.

FRAGMENTING THE METROPOLITAN REGION:
DIVIDING THE INDIVISIBLE

Something indeed is new in the cities, but it is not social. It is not the development of suburbia and megalopolis, and it is not the sudden end of the pluralistic process of integration. The city was never a melting pot. It was always a boiling pot. Americans have reason to be proud of their social history because they have had so much to adjust to, but there was never a period free of problems with what we now euphemistically call intergroup relations. Many problems were indeed settled peacefully. For many others violence was required; it was an integral part of urban life from the start. Still more often problems were solved neither by peaceful adjustment nor by confrontation. The pot simply, and quite literally, boiled over. For many escapees there was the West, but for most there was escape to the suburbs. In no sense is this a new pattern.

Cities have always grown at their peripheries. Escape from the city is almost as old as city growth itself. Park and Burgess plot out the fossil remains of outward movement in their concentric circle theory of Chicago. Between 1910 and 1930 the old city of St. Louis along the Mississippi lost 50,000 inhabitants, while the greater city was growing. And so on.

Closer examinations of the makeup of the earlier movements suggests that the reasons for growth through escape to the periphery were also the same, even before the Automobile Age. The reasons are hate and fear, an age-old treadmill. Yankees hated Germans and Irish, and Yankees escaped to whatever was a suburb at the time of the escape. Germans and Irish hated and feared Jews, Italians, Bohemians, Poles, and Greeks —and they escaped. All of them hated and feared the varieties of poor white trash, who inherited the third and fourth generations of central ruins in the wake of their escaping predecessors. Common fear and hatred of the Negro is one more turn in the cycle, and it can hardly be the last turn, for the Negro middle class is not altogether at rest with any of the lower classes. As one Chicago comedian put it, "The black and the white walk shoulder to shoulder, against the lower classes."

If the overall social pattern is about the same now as before, then we are left with a very limited number of reasons for the undeniably inferior adjustment the Negro has been making to it. The first possibility, that the Negro is racially inferior, we must reject—at least until every other possible explanation is exhausted. The second is that the Negro has deliberately chosen disorder, destruction, protest, burning, pillaging, narcotics, numbers, gang warfare, and rule by extortion, and that Negro adjustment is simply a question of his espousal of something other than middle-class white values. This, too, must be rejected. Many black militants do wish to cop out from the white value system, but none can prefer the self-destructive and self-defeating turn the present crisis has taken, and the largest majority of Negroes themselves probably define the present adjustment as inferior. We are led then to the third possibility.

Somewhere about thirty years ago, something much more important than Negro northern immigration or the automobile happened to the social process of the cities. At about that time the residents of the outer periphery of virtually every city in the country began to erect political barriers to the city's development. The suburban city fathers did the impossible: They divided the indivisible. Until the 1920's the city as a political and governmental entity grew along with its population. Governmental jurisdiction went wherever the escaping classes went, and the governmental city remained nearly coextensive with the social and economic city. The legal city was about the same as the real city; city problems were hardly larger than city power and city resources.

Between the two world wars governmental jurisdiction became as selective as the escape pattern itself. In the real city of the 1930's there emerged several important political jurisdictions where once there had been only one or two. In short order each developed its own interest and sense of integrity, for in each case the city fathers knew what they wanted. Incorporation as a legal city gave them the power to zone their properties in ways that could keep out unwanted classes. More generally, it gave them power to enact and to protect their version of the American Way of Life. This was new. If other things were new too, this power was the most important of them. Obviously it put an entirely new light on the meaning and consequences of the regular practice of suburban escape.

In brief, the new pattern of political subdivision of the metropolis closed the city off from its best human and material resources. Cities are the source of the American dynamism. But cities also specialize in another function absolutely vital to the society. Cities specialize in immigrants, in lower classes, in induction of new peoples into the culture, in care for those about to leave the culture, and in all the flotsam and jetsam of industrial society. That is to say, the American city specializes in care for all peoples in greatest need of attention. These people must collect somewhere to be dealt with, and in the United States that place is the city rather than the family, the tribe, the neighborhood, or the internment camp. *Yet as each city incorporates more and more of these needy people it becomes less and less successful in keeping up with its most successful residents*—those who chose to escape from Hyde Park to Glencoe, from Brooklyn to Scarsdale. The Curves of Despair show a strong and inverse relation between city needs and city capacity.

Diagram a. shows how strongly the factor of age can kill a city. Among the 35 cities of most recent vintage, over 20% of their growth between 1950 and 1960 was attributable to annexation. This means that the pattern of escape did not have overwhelmingly negative value to the city; it continued to mean merely a shift of population. Note in contrast how the 49 oldest cities grew through annexation by an average of less than 5 per cent.

Diagram b. adds a special note of desperation to Diagram a. because educational composition is a strong index of a city's capacity to prosper and of its citizens to prosper without public assistance. Here we see that educational composition exacerbates the problem of city age, for the city whose typical adult was badly educated had a poor record of keeping up with its best-educated adults. Among the 40 cities whose adults were largely high school and college graduates, nearly 25 per cent of their population growth was attributable to annexation of new territory. In contrast, in 36 cities in which the typical citizen was a school drop-out, population growth through annexation of suburbs accounted for less than 5 per cent of total growth.

Diagram c. makes abundantly clear that the socially significant pictures presented in the first two diagrams are not spurious. The factor of city size, which most discerning observers would assume is of great importance, plays almost no role in explaining why the old cities and the poorer cities have had such bad luck in keeping up with their escaping middle classes. Cities of over 500,000 population did almost as well as cities of only 80,000 and actually better than cities of around 100,000. It is obvious that when suburbanites resist the giant it is for fear of his smell and size.

All of this points to the simple truth about suburbs and what is really new about them. They are fictions. Literally, they are legal fictions. They are that part of the real city that chose to stay apart and to perpetuate its apartness in the law. A suburb is ultimately an instrument by which the periphery can exploit the center. The suburb is a parasite whose residents can enjoy the benefits of scale and specialization without sharing in the attendant costs. What would the Kenilworth house be worth if suddenly it were transported to the real estate market of Watertown, South Dakota?

The true city, the socioeconomic city, is the entire six-county region of Chicago, the entire fifteen-county region of New York, and so on. Fear found a means, *through government,* to divide the indivisible unit into an incapacitated marketplace of publics. There are now many publics, but there is no polity. Some years ago Robert Wood counted 1,400 governments in the "city" of New York. In a more recent count for the smaller

A. ANNEXATION AND CITY AGE

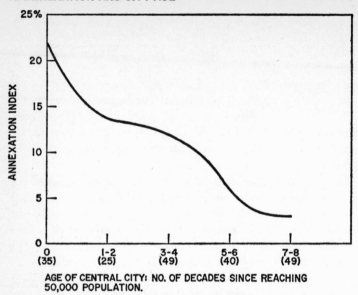

AGE OF CENTRAL CITY: NO. OF DECADES SINCE REACHING 50,000 POPULATION.

B. ANNEXATION AND LEVEL OF EDUCATION

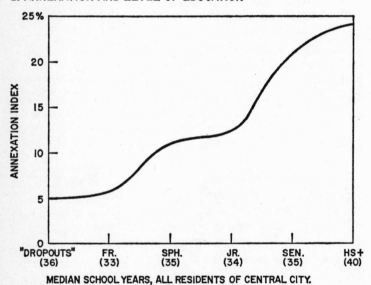

MEDIAN SCHOOL YEARS, ALL RESIDENTS OF CENTRAL CITY.

FIGURE 7.1. The Curves of Despair *

C. ANNEXATION AND SIZE OF CITY

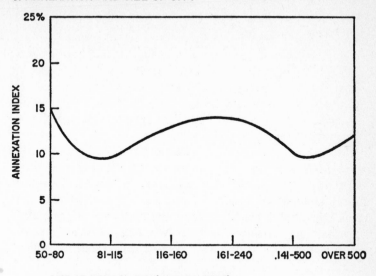

FIGURE 7.1. The Curves of Despair (*continued*) *

* Data drawn from research of Professor Thomas R. Dye ("Urban Political Integration: Conditions Associated with Annexation in American Cities," *Midwest Political Science Quarterly* (Nov., 1964), 430–46), who does not necessarily agree with the conclusions here. Numbers in parenthesis represent the actual number of cities in each category. The total, 213, constitutes all of the Census Bureau's "urbanized areas" in 1960. The Annexation Index is a simple expression of the proportion of a city's growth of population between 1950 and 1960 which was attributable to annexation of new territory.

"city" of Chicago, there proved to be 1,060 governments, of which 995 were substantial enough to have the power to tax. In the country at large there has been a tiny reduction in the total number of governments, but this is not true in the largest metropolitan areas. In Chicago, for example, three more governments have been added since 1960, and none have disappeared. (The village of Weston will ultimately disappear because the United States will soon build the world's largest atomic accelerator on top of it.)

FRAGMENTATION OF THE OLD CITY: EMERGENCE OF
THE NEW MACHINES [3]

Even if the metropolitan city had not become hopelessly divided, patterns in the original central city suggest a developing incapacity for governing. When cities gave up political machines—or adopted measures to prevent their emergence— they undoubtedly became better-run systems. But they did not necessarily become better-governed systems.

Modernization has meant replacement of Old Machines with New Machines. The New Machines are the professionalized administrative agencies that now run the cities. The career bureaucrat is the new Boss. He is more efficient, honest and rational than the old amateur Boss. But he is no less political. If anything, the bureaucrat with his New Machine is more political because of the enormously important decisions we entrust to him.

Sociologically, the Old Machine was a combination of rational goals and fraternal loyalty. The cement of the organization was trust and discipline created out of long years of service, probation and testing, slow promotion through the ranks, and centralized control over the means of reward. Its power in the community was based upon services rendered.

Sociologically, the New Machine is almost exactly the same sort of organization. The definition of the Old Machine needs no alteration to serve as the definition of the New Machine. There are many New Machines where there used to be only one or two Old Machines. They are functional rather than geographic in their scope. They rely on formal authority rather than upon majority acquiescence. And they probably work with a minimum of graft and corruption. But these differences do not alter their definition; they only help to explain why the New Machine is such a successful form of organization.

The New Machines are machines because they are relatively

[3] *Cf.* the longer treatment in my Foreword in the new edition of Harold F. Gosnell, *Machine Politics: Chicago Model* (Chicago: University of Chicago Press, 1968).

irresponsible structures of power. That is, each agency shapes important public policies, yet the leadership of each is relatively self-perpetuating and not readily subject to the controls of any higher authority.

The New Machines are machines in that the power of each, while resting ultimately upon services rendered to the community, depends upon its cohesiveness as a small minority in the midst of the vast dispersion of the multitude.

The modern city is now well run but badly governed because it is now comprised of *islands of functional power* before which the modern mayor stands impoverished.[4] No mayor of a modern city has predictable means of determining whether the bosses of the New Machines—the bureau chiefs and the career commissioners—will be loyal to anything but their agency, its works, and related professional norms. Our modern mayor has been turned into the likeness of a French Fourth Republic premier facing an array of intransigent parties in the National Assembly. The plight of the mayor, however, is worse: at least the premier could resign. These modern machines, more monolithic by far than their ancient brethren, are entrenched by law and supported by tradition, the slavish loyalty of the newspapers, the educated masses, the dedicated civic groups, and, most of all, by the legitimized clientele groups enjoying access under existing arrangements.

The typical reformer's response to the possibility that there could be an inconsistency between running a city and governing it is the assumption of the Neutral Specialist. This is the bureaucratic equivalent to law's Rational Man. The assumption is that if men know their own specialties well enough they are capable of reasoning out solutions dispassionately to problems they share with men of equal but different technical competencies. That is a very shaky assumption indeed. Charles Frankel's analysis of such an assumption in Europe provides an appropriate setting for a closer look at it in the most modern of cities, New York: "[D]ifferent [technical] elites disagree with each other; the questions with which specialists deal spill over into areas where they are *not* specialists, and they must either

[4] Compare Sayre and Kaufman, *op. cit.*, pp. 710 ff.

hazard amateur opinions or ignore such larger issues, which is no better. . . ." [5]

During the 1950's government experts began to recognize that, despite vast increases in efficiency flowing from defeat of the machine, New York city government was somehow lacking. These concerns culminated in the 1961 Charter, in which the office of mayor was strengthened in many impressive ways. But it was quickly discovered that no amount of formal centralization could definitively overcome the real decentralization around the mayor. It was an organized decentralization, and it was making a mockery of the new Charter. The following examples, although drawn from New York, are virtually universal in their applicability:

(1) Welfare problems always involve several of any city's largest agencies, including Health, Welfare, Hospitals, etc. Yet, during more than forty years, successive mayors of New York failed to reorient the Department of Health away from a regulative toward a more service concept of organization.[6] And many new aspects of welfare must be set up in new agencies if they are to be set up at all. The new poverty programs were very slowly organized in all the big cities—except Chicago.[7]

(2) Water pollution control has been "shared" by the Departments of Health, Parks, Public Works, Sanitation, Water Supply, and perhaps one or two others. No large city, least of all New York, has an effective program to combat even the local contributions to pollution. The same is true of air pollution control, although for some years New York has had a separate department for such purposes.

(3) Land-use patterns are influenced in one way or another by a large variety of highly professional agencies. It has proved virtually impossible in any city for any one of these agencies to impose its criteria on the others. In New York the opening of Staten Island by the Narrows Bridge, in what may be the last large urban frontier, found the city with no plan for

[5] Charles Frankel, "Bureaucracy and Democracy in the New Europe," *Daedalus*, Winter, 1964, p. 487.

[6] Sayre and Kaufman, *op. cit.*, p. 274.

[7] See below, Chapter 8.

the revolution of property values and land uses in that borough.

(4) Transportation is also the province of agencies too numerous to list. Strong mayors throughout country have been unable to prevent each agency from going its separate way. For just one example, New York pursued a vast off-street parking program, at a cost of nearly $4,000 per parking space, at the very moment when local rail lines were going bankrupt.

(5) Enforcement of civil rights is imposed upon almost all city agencies by virtue of Federal, State, and local legislation. Efforts to set up public, then City Council, review of police processes in New York have been successfully opposed by professional police officials. Efforts to try pairing and busing of school children on a very marginal, experimental basis have failed. The police commissioner resigned at the very suggestion that values other than professional police values be imposed upon the Department, even when the imposition came via the respected tradition of "legislative oversight." The superintendent of schools, an outsider, was forced out. He was replaced by a career administrator. One education journalist at that time said: "Often . . . a policy proclaimed by the Board [of Education], without the advice and consent of the professional, is quickly turned into mere paper policy. . . . The veto power through passive resistance by professional administrators is virtually unbeatable. . . ."

The decentralization of city government toward its career bureaucracies has resulted in great efficiency for the activities around which each bureaucracy was organized. The city is indeed well run. But what of those activities around which bureaucracies are not organized, or those which fall between or among agencies' jurisdictions? For those, as suggested by the cases above, the cities are suffering either stalemate or elephantiasis—an affliction whereby a particular activity, say urban renewal or parkways construction, gets pushed to its ultimate success totally without regard to its balance against the missions of other agencies. In these instances the cities are clearly ungoverned.

Mayors have tried a variety of strategies to cope with these situations. But the 1961 mayoral election in New York is the ultimate dramatization of their plight. This election will some day be seen as one of the most significant elections in American urban history. For New York it was the culmination of many long-run developments. For the country it may be the first of many to usher in the bureaucratic state.

The primary significance of the election can be found in the spectacle of a mayor attempting to establish a base of power for himself in the bureaucracies. The "organization" of Mayor Robert F. Wagner included the following persons: His running mate for president of the City Council had been commissioner of sanitation, a position which culminated virtually a lifetime career in the Department of Sanitation. He had an impressive following among the sanitation workers, who, it should be added, are organized along precinct lines. The mayor's running mate for comptroller had been for many years the city budget director. As a budget official he had survived several administrations and two vicious primaries pitting factions of the Democratic Party against one another. Before becoming director he had served a number of years as a professional employee in the Bureau. The leaders of the campaign organization included a very popular fire commissioner who retired from his commissionership to accept campaign leadership and later to serve as deputy mayor, and a former police commissioner who had enjoyed a strong following among professional cops as well as in the local reform movement. Added to this coalition was a new and vigorous party, the Brotherhood Party, composed in large part of unions with broad bases of membership among city employees. Before the end of the election most of the larger city bureaucracies had political representation in the inner core of the new administration.

For the 1961 election Mayor Wagner had put his ticket and his organization together just as the bosses of old had put theirs together. In the old days the problem was to mobilize all the clubhouses, districts, and counties in the city by putting together a balanced ticket about which all adherents could be enthusiastic. The same seems to have been true for 1961, except that by then the clubhouses and districts had been replaced almost completely by the new types of units of the New Machine.

Destruction of the Old Machine and streamlining of city government did not, in New York or elsewhere, elevate the city into some sort of political heaven. Reform did not eliminate the need for political power. It simply altered what one had to do to get it. In the aftermath of twenty or more years of modern government it is beginning to appear that the lack of power can corrupt city hall almost as much as the possession of power.

Local government reform is another part of the pluralist approach to government. Traditionally, the reform cry was populism, technocracy, and decentralization, but its results are pluralistic—with predictable consequences. Reform was based on an assumption that the city needed to make no hard policy choices but only to set up a process by which agencies and clientele would make the laws. The public interest would emerge from interactions between elites of skill and elites of interests. The actual result has been stalemate, because in the process of reform no care was taken for preservation of ultimate authority. Thus, Chicago with its Old Machine is no worse off than New York with its New Machines.

All cities have traffic congestion, crime, juvenile delinquency, galloping pollution, ghettoes, ugliness, deterioration, and degeneracy. All cities seem to be suffering about equally with the quite recent problems of the weakening legitimacy of public objects, resulting in collective violence and pressures for direct solution to problems. All cities seem equally hemmed in by their suburbs and equally prevented from getting at the roots of many of their most fundamental problems. Nonpartisan approaches, even the approaches of New York's Republican mayor to Republican suburbs and a Republican governor, have failed to prevent rail bankruptcy in the vast eastern megalopolis, to abate air or water pollution, to reduce automobile pressure, or to ease the pain of the awakening Negro.

The problems of the city seem to go beyond all the known arrangements for self-government. This is, however, less a cause for despair than a moment for realizing that some city problems require substantive law, not procedural tinkering and marginal incrementalism. Unfortunately, all the tinkering of the past, however honest and efficient its bureaucratic results, seems to have ended in an institutional incapacity to make law. Thanks to reform, cities are no longer problems of management. They are problems of morality, and morality is not a question of technology.

WHY FEDERAL IDOLS BROKE

This is, then, the new situation in which the cities find themselves. There is no Negro social dissolution in any particularly new extreme. Some would even argue that the Negro ghetto has become overorganized. Instead, there is political dissolution of the city in which the Negro finds himself. The one essential factor facing the Negro that was not facing his lower-class white predecessors is the failure of political institutions. In the new city there are many publics but no polity, therefore little law. In the old city at the center the polity has been carved up into rigid technocratized domains, so that functional power increases at the expense of substantive authority. The crisis in the cities is one of political efficacy and governmental legitimacy. The black revolution is merely showing it up for what it really is. The city began to fail its residents, black and white, as it fragmented itself. Cities can move mountains of earth and stone to build, but they seem no longer to possess the capacity to reach the basis of decay. Whether the issue is pollution, transportation, or integration, there can be no policy for the city without a *polity of the city*.

Respect for public objects and symbols has thus reached a new low among Negroes. While rioting cannot be condoned, at least it can be properly understood in this context. There may be a randomness and an urgent desperation in the black riots of recent years, but it is no coincidence that the riots and the near-riots tend to be literally triggered off by a minor involvement with the men in blue. It is also no coincidence that when the riots do become focused on an attack, this attack seems to be against cops and firemen. It is not upon the "white devil" as such. White merchants in the ghetto suffer, but that is part of the self-destruction of ghetto life itself. When the riot moves to the attack it moves against authority and the symbols of authority. Phrases like "black power," "the power structure," "green power," and "Black Nationalism" constitute a political rhetoric because the immediate crisis is a political one.

WASHINGTON: RISE AND DECLINE

In the midst of longstanding fragmentation and stalemate, the cities began to turn to Washington even before World War II. The response in Federal programs with special relevance to the cities slowly began to expand in the late 1940's, but the real expansion came after 1957, following the Little Rock and Sputnik crises, the urban-liberal takeover of Congress in 1958, and the return of the Democrats to Executive control in 1961.

It would be impossible to construct an authoritative list of Federal urban policies. Many of the most important Federal programs in the cities are not, strictly speaking, urban but merely have special urban relevance. The following list is therefore selective and informal. However, it does provide a good context for grasping the scale and the problem of Federal involvement in urban life.

The pattern that comes out most clearly is that Federal policies that are directly and exclusively urban in intent are of relatively recent vintage. Primarily they are the housing, transportation, and health programs of the 1949–50 and 1958–62 periods, and the new "urban welfare" programs of the most recent period. These direct and exclusive urban-oriented programs are not only the most recent, but are governmentally weak in a way that prevents them from answering the real cries of the cities. Because of their weaknesses they will continue to constitute an inadequate response, no matter how greatly they may be expanded and how sincerely and efficiently they may be implemented. At present they are making a palpable contribution not to the quieting but to the intensification of those cries.

The older policies, established primarily in the 1930's, had

TABLE 7.1

FEDERAL PROGRAMS OF RELEVANCE TO
URBAN LIFE *
BUDGETED (IN MILLIONS) FOR 1967

Department of Commerce	$
Economic Development Administration and other planning assistance	84.1
Federal Aviation Agency: Federal aid to airports	60.0

Department of Housing and Urban Development

Low-income housing demonstration program	1.9
Low-rent public housing program	253.6
Urban planning grants	22.0
Open space and urban beautification program	29.1
Grants for water and sewer facilities	50.8
Grants for neighborhood facilities	12.5
Demonstration city grants	5.0
Urban renewal	373.5
Urban transportation assistance	65.0
Other aids for urban renewal and community facilities	2.4

Department of Health, Education, and Welfare

1. Health

Community health, hospital construction	221.1
Other community health activities	140.0
Environmental health	10.5
Mental health	71.8
Regional medical programs	35.0
Water pollution control	107.0

2. Welfare

Maternal and child welfare	146.0
Medical care for the aged (public assistance)	288.8
All other public assistance (old age, aid to dependent children, aid to the blind, and aid to totally disabled)	3,306.2
Vocational rehabilitation	259.8

* Source for all figures except those on insurance and credit programs: *A Fiscal Program for a Balanced Federalism* (New York: Committee for Economic Development, June, 1967), Appendix IV.

TABLE 7.1 (*Continued*)

3. Education

Aid to impacted areas program	252.0
Elementary and secondary school aid	1,200.0
Higher education facilities construction, etc.	176.6
Vocational education and other problem area teaching	209.7
Community services and National Teacher Corps	15.0
Civil rights educational activities	2.9

War on Poverty (appropriations direct to President, for Office of Economic Opportunity)

Community Action Programs	644.1
Neighborhood Youth Corps	247.0
Work experience program	138.7
Other	60.0

Department of Agriculture

School milk and lunch program	202.3
Food stamp program	126.5

Department of Labor

Manpower development and training programs	57.6
Administration of employment and social security programs	500.6

Insurance and Credit Programs

Social Security (trust funds) †	23,675.0
FHA mortgage loan guarantees ‡	5,513.0
VA mortgage loan guarantees ‡	3,045.0

† This figure is for fiscal 1966 and includes payment of the Federal share in the insurance trust fund for old age and disability (OASDI) insurance and unemployment compensation. It does not include payments made under the new Medicare coverage.

‡ Figures for FHA and VA are for 1964, taken from *Congress and the Nation* (Washington: Congressional Quarterly, 1965), pp. 463 ff. Over 250,000 units of nonfarm housing were financed under FHA, and 59,000 nonfarm units were financed under VA. This amounts to 14% and 4%, respectively, of all housing starts of 1964.

two very important common features. They were general, problem-oriented programs that simply had a special relevance to urban life. That is, they constituted an attack on the problems of industrial society as these were finally beginning to be understood. Second, they tended to be non-discretionary.[8] Admittedly there are variations of degree, but it is nonetheless true that the older programs were clearer in their definition of the problem and more ministerial (i.e., almost routine) in implementation. Some of the older programs were more discretionary, but, as we shall see, they share the weaknesses of the newer programs. The older programs—like the Social Security titles, public health, research, highway construction and so on —sought to achieve their generality by defining a category and applying the law—aids or restraints—to the entire universe of persons, practices, resources, or symptoms within the category. There was necessarily some discretion within which the administrator could deal with unanticipated cases; however, there was also considerable amount of statutory guidance. So much is this the case that these programs became systematized as part of the everyday structure of public life. This was also true of the first fiscal policies, which quickly became the "automatic stabilizers." [9]

The newer urban-oriented programs tend to turn these criteria on their heads. The new programs try to achieve their generality by delegation rather than by definition. They are very general only in the sense of being vague as to jurisdiction, methods, scope, objects, and any other dimension in which an administrator requires guidance. Having settled on the urban context as the specific situation (rather than the specific problem to be solved) the argument for delegation becomes unavoidable. True, we cannot know the future of each city. True, each problem area is too complex and subject to change, espe-

[8] This distinction and the following analysis are applications of criteria developed in Chapter 5. For further treatment of welfare in particular, see below, Chapter 8.

[9] Another good criticism of the liberal theory of delegation: There is more good law to be found in the new social legislation of the 1930's than in the older and better established regulatory programs discussed in Chapter 5, above.

cially since it will be different in each city and in each section of the country. True, interested persons on the scene know the most about the problems in which they are most interested. Thus, it now follows that the administrator and the Executive must be left almost complete discretion, for how else could government adapt as conditions change, and how else could the most interested local persons have a chance to shape Federal power?

WHY EFFECTIVE URBAN POLICIES CANNOT BE MADE BY MODERN PRESIDENTS

The conversion of Federal policies from problem-oriented and ministerial to urban-oriented and discretionary is not merely a fact. It explains why the Federal government changed from helpful associate to harmful partner. There are three reasons why this is true and will continue to be true until urban-liberal concepts of policy-making are changed for something else:

First, the national government is precisely a national government. Since each city is special, a Federal policy oriented toward cities as such can be general only insofar as it is vague. This type of "enabling legislation" has been made a virtue of in the present public philosophy, but obviously it can often become so vague as to be totally meaningless. What then? In allowing for regional and local variation and for bargaining, the Federal government merely enables the cities to reinforce local patterns and practices.

Second, this broad, enabling legislation renders the national government politically incapable of applying it effectively to specific urban problems. Discretion to the Executive means an increase in power for the President and for those to whom implementing power is subdelegated. However, discretion also means a commensurate increase in personal responsibility, and that ultimately means weakness rather than strength in implementation. While this is true in general, it is true with a vengeance in urban policy. The political power of the President, be he Republican or Democrat, rests heavily in the urban areas, and it will remain there so long as the Electoral College is weighted in favor of urban States and so long as organized, urban interests can tip the scales in closely contested elections. To interest-group liberals, this special urban relationship has always been one of the appeals of the Executive over Congress. But the new urban programs alter the meaning of that relationship almost completely. Who is to be responsible for a decision that might affect a local situation? In 1965, for example, the Office of Education decided to withhold around $30 million from Chicago's Board of Education pending investigation of charges of *de facto* violation of civil rights laws. A combination of Mayor Daley's special access to the White House and Mayor Daley's control over both the congressional delegation and the delegates to future national nominating conventions proved too much for the combined strength of the Office of Education and the Presidency of the United States. The prostration of the mighty Washington before a scrappy mayor is merely suggestive of the problem.

Third, the urban orientation tends to destroy clarity and true legal generality even when it can be shown already to exist. To be quite specific, urban orientation took the civil rights out of civil rights. In order to reach a level of generality above the morass of individual cities Presidents Kennedy and Johnson defined the problem of urban living as economic. That is to say, not only were definitions made broad enough to "cover in" every city, the problem was given an *apparent* common denominator—apparent because in actuality, as everyone knew, the problems were not economic at all but moral and, therefore, political. Civil rights laws, the most moral of governmental acts in our time, define the root and foundation of the problems of American life in the 1960's, just as welfare and labor legislation defined the problems in the 1930's. Civil rights laws are not urban legislation. But unfortunately most civil rights law was enacted with distinctly nonurban—i.e., southern —practices in mind. Due largely to the political foundation of the Presidency and the fatal recourse to the urban orientation, the civil rights acts became the urban War on Poverty when the social revolution shifted to the North. The cries of the cities are the cries of the President's constituency. Given the structure of government and policy provided him by interest-group liberalism, the President was forced to answer the cries of the cities with cash. In going the urban route and abandoning the older welfare route, *Federal policy became a matter of indemnifying damages rather than righting wrongs.*

CHAPTER 8

INTEREST-GROUP
LIBERALISM AND POVERTY
The End of the Welfare State

Poverty is all relativity. One can draw the cutting line for the poor anywhere he wishes, depending only upon one's propensity to sympathize. When Marie Antoinette said "Let them eat cake," all she probably meant to say was that she assumed most of the poor were well enough off to buy cake when there was no bread to be had. On the other hand, the line can be drawn harshly at the level of actual physical survival, as Ricardo and the gloomy nineteenth-century Liberals tended to do. But even here there is some arbitrariness, for subsistence changes with medical advances and according to prevailing definitions of survival. The leadership of the 1960's has chosen to draw the line at around $3000 of family income per year. Such a criterion has important policy implications, because it defines as poverty-stricken and in need of public assistance nearly one-fifth of the population of the United States. There are many technical objections to this criterion, especially to basing it upon money income.[1] But there is nonetheless no

[1] See the excellent remarks of Professor Margaret C. Reid before the Poverty Subcommittee of the House Committee on Education and Labor,

principle by which one can object to the high cutting point as such. The generosity of the contemporary American definition is somewhat exhilarating, especially given the tardiness with which Americans agreed to discuss the issue in public at all.

Almost from the dawn of the industrial revolution poverty was recognized as one of the new problems. There had always been poor people, but never before industrialization had there been a permanent stratum of propertyless, dependent paupers (i.e., dependent persons outside almshouses and other institutions).[2] The mechanism by which industrial poverty was created may not have been the poor redistribution of Henry George's "unearned increment" on land; nor need it have been deliberately created by capitalists to instill the will to work. But undeniably poverty did not disappear with progress.

As industrial States became industrial democracies poverty became an intolerable condition rather than merely an established fact. At first, industrial poverty in the United States was taken care of—haphazardly but rather well in relation to contemporary attitudes—by personal, family, and local resources. Organized philanthropies, neighborhood and fraternal organizations, settlement houses, and other more or less formal organizations were soon to join in. Only at the end of the nineteenth century were State and local governments to begin picking up a significant share of the costs. State and city departments of charities were soon set up to dispense aid directly and to participate indirectly through grants in support of existing private institutions. Once the pattern was established, growth was probably inevitable. A public aid lobby developed under the leadership of such visionaries as Frances Perkins in New York and Edwin Witte in Wisconsin. Public aid appropriations expanded. Methods of administration were invented. Concepts, definitions, and means tests were invented. A whole new profession of Welfare Administration emerged. In 1928, at

April 24, 1964, pp. 1427 ff. Reprinted in *Poverty American Style*, ed. Herman P. Miller (Belmont, Calif.: Wadsworth, 1966), pp. 231 ff.

[2] For an excellent treatment of the relation of poverty and pauperism to industrialization, see Polanyi, *op. cit.*, Chapters 7–9.

the height of prosperity on the eve of the Depression, 11.6% of all relief granted in fifteen large cities came from public funds.[3] A meager proportion by present standards, but by that time the basis for the welfare revolution had been established. Even the meaning of being poor had been redefined, as is suggested early in the game by the almost universal change of designation from "Department of Charities" to "Department of Public Aid" and then to "Department of Welfare." (Still another revision is in the offing: "Department of Human Resources.")

These rudimentary welfare systems of the early part of the century were probably adequate for their times, just as private methods may have been sufficient for the early periods of industrialization. While they met only a fraction of the need, by any definition, these agencies worked among people who expected far less (whole populations were poor according to present definitions), who could return to the family farm, and/or who lived amidst a self-conscious ethnic or regional group. It is hardly necessary to report that the 1929 Depression changed all this. The scale of industrial failure made nationalization of welfare necessary. The degree to which it rendered poor many thousands who had never known poverty before also meant that all lingering notions about individual guilt for poverty would be forever eliminated. The Depression revealed that capitalistic poverty is systematic. Obviously this meant that something systematic should be done about it.

However, recognition of national responsibility for poverty is only one half of the problem, perhaps the simpler half. How one proceeds to discharge that responsibility is quite another matter. America's initial response was the social security system of the 1930's—by 1965 this was "Old Welfare." Once it established itself as a basic part of the American way of life its inadequacies came to be stressed. Since no amount of revising categories of aid or liberalizing benefits could meet all criticisms, a search for an entirely new concept of welfare was initiated in the early 1960's. The conclusion of this search is the

[3] From a WPA study by Anne E. Geddes, reported in Fainsod *et al.*, *op. cit.*, p. 769.

New Welfare. Old Welfare was a creation of Old Liberalism, which took capitalism for what it was and sought to treat the poor as the inevitable, least fortunate among the proletariat. It was a good system. It is in danger today only because of efforts to make welfare policy do more than it can possibly do. New Welfare is a creation of New Liberalism, interest-group liberalism. While New Welfare defines poverty in simple economic terms, it rejects the notion of poverty as a natural and inevitable sector of economic life. It seeks to humanize poverty. It seeks to organize poverty as though it were a human characteristic comparable to any other "interest" around which interest groups form. The results, for the poor and for the society at large, are far from what liberalism in any form could possibly desire. New Welfare is self-defeating because it seeks to apply notions like welfare and poverty to entirely alien phenomena. The real poverty problem of the 1960's could have been dealt with entirely by mere liberalization of Old Welfare. The new problem of the 1960's, for which New Welfare is a total misapplication, is the problem of justice. The interest-group liberal approach proves useless for that.

THE OLD WELFARE SYSTEM—1935

The Federal social security system was framed in a context of fear. There was fear for the economy, and there was fear that even if prosperity returned it would never wipe out large-scale dependency. There was fear of the repercussions of unrest left too long unattended. Huey Long was only one of many popular figures with a crackpot scheme. Frances Perkins reported how she was cornered in a hall at the White House by her friend Adolph Berle, in the spring of 1933, and was urged by Berle to leave Washington before summer if she possibly could. Berle feared widespread violence in Washington and New York.[4] Fear had made a welfare program of some sort necessary; fear had also made it politically possible. As Miss

[4] From conversations between Miss Perkins, the author, Laurence Pierce, and Michael Schwartz, Cornell University, April 14, 1965.

Perkins put it, "we would not have had Social Security without the crisis of the depression." [5]

BUREAUCRATIZATION OF ROUTINE FUNCTIONS

Out of these conditions came a clear view of the problem. First, it had become supremely clear that poverty was national, because the economic system that made poverty the sort of problem it is was national. Second, it had become clear that in addition to age, unemployment, injury, and disability were the key causes of poverty, and obviously these were conditions into which a man falls most often through no fault of his own. In our day these conditions had become the normal "cost of doing business." [6] Through the heat of depression and the fear of insurrection, we had changed our ideology so fundamentally that we were now prepared to see poverty as a social rather than a personal condition. The depression destroyed once and for all the old puritanical concept of poverty as the wages of sin, sloth, and stupidity. Grinding poverty had hit thousands of temperate and sturdy workers in 1930 and was not showing much of a tendency to lift by 1934. Industrial poverty could hit anyone, and industrial society poorly equipped its finest specimens for its own occasional lapses. After the third and fourth generation of industrialization, industrial man has no skills for producing a whole product; neither has he an original homestead and would not know how to farm it if he did have one. Industrial poverty is also random as well as inexorable. The poor in 1934 were not a select group. The poor were all those people whose jobs and abilities were affected by the market. Industrial poverty was indeed a random harvest. It was an objective socioeconomic fact that required an objective politico-economic solution.

In 1935 Congress marked the "passing of the old order" with the Social Security Act. It was the result of a year of careful research and drafting, done primarily by academic and government technicians in the Executive branch. One or two im-

[5] *Ibid.*

[6] Frances Perkins, *The Roosevelt I Knew* (New York: Viking, 1946), p. 290.

portant changes in the original version were made in the House Committee on Ways and Means, but these were ratifications of compromises made between Treasury Secretary Morgenthau and Labor Secretary Perkins. After very unspectacular debate the House voted 371 to 33 and the Senate 77 to 6 for passage. The Act that virtually ushered in the Welfare State had been prepared, drafted and passed with incredible calmness as well as speed. To be sure, several serious issues were settled only after protracted controversy. However, the controversies were contained within the President's Committee on Economic Security (headed by Frances Perkins) and its Technical Board (headed by Professor Witte). Congress' major contributions were (1) reduction of the degree to which the Act would redistribute wealth by holding out for Secretary Morgenthau's scheme for joint contribution by employee and employer in old-age and survivors insurance, and (2) holding out for a Federal-State rather than a national scheme of implementation.[7]

In the 33 years since its passage, the Act has held up well. It has been expanded; its systems have become more intricate. But its assumptions and its basic structures remain unchanged.[8] Social Security was what is called an Omnibus Act. The statute contains eleven titles; seven titles deal with separate but strongly related programs. However, Social Security is an Omnibus Act in a very special sense. Each of the titles is carefully defined in relation to the others, and the several parts were to be interrelated and to add up to something of a relativly comprehensive package of welfare. In this sense it is better to call Social Security "categoric" rather than "omnibus."

The primary distinction in the Act is between two groups of beneficiaries—those who contribute and those who do not. The first is the base for an insurance system, from which pay-

---

[7] No book-length study of the important Act exists. The best sources are: Perkins, *op. cit.*; Edwin E. Witte, *The Development of the Social Security Act* (Madison: University of Wisconsin Press, 1962); and Paul H. Douglas, *Social Security in the U.S.* (New York: Whittlesey House, 1936).

[8] *Cf.* Gilbert Y. Steiner, *Social Insecurity: The Politics of Welfare* (Chicago: Rand McNally, 1966), p. 6.

ments are received as a matter of right by virtue of contributions made during one's income-earning life. The other is the base for a system from which payments are made to all needy persons after determination of the actual degree of individual need. The former, the contributory or insurance scheme, is probably what most people have in mind when they refer to "social security." The latter is generally known as "public assistance." Both were set up in the original act. (See the outline below.)

Within each of these groups of beneficiaries there are categories of welfare activity. Each category is designed to deal with a primary type of dependency, whether of disability or of reduced income. Take first the insurance group, because it was expected to become the overwhelmingly predominant group after prosperity returned. The Act set up two categories for treatment by insurance: (1) aged persons and their survivors, and (2) temporarily unemployed persons. Insurance is actually a misnomer, for it implies an ideal of actuarial soundness— meaning that sufficient funds should be collected from all beneficiaries to cover, after interest is added, the payments drawn out of it as they come due. Indeed, an Old-Age and Survivors Trust Fund was created to receive all Federal employment tax revenues, and this implied actuarial soundness (Title II, Sec. 201 of the Act). But the rates were never set high enough to guarantee such soundness. As the population grew older and benefits and coverage were increased, especially after 1958, the subsidy to the Trust Fund from general revenues began to increase.[9] However, the "financial integrity" of the system is not at issue here. A good argument can even be made against rigid adherence to sound financial principles for social insurance, because a sound fiscal system for the whole economy must be able to take into account the total flow of cash between government and the public. It is safer to call the retirement and the unemployment systems contributory rather than real insurance plans.

[9] James M. Buchanan, *The Public Finances* (Chicago: Richard D. Irwin, 1960), pp. 321 ff. The Act also established an Unemployment Trust Fund (Sec. 904, Title IX), but no such actuarial expectations seemed to be applied to it.

The second group of beneficiaries comes under the general rubric of noncontributory welfare, but within that the law specified at least six distinct categories of welfare. The latter three (II. D., E., and F.) are service activities, involving no payments but only services that are available to all but primarily focused upon the poor. The first three comprise the "public assistance" categories of the Act. The Act achieved something of a guarantee of state public assistance by provision of matching grants for states whose welfare programs were designed according to the categories defined in the Federal law.

TABLE 8.1

PROGRAMS UNDER SOCIAL SECURITY ACT OF 1935

I. Contributory (Insurance) System

A. OLD AGE & SURVIVORS—TITLE II. National system financed by taxes on employer and employee, plus subsidy from general revenue.

B. UNEMPLOYMENT—TITLE III. State systems, National Trust Fund with state accounts. Financed by tax on employers of eight or more persons, 90% of which is credited against contributions to an approved state program (Secs. 903 and 902, Title IX).

II. Noncontributory System (Public Assistance)

A. OLD-AGE ASSISTANCE—TITLE I. Grants to states for one-half of all payments of up to $30 per month to individuals of 65 or over, if state program is approved by social security board.*

B. AID TO DEPENDENT CHILDREN—TITLE IV. Grants to states for one-third of payments of up to $18 per month for first child and $12 for each additional child.†

C. AID TO THE BLIND—TITLE X. Grants to states for one-half of payments of up to $30 per month, subject to approval by social security board.

* Federal grants were made quarterly and could be stopped at any time violation of Federal standards were discovered. The ceiling and the rates have changed many times since 1935. In the 1960's ceilings for Federal participation are up to $75, and the Federal share for the

TABLE 8.1 *(Continued)*

D. MATERNAL AND CHILD WELFARE—TITLE V. Non-monetary welfare. Payments based on number of births and financial need to states providing hospital, nursing, and public health services under plans. By Secretary of Labor and children's bureau, up to one-half of cost of services.

E. VOCATIONAL REHABILITATION—TITLE V. Extension of act of 1920. Non-monetary welfare.

F. PUBLIC HEALTH—TITLE VI. Non-monetary welfare. Grants to states for improved services, personnel, or sanitation.

first $30 has passed the three-quarter mark. (See Steiner, pp. 24, 49, and *passim.*) However, the structure of the program remains the same.

† Supervision and sanction of State programs are the same as for old-age assistance. In 1966, the Federal share was about three-quarters of the first $32 of monthly payments.

The three noncontributory programs plus the two contributory programs include within Federal-State responsibility virtually every type of honest dependency known to man: age, disability, unemployment, abandonment, desertion, and blindness. These programs are seldom administered to the full satisfaction of anyone, and there is grave doubt that payments are realistic. However, even from this brief review it is possible to support the following propositions: (1) Poverty was not discovered in 1964: "The poor" have been recognized wards of the Federal government for 30 years. (2) Charges of bureaucratization are hurled against these programs constantly—charges that there is delay, waste, formality, and irresponsibility. However, it seems clear that the greater flaw is *insufficient* bureaucratization, because the perfect bureaucracy (See Chapter 2) would minimize delay and waste, and the perfect bureaucracy would be formal in order to maximize services to real clients, eliminate service to the ineligible, and minimize errors and irresponsible behavior toward needy clients. (3) Programs, especially the three based on means tests, are criticized for being unduly harsh. But that is only a sign that the local administrators are obeying laws clear enough in intent to require obedience. It is the laws that are unsympathetic, not the intrinsic character of the programs of Old Welfare. Such laws can be made less harsh without changing the character of the system itself.

THE INTEGRITY OF OLD WELFARE

Charges of inadequacy, bureaucratization and arbitrariness are hurled by the ignorant at those flaws of the welfare system that mere reform could have remedied. Even a formal review of Old Welfare reveals its basic integrity. Despite its lack of actuarial soundness—or perhaps because of it—Old Welfare has fiscal integrity. It builds up very large, anti-inflationary funds without being rigidly deflationary. The system of contributions is regressive, but that is a minor point on which disagreements can never be settled. It has fiscal integrity from the standpoint of the economy as a whole. Not only has the system relieved much of the suffering of the poor, it is the key variable in counter-cyclical compensatory policy. Its outlays are automatically cranked up as private mechanisms run down. The increase of buying power automatically effected by Federal social transfer payments during economic decline regularly makes up a large proportion of the decrease of buying power due to layoffs and cutbacks in the private sector. This aspect of the system is not only fundamental to the modern consumer economy: It cannot work at all unless it is highly bureaucratized.

Despite abuses, the organizational integrity of the system is also clear. The categories of poverty are clearly identified. A person is either old or not, blind or not, unemployed or not, dependent or not, and so on. Each condition is a standardized source of poverty and can be routinely met with food, shelter, clothing, or the guidance and wherewithal to secure them. Any function that can be dealt with routinely ought to be administered; it must be bureaucratized as much as possible. Charges against the system, like "red tape," are usually the result of insufficient bureaucratization.

Finally, Old Welfare has a very notable legal integrity. The Social Security Act is a distinctly modern piece of legislation in that it operates through broad delegations of power—in this case to State legislatures and, thence, to State administrative agencies. But legal integrity is achieved by specification of standards very much lacking in regulatory policy (Chapter 5). The first, and principle, standards to guide the administrators can be found in the categoric structure of the Act itself. While the Act left to the States the discretion to be as generous as they wished, they were clearly prevented from (1) going below certain minimum payments and (2) establishing any types of aid or conditions to aid as they saw fit. The act identified basic sources of objective poverty and saw to some provision for each.

Relatively clear standards also accompany each category or title within the Act. The age of 65 was set for eligibility under old-age assistance. The Act also set citizenship and residence requirements, as well as procedures for settling the inevitable disputes that arise over questions involving eligibility. It set down several principles for financing and administering the programs, and clear guidelines for investment of trust funds by the Federal Treasury. One of the harsher standards was that of limiting eligibility for annuities strictly to those who had ceased to be employed (Sec. 202 d). However, it is a clear policy choice and can be changed in the same manner.

Public policy in the Act was also careful with jurisdictional and procedural standards in the unemployment title. While it was silent on the duration of unemployment necessary for eligibility (in most States the waiting period is a week), the Act was more than clear on other features of the category. For example, persons were required to take new work if available, but not if the job offered were vacant due to a strike or other labor dispute, not if the wages, hours, and conditions were substantially less than the going rate, and not if the condition of employment included the obligation to join a company union or to refrain from joining a bona fide union (Sec. 903). Standards for State administrative procedure were set, as were procedures for review of decisions involving denial of compensation. States were free to determine the length and size of benefits but not to change the minimum conditions of eligibility.

The Aid to Dependent Children Title attempts to establish a category of assistance more difficult to identify than old age, unemployment, blindness, and so on. However, the category is defined in terms quite elaborate enough to begin the task of guiding administration. "Dependent child" is defined (by Sec. 406) as "a child under the age of 16 who has been deprived of parental support or care by reason of the death, continued absence from the home, or physical or mental incapacity of a parent, and who is living with his father, mother, grandfather, grandmother, brother, sister, stepfather, stepmother, stepbrother, stepsister, uncle, or aunt, in a place of residence maintained by one or more of such relations as his or their own home." The Title, although somewhat shorter than those preceding, also established a series of important administrative obligations for the State to uphold, including the requirements that there be a single responsible State agency and that the State program be uniformly in effect in all subdivisions of the State (Title IV). These were particularly important in the days when few States had any modern machinery by which to process or serve needy clients.[10] There were also in the title strict eligibility rules. The purpose of the title was to help keep the family together following loss of the primary breadwinner or some other disabling blow.

Though meagre in support and harsh in eligibility, these titles, and the others not singled out for treatment here, are undeniable statements of public policy. They are not mere expressions of general public sentiment. However, there is still more to the legal integrity of Old Welfare. The existence of fairly clear rules, standards, and definitions in the organic Act gave rise to considerable administrative rule-making (in this case, State rule-making) down the line. This means that the highest line agency—in this case the State legislature—was forced to enter into the spirit of the Act by passing further rules, standards and definitions. State welfare law as a conse-

[10] *Cf.* Douglas, *op. cit.*, pp. 185–96.

quence may be a thicket to the uninitiated and a nuisance to
the operating case worker. But it is, for all that, an effective
guide to administrative conduct. It makes a reality out of the
myth of the Neutral Administrator acting "in accordance with
law." And as usual law begets law. The wide latitude left to
the States was ultimately narrowed by the States because there
were clear legal issues to begin with. New York State welfare
law, for example, is nearly 600 pages in length, yet covers only
the public assistance categories. Two pages—sixteen
subsections—are devoted to the definition of "child," "dependent," and other features of the ADC category (Sec. 371). Still
further specification of the category is provided in Sec. 349, in
which parent eligibility is dealt with. This hardly exhausts the
guidelines.

Some have objected that no full-scale reexamination of the
system took place for 27 years.[11] That is not exactly true. At
the Federal level there was no basic revision because until the
1960's, during war, postwar, reaction, and recession, there were
neither financial resources nor political support for it. But
meanwhile serious changes in the law were taking place frequently in every State. When that reexamination did come the
eventual attack was on the very legal and organizational integrity of the welfare system itself. The interest-group liberal
leadership chose to improve and then to supplement the welfare system with non-law—discretion and bargaining. The
onset of decline of the welfare state can be dated by those
efforts.

New Welfare

John F. Kennedy ran into poverty for the first time in his priv-
ileged life only as he was preparing to run the country. To
him it was a real discovery, and he carried it to Washington as
part of that virgin territory, the New Frontier. His entire Administration was imbued with dedication to service, inspired

[11] See Steiner, *op. cit.*, p. 34, for example.

by a glowing sense of their own efficacy, and infinitely confident of the great American system. They set themselves the heroic task, among many others, of eliminating poverty. Alleviation was for sissies.

Getting down to political realities, alleviation was also costing too much. Worse yet, too much of it was going to the wrong people. Still worse, the size of the welfare portion of public expenditure did not seem to show any downward responsiveness to prosperity. A closer look at these realities helps explain why the established welfare system came in for a serious reexamination in the 1960's.[12] However, it should be made clear before reviewing these factors that they do not explain the particular response the New Frontier and the Great Society finally formulated. Only the new public philosophy can explain that.

NEW FACTS ABOUT OLD WELFARE

The first politically relevant fact about the old welfare system was that after 30 years the several noncontributory, public assistance categories had not even begun to "wither away." [13] From the beginning, most experts and political leaders were confident that as the insurance features expanded the public assistance features would contract. After fifteen years of operation, this expectation was still expressed, although surely by this time it was totally mythological. At the time of a significant expansion of old age insurance benefits President Truman could say, "the basic purpose of public assistance . . . is and has always been to supplement our social-insurance system. Our aim has been to expand coverage of social insurance and gradually reduce the need for supplementary public assistance programs." [14] On through the Eisenhower Administration the same theme was expressed, by enthusiasts outside and by the hesitant inheritors within the Administration, who on

[12] In this I am most indebted to the excellent research of Gilbert Steiner and Sar Levitan, neither of whom probably would agree entirely with the conclusions I draw.

[13] Steiner, *op. cit.*, Chapter 2.

[14] Quoted in Steiner, *op. cit.*, pp. 21–22.

this faith incorporated disability insurance into the old-age insurance system and significantly expanded its coverage.[15]

Rather than wither away, public assistance payments have gone rather steadily upward. And, since the Federal share of

TABLE 8.2

WELFARE EXPENDITURES, 1929–1962 *

	Public Assistance			Social Insurance		
	TOTAL (IN MIL- LIONS)	FEDERAL PER- CENTAGE	STATE AND LOCAL PER- CENTAGE	TOTAL (IN MIL- LIONS)	FEDERAL PER- CENTAGE	STATE AND LOCAL PER- CENTAGE
1929	$500	1	99	$340	21	79
1935	2,998	79	21	384	26	74
1940	3,599	63	37	1,216	29	71
1945	1,031	41	59	1,388	53	47
1950	1,496	44	56	4,911	42	58
1955	3,003	50	50	9,845	65	35
1960	4,101	52	48	19,292	74	26
1962	4,441	53	47	22,357	72	28

* Source: U.S. Department of Health, Education and Welfare, 1963; quoted in Dye, *op. cit.*, p. 118.

the payments has also increased, the actual Federal outlay has increased significantly, while that of the States has remained constant but at a high level. Between 1960 and 1962, Federal outlays for public assistance categories alone increased by over $200 million, from $2.13 billion to $2.35 billion. In 1965 the Federal share had gone up to $2.79 billion, and the appropriation for fiscal 1967 was for $3.31 billion. These latter figures do not include outlays for the inauguration of Medicare ($288 million for fiscal 1967).[16]

[15] *Ibid.*, pp. 21–23. Mrs. Oveta Culp Hobby, Secretary of Health, Education, and Welfare, testified: "It really happens much faster than you think, as the federal old-age and survivors' insurance really begins to do its job, the need for public assistance would deteriorate."

[16] Source: Committee for Economic Development, *op. cit.*, p. 65.

The second relevant political fact is that the composition of the public assistance rolls has shifted toward the least influential and least admired of humanity. Assistance to the aged, the most popular of the categories, has actually declined, relatively speaking, as a proportion of the increasing number of older persons in the population.[17] The culprit has been Aid to Dependent Children (ADC), which has grown steadily in cost and coverage since 1946. The plain and simple truth is that the typical ADC recipient is coming to be a Negro woman with one or more children, to wit: As of 1961, Sar Levitan reports that 1 out of every 5 children on ADC was illegitimate, and double that many were children of broken homes and estranged parents.[18] At that time just below one-half of all ADC children (1,112,106) were Negroes and half of them were sufficiently concentrated in our largest cities to constitute three-quarters of the ADC recipients there.[19]

The first response of President Kennedy to the problem of poverty was the result of his own apparent preference for government manipulation of aggregate demand, and this was reinforced by the conditions of mild recession and gold outflow which surrounded his election. However, his success seemed only to underscore the fact that prosperity is no antidote for poverty. If the bulk of public assistance is for unemployables, neither it nor the poor will be eradicated by an economy heated up even to 98 per cent of full employment.

Given these unmistakable tendencies in the development of Old Welfare public assistance categories, the initial attack by the New Frontier is incredible. President Kennedy, HEW Secretary Ribicoff, and most of their welfare advisers produced the 1962 Amendments to Social Security, which were the culmination of a massive reexamination. These were hailed as "landmarks"—"the most far-reaching revision of our public-welfare program since it was enacted in 1935." This bold revision amounted to nothing more than the provision of matching

[17] Steiner, *op. cit.*, p. 23.

[18] In Miller, *op. cit.*, p. 170. Cf. Steiner, pp. 26 ff.

[19] Daniel P. Moynihan, "Employment, Income and the Ordeal of the Negro Family," *Daedalus,* Fall, 1965, p. 762.

grants (up to one-fourth of State costs) as an incentive for the States to undertake rehabilitation programs in conjunction with ADC casework. How this was more bold than the Eisenhower self-help effort is hard to imagine.[20] It is significant only because it is a tip-off to the interest-group liberal approach to welfare that matured only three years later. The 1962 effort was an attempt to solve the real problems of ADC, a nondiscretionary program, merely by making it discretionary. ADC was and continues to be in need of serious reform. But the means chosen in 1962 were the worst possible ones: simply to state a general national goal of getting people off the welfare rolls (a goal ardently shared by the Republicans) and to delegate the achievement of this goal to the State ADC programs and the public assistance caseworkers.

The liberal solution, thus, seemed to be the incantation of some bold new words and the allocation of funds to provide incentives for each State to give real substance to the words. *Administrators far down the line were being told to make law. Further, local personnel were being assigned the personal responsibility for making Federal law.* The fact that these increasingly strike-prone caseworkers were already overworked even without these new functions, that they were in no way professionally equipped to carry out the new rehabilitation and family service work anticipated in the Amendments, that by the very definition of their local status they could never make laws only shows how impossible the entire situation was.

The choice made by the President, his advisers, and Congress in 1962, after due consideration of impressive technical services, was to make no choice. All they did was to create a new function and a new set of powers, and then to set the political process going round them. Increments of change in the State ADC agency resulting from interactions among the agency, the interests, and the clientele would, it was hoped, ultimately result in a new program. This explains the 1962 Amendments and the *modus operandi* of interest-group liberal-

[20] For evaluations, see Steiner, *op. cit.*, pp. 34 ff. Steiner is himself critical but provides an excellent list of sources for those who would try to defend the 1962 Amendments.

ism in the entire field of welfare. The "bold" 1962 package of Amendments constitutes only a warm-up. The New Welfare of interest-group liberalism came into full maturity in 1964 with the War on Poverty.

THE WAR ON POVERTY—UNDERLYING ASSUMPTIONS

Despite publicly expressed faith that the 1962 Amendments constituted a "new spirit" and a "completely new philosophy . . . in welfare," actions inside the Kennedy Administration by mid-1963 indicated an entirely different private attitude. Kennedy had already used the phrase "war on poverty" in his 1960 campaign, and as it became increasingly clear that neither prosperity nor rehabilitation were going to wipe out his memory of and his promises to West Virginia, he ordered further "basic soul-searching" by the Council of Economic Advisers (CEA).[21] Soul-searching led to a flow of technical papers by Council, Budget Bureau, and White House personnel, but without inspiration. In early November, Council Chairman Walter Heller issued a formal request to all the heads of domestic Departments and major independent agencies to examine their existing programs as a means of generating new program suggestions.

The response to Heller's request was overwhelming, and probably not a little distressing. More than 100 distinct proposals were made. However, each agency tended to see a new war waged by expansion of its own programs. All the CEA could do at this point was to seek the President's encouragement to plan toward a statement for one of the January messages to Congress.

One of President Johnson's earliest decisions upon taking office was to press for an antipoverty program: "That's my kind of program. It will help people." But the gnawing problem was that there had already been an unbelievable proliferation of uncoordinated programs "helping people." Each was in

[21] Facts on the pre-history of the War on Poverty are taken from: John Bibby and Roger Davidson, *On Capitol Hill* (New York: Holt, Rinehart and Winston, 1967), Chapter 7; Brian Henry Smith (Unpublished Master's thesis, Columbia University, 1966); and Isaac Balbus (Unpublished Master's thesis, University of Chicago, 1966).

justifiable need of expansion because each was, indeed, already an attack on poverty. The Bureau of the Budget was called in to help process and evaluate the proposals in a manner not unlike its normal budget review. Unfortunately, however, this was neither normal budget review nor normal legislative clearance of individual agency proposals for legislation. It was full-scale program development—planning and policy-making at its highest level. The question here then becomes, how do interest-group liberal policy-makers go about their jobs when there is a large substantive (one is tempted to say *critical*) issue rather than several discrete, *incremental* issues? The answer is, *incrementally just the same, which means they make no substantive decision at all.* How can those who discover incrementalism at the top accept it as the reality of politics and not see it for what it really is—the implementation of an ideology?

It is not always easy to make a decision that is not a decision, but in the fall of 1963 such a solution was discovered. It was then that the Bureau of the Budget hit upon the notion of the "Community Action Program." Since there was to be a mere $500 million above existing program commitments for this antipoverty war, each agency feared loss of important roles in the war. One would think that under the circumstances a way would have to be found to make hard choices from an actual priority listing of public activities. But this is not only extremely difficult to do: according to prevailing public philosophy it is positively undesirable. The Community Action Program idea provided just the right tactic for avoidance. Priorities would be found not at first but at last.

The Community Action idea had been developed in the 1950's by Ford Foundation teams in "gray areas" of cities as a means of extending civic education. President Kennedy's juvenile delinquency program had made use of the same self-help idea in a small series of experimental efforts. The purpose of Community Action in the far larger War on Poverty was to provide a coordinated and comprehensive approach to poverty without basically altering existing Federal patterns. It seemed to have dual virtues. It could involve the clientele and thus be self-educative as well as self-executing. And it would provide a method of substantially coordinating existing programs *out in the field;* that is, it provided a means of blasting loose a generation of professionally supported incrementalism at the bottom without bothering the top at all.

But why is coordination good at the local level and not good among the parent agencies at the center? Why do "power structures" need shaking up in Washington State but not in Washington, D. C.? Why was there talk of substantive policy in the cities and not in the Federal government? A close look at the statute suggests that there was no perceived inconsistency between the two. The framers sought no revolt against the separated and stalemated "power structure" in Washington, D. C., not because they lacked the courage but *because their ideology blinded them to the need.*

The New Welfare, perhaps more than any Federal activity today, is a systematic expression of interest-group liberalism. It is a classic example of provision of official routes to official recognition of private decisions reached by a process dimly specified in the statute. It is an ultimate in efforts to deliberately fulfill the pluralist conditions of groups-with-countervailing-groups. It is a paragon of policy-without-law.

New Welfare is not only hostile to law. In implementation it is antithetical to rational and responsible administration, because the principle of representation is antithetical to the principle of administration. The further down the line one delegates power, the further into the administrative process one is forced to provide representation. While much of this is unavoidable, formalizing the fusion of administration and representation is a way of discrediting both. The worst results of interest-group liberalism in general and New Welfare in particular follow from this. Let us look more closely at these tendencies.

NEW WELFARE IN LAW: ULTIMATE INTEREST-GROUP LIBERALISM

The Economic Opportunity Act of 1964 is an Omnibus Act composed of seven titles in which there are approximately ten programs—approximately because the number can shift according to the definition of a program. Some programs were new and distinct, like Job Corps, work-study, and Volunteers in Service to America (VISTA). Others involved expansion of existing programs—work-training, adult education, work-experience,[22] business incentives, and rural assistance (a tripartite feature of Title III). The total number depends especially upon how one counts the Community Action Title (II) and the Office of Economic Opportunity (OEO, Title VI), because in these no programs were created but important powers were conferred.

Delegation of power is the order of the day in this statute. Operative standards are almost impossible to find anywhere in it. In contrast to the Social Security statute, this Act reflects care to avoid the identification and definition of categories and to avoid cumulation of these into some kind of interrelated package. The most important sources of standards in Old Welfare—definitions, lists of examples, exceptions, exclusions, prerequisites—are almost absent here. In its place one finds a grab bag. This was to be a war ending in the total elimination of poverty. The partisans praised it by condemning Old Welfare for dealing only with symptoms and not with causes. Yet, strangely enough, it is a war in which neither the enemy nor the methods are positively determined. It is a campaign waged without placing any strong imperatives to action upon the front-line, the administrators. Instead it is a catchall of job-creating, job-training, and money-providing programs aimed largely at making lower-class life a bit more comfortable for the present lower classes. Some object that it would be paternalistic to have a program in which administrators had clear goals which they were obliged to seek. But nothing is more paternalistic than Job Corps, VISTA, and training for manual and semiskilled labor, however benevolent and permissive they may appear. Worse, and more directly in point here, the absence of central direction and guidance simply deprives the

[22] This was a small boost for the almost-forgotten "bold new philosophy" Public Welfare Amendments of 1962.

disappointed of something to shoot against.[23] This is a paternalism that demoralizes.

Within each category, the statutory directives are almost completely "end-oriented," but only in the sense that they express sentiments. Examples of ends that constitute sentiments rather than standards abound in the Act. The director (of OEO) is empowered to arrange for the "education" and "training" of enrollees and to provide programs of "useful work experience." The VISTA volunteers are directed to "combat poverty"—with the consent of the governor, another completely undefined role. The climax comes in the formulation of community action, the real work component of the program, the core that was to draw the otherwise unrelated programs into a unity. The Community Action Program, which received its purest definition in the original Administration draft presented to Congress, is one:

(1) which mobilizes and utilizes resources, public or private, of any urban or rural, or combined urban and rural, geographical area (referred to in this part as a "community"), including but not limited to a state, metropolitan area, county, city, town, multicity unit, or multi-county unit in an attack on poverty;

(2) which provides services, assistance, and other activities of sufficient scope and size to give promise of progress toward elimination of poverty or a cause or causes of poverty through developing employment opportunities, improving human performance, motivation, and productivity, or bettering the conditions under which people live, learn, and work;

(3) which is developed, conducted, and administered with the maximum feasible participation of residents of the area and members of the groups served; and

(4) which is conducted, administered, or coordinated by a pub-

[23] In a perverse way, the case of the South and civil rights makes the same point. The fact that southern states had actual laws governing racial privileges made it easier for civil rights movements to get under way and helped bring about quicker changes. The northern situation, in which power over race relations is delegated to public and private agencies, is more subtle, more permissive, less paternalistic only on the surface, and far more demoralizing. One need only note the failure of Martin Luther King's movement in Chicago.

lic or private nonprofit agency (referred to in this title as a "community action organization") which is broadly representative of the community.[24]

Paragraph (1) defines location, which could be anything, and it is certainly *not* limited to all of the principalities and combinations of principalities known in the United States today. Paragraph (2) defines jurisdiction, which, other than limiting the focus to poverty, could be anything, and certainly is *not* limited to all of the sources of poverty and all of the ways of improving conditions known in the world today. Paragraph (3), of which more in a moment, defines one special condition regarding how poverty policy should be made. However, Paragraph (4) makes clear that (3) is inclusive rather than exclusive by requiring the participation of any and every other relevant group besides the immediate clientele groups.

These features reveal the meaning of the poverty program in no uncertain terms. The Act is, especially in its most important and most novel titles, completely process-oriented non-law. It speaks of reaching the causes of poverty, but this is almost entirely rhetorical, for there is nothing in these clauses of the statute and official records that even the most legally-minded bureaucrat need feel guided by. There is no guidance because all the apparent guidance is suggestive and permissive. Categories are open-ended; they are lists always introduced with "not limited to" or "such as." The following example is Mr. Shriver's important elaboration of the Community Action Program and how it would unify the effort to eliminate poverty:

> The local organization applying for a community action program grant must satisfy only one basic criterion: it must be broadly representative of the interests of the community. It may be a public agency. . . . *Or it may be* a private nonprofit agency which has the support of *the relevant elements* of community government. . . .
>
> Communities will have wide discretion in determining what program activities should be undertaken. . . . [I]t *is likely* that

[24] U.S. Congress, House, *To Mobilize the Human and Financial Resources of the Nation to Combat Poverty in the United States,* 88th Cong., 2d Sess., 1964, H.R. 10440, pp. 17–18.

community action programs will include activities *such as* the following, all focused on the problems of poor people:

1. Services and activities to develop new employment opportunities;
2. Strengthening the teaching of basic education skills, especially reading, writing and mathematics;
3. Providing comprehensive academic counseling and guidance services and school social work services;
4. Providing after-school study centers, after-school tutoring, and summer, weekend, and after-school academic classes;
5. Establishing programs for the benefit of preschool children;
6. Reducing adult illiteracy;
7. Developing and carrying out special education or other programs for migrant or transient families;
8. Improving the living conditions of the elderly;
9. Arranging for or providing health examinations and health education for school children;
10. Rehabilitation and retraining of physically or mentally handicapped persons;
11. Providing health, rehabilitation, employment, educational, and related services to young men not qualified for military service;
12. Providing community child-care centers and youth activity centers;
13. Improving housing and living facilities and home management skills;
14. Providing services to enable families from rural areas to meet problems of urban living; *or*
15. Providing recreation and physical fitness services and facilities.[25]

Compare the language of the Social Security Act with the extremely informal and inclusive language of the Economic Opportunity Act, bearing in mind that the great bulk of Social Security law is in State-implementing statutes. In New Welfare, the Economic Opportunity Act, including implementing documents such as Shriver's, *is all the law there is.*[26] Old

[25] *The War on Poverty*, Senate Document No. 86, Committee on Labor and Public Welfare, 88th Congress, 2nd. sess. (Italics added.)

[26] In the OEO's *Community Action Program Guide* and in various official statements, the OEO people have been extremely reluctant to specify standards even about the process itself. See, e.g., Barbara

Welfare obviously works through law, New Welfare through delegation.

Finally the poverty program gets at causes no more, or no better, than, the Social Security Act. In both the assumption is that the cause of poverty is "being poor." The difference is that the Social Security Act recognized that and went after it as a matter of law and appropriate bureaucratization. In contrast, the poverty program assumes, rightly, that something else is behind being poor. But rather than identify what it is, the Act simply delegates to public and private "groups" the task of finding it out; and the causes are expected to vary from one city to another. Granted, the War on Poverty anticipates a wider array of palliatives than Social Security does or could. But even on this narrow plane, one wonders how distinctive it is. Employment agencies established by the 1935 program have put a lot of needy people in jobs. Is is not possible that this, plus an expansion of regular education, amounts to all the War on Poverty can ever be as a welfare program? If not, and if there are causes of poverty untouched by Old Welfare, why were the framers of New Welfare so reluctant to identify them?

These last questions point to the primary features of the War on Poverty and how these are the direct and necessary expression of interest-group liberalism: (1) It is better not to state hard policy but only to start a process. (2) Everything is good to do. Make everything available and the bargaining process will provide the appropriate mix. (3) It is not desirable to distinguish too clearly between public and private agencies. Authority hampers the bargaining process. (4) The distinction between public and private is in general undesirable because it interferes with delegation of power by specifying goals and responsibilities; and you cannot have a real policy-making process without broad delegation of power. These sound familiar because this is the logic of interest-group liberalism whenever and wherever it operates as a guide to the public function.

Carter, "Sargent Shriver and the Role of the Poor," *Reporter*, May 5, 1966, p. 18.

As the final section will document, interest-group liberalism has produced two important consequences in New Welfare. First, New Welfare misses the new causes of poverty more than almost any conceivable program could. Second, New Welfare has demoralized the civil rights movement just as it will demoralize any mass effort to redress injustices. Interest-group liberalism has thus produced two major antilibertarian consequences far more surely than if these consequences had been heartfelt intentions. These consequences were produced because of the refusal of interest-group liberalism to make moral choices and set clear legislative standards. Prosperity is a real problem. When everything is good to do nothing seems compelling.

THE END OF NEW WELFARE

Although New Welfare has been in full-scale operation for only a short time, the results anticipated from a plain reading of the statute are already plain to see in the field. Hardly 18 months after the War on Poverty was declared, its most important ally and influential lobby, the Citizens Crusade Against Poverty (CCAP), held its national conference in Washington. Already on record for maximum feasible participation (its executive director is credited with the invention of that famous phrase), its purpose in holding the national conference was to whip up support for maximum participation and against government interference. Suddenly the CCAP found itself swept by a storm from within. During a speech by OEO Director Sargent Shriver, in which he was praising the revolutionary aspects of the program, the meeting fell into an uproar. Shriver hastily departed, and the floor was seized by angry militants who expressed their hatreds, one after the other, for one aspect of the program after another. One speaker was inconsistent with another, and it seemed to make no difference that their attack was upon an organization whose goals they themselves espoused.

The message seems to be clear.[27] Hope had curdled into in-

[27] *Cf.* Morton Kondracke, Chicago *Sun-Times,* April 17, 1966.

dignation. Such expressions characterized outbursts in many meetings all over the country, because frustrated hope is sewn into the War on Poverty. Early returns from several cities tend to bear this out. [28]

THREE YEARS OF COMMUNITY ACTION

New York City represents one extreme of experience with New Welfare, an extreme in the degree of real, maximum participation. Many participating groups already existed; others were created with government assistance. Developments in New York from the beginning have revolved mainly around fights among groups and leaders for recognition. The results: maximum participation and minimum appropriations of actual funds to the poor and their projects. The Harlem program, upon which so many hopes were pinned precisely because the makings of a good "group process" were available, was something of a disaster. Not a tenth of originally expected Federal and local funds became available, and for a time new money was stopped and leadership was totally in abeyance while the executive director took a leave to trace the whereabouts of an unaccounted-for $400,000. One leader and one element of the Negro community, in Harlem and elsewhere in New York, was set off against another, culminating in strenuous battles to create peace. A real "culture of poverty" is in the making.

Chicago represents the other extreme. Here the experience has been minimum feasible participation and maximum appropriation of funds to the poor. In New York the sense of futility came from stalemate. In Chicago it came from paternalism. Mayor Daley's immense success in getting poverty funds seems equalled only by his ability to use them in support of (or without hurting) the Democratic organization of Cook County. On paper his CAP organization scheme looks like an ideal design for such a program. But all the directors are handpicked and

[28] I am grateful in particular for the research of Paul E. Peterson, whose doctoral dissertation so thoroughly covered CAPs in New York, Philadelphia, and Chicago ("City Politics and Community Action," University of Chicago, 1967). Unless otherwise cited, my source is very likely this research. However, Professor Peterson does not necessarily share my conclusions.

the local CAP representatives are appointed with all due political care. The Mayor appoints the executive director, and the executive director appoints the directors of the neighborhood Urban Progress Centers, who appoint the neighborhood advisory committees—whose chairmen are appointed by the executive director. In New York City, politics is fragmented; New Welfare reinforced the fragmentation. In Chicago, politics is tightly controlled by a political machine; New Welfare reinforced the machine.

The situation in Philadelphia has located itself somewhere between the two extremes, but it also seems to have combined the worst features of both Chicago and New York. There is evidence of some appropriation of funds and a modicum of real participation; however, upon a closer look, the appropriation of funds has been used to co-opt the support of the leading participants.[29] Thus, Philadelphia's program encourages direct participation but managed to involve, during its first two years, less than three per cent of the residents of the neighborhoods served. Here again the sense of futility, not only because participation and influence are necessarily so slight but because there is evidence that much of Philadelphia OEO appropriation has served mainly the representatives and their families and friends. This is an aspect of "job creation" that was probably not anticipated. Nepotistic patronage can be just as demoralizing as party patronage.

Los Angeles is on par with New York. There has in fact been even less success in getting OEO funds down into the neighborhoods, as outright gifts or as continuing programs. After the Watts riots the appropriations and programs increased, but this is a rather corrosive form of representation. It is a bit like chasing one's tail. After the crisis the increase of Federal funds appeared as blood money. The spontaneity of the programs was lost, or had never existed. Federal involvement became a case of "damned if you do and damned if you don't."

[29] *Cf.* Paul E. Peterson, "Strategies for Educational Reform: The War on Poverty Experience," paper presented to the 1967 Convention of the American Orthopsychiatric Association: In Philadelphia, ". . . formal representation of the poor, by and large, scarcely altered community action proposals . . ." (p. 10).

Lest it be thought that rioting before the program began made Los Angeles special, there is the case of Detroit. Here was another city relatively faithful to the process principles of the Economic Opportunity Act. Here there was no preliminary riot. Yet here it was "damned if they did." Detroit was as participatory as New York and as successful in getting Federal funds as Chicago—it had one of the best records in the country. Yet at the very same time Mayor Cavanagh's stock with the ghetto Negro, a vital factor in Cavanagh's own mayoral election, was declining precipitously. When rioting came to Detroit it was especially severe. Opening up such functional representation had served only to intensify the Negro's awareness that he had only one representative on Detroit's nine-man, reformed, nonpartisan Common Council. Likewise for another riot-torn city—Newark—where City Hall had been so conscientious as to let itself be frozen out almost altogether in the formation of maximum participation in the rawest extreme.[30]

The Syracuse program brings all these various tendencies best into focus. Here OEO took maximum participation seriously enough to grant $483,000 to help organize the official poverty agency (Crusade for Opportunity) and then to grant $314,000 to a joint university–Saul Alinsky group (the Syracuse Community Development Association—SCDA) to organize the poor independently for purposes of representation on the Crusade. An early effort, Syracuse was also an early case study in the results of adding the element of broad discretion to welfare. Such discretion, coupled with organizations deliberately set up to exploit it, led to creation of inconsistencies between the poor and the government that did not necessarily exist before. It created the myth of a unitary "power structure" despite the fact that most large cities are plagued with multiple rather than single power structures. It created a conflict in the Mayor's mind about how he should work. In fact, *it made him look at the Federal poverty funds as co-optative resources whether he wanted to or not.*[31]

[30] *Cf.* accounts in the *New York Times Magazine*, August 27, 1967, p. 51; in Carter, *op. cit.;* and Witcover and Knoll, "Politics and the Poor," *op. cit.,* p. 24.

[31] *Cf.* Witcover and Knoll, *op. cit.;* see also, by same authors, "Organizing the Poor," in Miller, *op. cit.,* pp. 247 ff.

Have the cities gained anything in return? Even as measured by standards relevant to the spirit of the Act—turnout in the CAP neighborhood elections—these efforts tend to discredit New Welfare: the turnout in Philadelphia for the 1965 elections for CAP representatives was less than 3 per cent. Is this a measure of failure to involve the residents of the affected areas? Other cities would tend to suggest at least that the program was not working to the best pluralist expectations. In mid-February, 1966, 5 per cent (8,287) of Kansas City's eligible adults turned out for a poverty election. This followed efforts by 276 candidates and 4,000 volunteer canvassers, and an official get-out-the-vote campaign contribution of $50,000. Later in the same month, the turnout in Cleveland amounted to 4.2 per cent despite thousands of manhours of campaigning, generous newspaper appeals, and babysitting services. Fewer than 1 per cent turned out in Los Angeles. If an outsider can empathize at all he must inevitably share a sense of futility and embarrassment in the midst of the incredible paternalism and the goody-goody character of the organizing efforts.

OLD WELFARE VERSUS NEW WELFARE

Welfare is a politico-economic conception appropriate to a special economic problem. *That problem is the problem of scarcity and of inefficient distribution of wealth under capitalism.* Old Welfare was a successful effort to come to grips with poverty caused by capitalist technology and capitalist methods of production and distribution. The purpose of Old Welfare was and is to make the march to the grave a bit more comfortable. Capitalist poverty is an objective thing; it is a random harvest. Therefore it possesses the virtue of being susceptible to treatment by general rules and by bureaucratization of their implementation. Nothing is wrong with Old Welfare that cannot be reformed by merely increasing redistribution or revising categories as capitalist organization changes. The criticism that Old Welfare must perpetuate poverty is an absurdity. The welfare dole is no more demeaning than the socio-economic conditions that made it necessary. Old Welfare was and is an immensely successful means of tending to the human exhaust of capitalism.

New Welfare is based upon a most meaningful, deliberate ignorance. Its creators sought to combat the poverty of their age as though poverty is poverty is poverty. But this is not true, and they would be incredibly obtuse to believe that it is. The phenomenon being called poverty today is not capitalistic poverty. The phenomenon we fight today is not a random thing, not a natural consequence of the objective weakness of economic or environmental forces. *The phenomenon we fight today is in fact not poverty at all.* The phenomenon is the injustice that has made poverty a nonrandom, nonobjective category. Poverty in this case is the merest epiphenomenon, and there is nothing at this level that Old Welfare could not and cannot do better than New Welfare. (After 15 months of operation Kansas City's CAP was unable to utilize the $2 million "handed to them on a platter.")

The real task of our time was to attack injustice and to change social rules and conduct in order that poverty become and remain a random thing, an objective category. The interest-group liberal approach—defining the effort as economic, attaching it to the welfare system, and making it almost totally discretionary—was not merely superfluous and redundant; it produced a whole array of unhappy consequences. These consequences were unintended, but they are not paradoxical. They arise out of features of the War on Poverty that were deliberately sought by the interest-group liberals. All but one of the consequences fit as various headings under the general rubric *conservatism.* I choose the word deliberately, despite Chapter 3, because it best evokes a sense of the very things to which traditional liberalism claimed to be most antagonistic. The last of the types of consequences is better termed *radical;* but that only confirms the character of the other consequences, because radicalism always tends to follow militancy against change.

Dulling the edge of civil rights: In general the War on Poverty has blocked change by falsely focusing the attentions of responsible persons sincerely committed to social change. In particular, it is astonishing how many Negro leaders have become taken in by the appeals of Community Action and the paltry extra sums of money forthcoming. The demand for civil rights declined as the demand for poverty money increased. The one cause was deserted for the other. Civil rights was for the South. Social injustice in the North was not to be rectified but only indemnified. For the South there was morality, for the North equity.

The "Peachum factor": The effects of the War on Poverty are also conservative in their pattern of implementation. Delegation of the program to private groups requires official recognition of groups and representatives. In the first round we may be impressed by emergence of new groups—and at least impressed by the amount of effort expended to bring new groups about. However, once the situation is stabilized by official recognition of groups and representatives, the situation tends to militate against emergence of still newer groups. Official recognition is a very conservative force; at the neighborhood level, Federal recognition becomes a valuable resource with which some groups can demoralize others. In South Chicago a gang called the Blackstone Rangers maintains its monopoly position through intimidation: "You belong to our gang or I'll knock your head off." Government recognition can work the same way: "Now we are official. If you don't join us you won't have any access." Official recognition tends to congeal social relationships. The latter instance differs from the Blackstone Rangers case only in the subtlety of the intimidation. And, as Peachum and MacHeath teach in "The Threepenny Opera," the poor are the easiest of all to intimidate, especially with symbols of authority.

The pseudo-Marxian factor: In order to overcome one kind of "false consciousness," the War on Poverty seeks to instill another; and it, too, militates against change. As the Syracuse case illustrates, Community Action organizing can create a conflict between the poor and the powerful that is neither natural nor inevitable. There is no necessary conflict of economic interest between the poor and the powerful. It depends on who the powerful are. Trying to give the poor, especially the Negro poor, a "correct consciousness" tends only to produce alliances between the rich and the powerful that may or may not have existed in the recent history of a given city. Behaving as though there is a single "power structure" helps create one and converts economic or racial issues into fights for the survival of the regime. The War on Poverty is tending to reunite social, economic, and political elites in the cities.

The conservatism of narrowed vision: Paul Peterson provides another insight into the conservative tendencies of Community Action in his research on OEO and education:

[E]ven where the OEO achieved considerable success, as in East Harlem, the organizations newly organized had such narrow constituencies that their demands were usually narrow and neighborhood-oriented rather than calls for broad reform which would improve education for all those in their class or ethnic group. . . . The East Harlem leaders sought neighborhood control, but neighborhood control, if applied equally throughout the city, would scarcely increase school integration. The East Harlem leaders sought a Negro or Puerto Rican principal for their school rather than insisting on changes in the general recruitment patterns for administrative positions that had effectively excluded minority groups. Even the compromise proposal sought quality improvements through a special arrangement with a university for a few East Harlem schools rather than a far-reaching program to improve quality of education in low-income areas throughout the city. The narrow constituency of the neighborhood organization made it an unsatisfactory vehicle for the articulation of broad demands necessary for major educational reform.[32]

The War on Poverty will never integrate the city, racially or culturally. Narrowed perspectives are created by and reinforced by the neighborhood concept. The call for decentralization is a sound of great joy to liberals. But decentralization is an absurdity at the beginning of a program whose major goal is (or ought to be) reeducation toward new social values. Decentralization in this case is abdication; worse, it provides additional powers of resistance.

The wasting of moral leverage: Even as it diverts attention from civil rights, so also does the War on Poverty militate

[32] Peterson, "Strategies," *op. cit.*, pp. 14–15. See also McConnell, *op. cit.*, for a general thesis on the effects of smaller versus larger constituencies.

against change by laying waste the real resources of the civil rights movement. The War on Poverty, with its emphasis on access and cash, is literally demoralizing. And it redefines the problem away from its most toward its least advantageous aspects. The political resources that impress Negroes most these days—numbers, organization, and "green power"—are admittedly important. But resources are not power; they must be exchanged for power, and the exchange is most effective where the moral claim is strong. The War on Poverty seriously weakens Negro political power by applying to it the pluralist notion that one set of ends is about the same as another. Everything is "interests." The War on Poverty took the heat off. Given the strength of the Negro's moral position and the guilt feelings of the white northern community, the revolution is selling out cheap for a War on Poverty.

Tilting the recruitment process: Organizing poverty groups in and for the ghetto, and making money and recognition available as systematic rewards, tends to reinforce the ghetto in a most systematic way. The rewards tend strongly to tip the balance arbitrarily toward those prospective leaders who are most strongly pro-ghetto, economics-oriented, and separatist. In a very important sense, the War on Poverty and especially Community Action helped bring on the black separatist movement itself by making black separatism the trait most favored in recruitment and promotion into leadership. Federal programs under New Welfare did not cause the attitude itself, but they seem to have helped make far more certain that those who are separatist become the key spokesmen and leaders. The fact that a few black spokesmen prefer segregation makes it no more acceptable and no less conservative.

Radicalism: No one can attend a conference or rally of community activists without being impressed with the simultaneous expressions of hope and frustration. New access has often led to disgust. The War on Poverty has contributed to these waves of sentiment by encouraging cynicism. Moreover, direct sponsorship by government has attached to personal cynicism a sense of the illegitimacy of public objects and their lack of efficacy in good causes. Government always depends

heavily upon the accidental strength of the congressional delegation, the role of the city in the upcoming election, whom you
know, how charismatic your spokesman is. However, when
these political tendencies are elevated to officially prescribed
criteria for making governments work, their meaning changes.
The War on Poverty removed hope that Federal power offers
another route. Radicalism is an expression of lost hope for the
existing order. Radicalism is usually what conservatism is put
to rest by.

WHO SHALL BE POOR?

Old Welfare was an enormously successful, even if belated,
act of social responsibility. New Welfare is an enormous misapplication of social responsibility resulting from derangement
of liberal ideology. New Welfare is sincere humanitarianism
gone cockeyed. A full generation after 1935, the crux of the
present crisis was human rights and the fact that the existing
rules were maintaining poverty as a nonrandom, unnatural
category. No War on Poverty can be won by eliminating the
poor—that is irresponsible rhetoric. It can be won only by
changing the rules that determine who shall be poor. This required hard choices and much social adjustment. Economic
incrementalism and pluralism cannot change rules. On the contrary, they operate on the assumption that the rules will not be
changed.

There is a rather large gulf between indemnifying damages
and righting wrongs. We are seeing this gap filled, first by disappointment and disbelief, then by cynicism, ultimately by
militancy. New Welfare sought merely to create a "culture of
poverty" rather than an orderly process of lawful integration,
and in so doing must have contributed to the decaying political
relationships in the nation. New Welfare stripped the Negro
revolution of its moral superiority. It is one of the tragedies of
our time that so many Negro leaders themselves took the War
on Poverty as their own. For their people they chose comfort
and mobility when they should have known that discomfort
and immobility for them were mere symptoms that would pass
away for most of them in a just society.

There will always be a stratum of discomfort. The yeast of revolt is not the discomfort but the declining propensity of members of that stratum to accept it as just. When the stratum is escapable, individuals will escape. When the stratum becomes to them unjust, they revolt, even if escape is made easier. Negroes had their Black Revolution. The only question was what they would do with it. Brought to leadership in an age of interest-group liberalism, they could not have chosen worse.

CHAPTER 9

FEDERAL URBAN POLICY—
WHAT NOT TO DO
AND WHAT TO DO
ABOUT *APARTHEID*

The War on Poverty is not a special case. It is only an extreme case of the way in which the liberal state typically responds to power centers and social crises in the United States. The arrangements worked out for the War on Poverty differ only superficially from those in the first large Federal endeavor —housing. Public housing, urban renewal, and the FHA-VA mortgage programs are, like New Welfare, enabling legislation: Public housing and urban renewal enable cities to remove Negroes and other undesirable lower classes from desirable locations. Public housing, with the help of urban renewal, enables the cities to relocate and to sift the lower classes into appropriate ghettoes. Federally backed credit then guarantees to every potential escapee from the city the right to a clean, single family home—provided he is able to buy and the sellers are willing to sell him the property. The framers of these programs almost certainly did not intend them to be used in this manner. But that is the most damning possible commentary short of evil intent itself. Such results make it absolutely impossible to continue supporting a public philosophy that makes a virtue of government by delegation at the center and government by bureaucratic lawmaking and interest group privilege in the field.

A close look at the actual impact of these Federal urban policies makes one wonder how there is any Federal political legitimacy left. Washington is over one hundred years away from *apartheid* policy, but after twenty years of serious Federal urban involvement, the social state of American cities could be only a little worse if all the Federal agencies had been staffed all those years with white secret agents from South Africa. The first part of this chapter is a simple case study of the implementation of Federal urban programs inside a city. In its perverse way, the case illustrates the effectiveness of planning when governments do define their goals clearly. If only good plans were formulated half as well as this city planned *apartheid*. The second part of this chapter presents a modest step toward a good social plan for guiding the revolution toward acceptable goals.

HOUSING POLICY IN IRON CITY: HAVE A PLAN WHEN YOU PLAN

Iron City is an urban-industrial area whose corporate boundary surrounds nearly 60,000 residents and whose true metropolitan area includes about 100,000. The name of the city has been fictionalized to avoid embarrassing the local officials. They are guilty as charged but no more so than thousands of mayors, councilmen, planners, realtors, and builders all over the country. Iron City presents a single well-documented case. The case situation itself is extreme and unrepresentative, but it will soon be clear that that is precisely why it offers an ideal laboratory for discovering the nature and limitations of modern Federal enabling legislation. Iron City is a southern city, and its official development plan promulgates a set of explicit racial goals. In so doing, however, Iron City officials only stated, as the innocent child in Hans Christian Anderson's "The Emperor's New Clothes," the awful truth about the land-use goals of cities all over the country. The explicitness of Iron City simply documents beyond doubt the extraordinary permissiveness of Federal urban policy; for these official development plans provided the local facts and proposals upon which the Federal allocations were based.

INTERLARDED NEIGHBORHOODS: *status quo ante*

In 1950, over 20 per cent of Iron City's population were Negroes. But there was something peculiar about these Negroes, peculiar at least to those acquainted only with northern cities. In 1950 they did not live in a ghetto. The largest concentration was in the north-central section, "across the tracks." (Note the shadings on the map.) There was another large neighborhood in the south-central section. However, there were neighborhoods of Negroes in virtually every section of town. There was a narrow strip along The River, and several strips in the west-central and western sections, in easy walking distance from the steel and textile mills.

This has been the typical Negro residential pattern in southern cities, especially stable, middle-sized cities. Beginning in the 1920's, relatively slow growth of the city and slow but steady immigration of Negroes from outlying rural areas contributed to a patchwork pattern. Rather than a single Negro section, there were interlarded neighborhoods of black and white.[1] This pattern was supported by the needs of the wealthier whites for domestic servants. "Close quarters" was literally the predominant feature. For example, the Negro neighborhoods east and the north of The Circle were surrounded on three sides by the wealthiest homes in Iron City.

Although the residents of Iron City tolerated the proximity of the races, in fact encouraged it in many ways, they could in no way be accused of living in an integrated community.

---

[1] Iron City extends to the east beyond The River as well as to the north. And Negro neighborhoods are interlarded with white ones in those sections as well. However, they need not enter significantly into the case here.

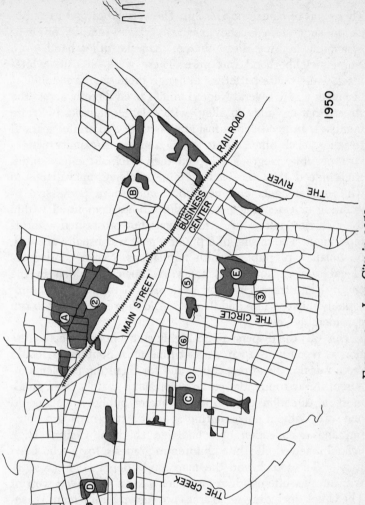

FIGURE 9.1. Iron City in 1950

There was of course no Harlem. The very word and its implications suggest the recency as well as the non-southern origin of
systematic housing discrimination. On the other hand, each
Negro neighborhood was pure. There were no black-white-
black-white house patterns (although there were a number of
instances where several Negro families lived directly across the
street from or "alley to alley" with a larger number of white
families). In good urban fashion, Negroes and whites learned
to ignore each other, yet to profit from the proximity where-
ever possible. Negroes accepted their back-of-the-bus status.
And indeed they received certain privileges unavailable to
whites. Merchants and newsboys were more permissive in
granting or extending petty credit. Crimes committed within
the race were not as a rule investigated or prosecuted with ut-
most vigor. The raising of a pig or a goat was usually allowed,
in violation of public health regulations. Negro bootleggers
(legal sale of liquor has for years been forbidden in the
county) had freer rein—and were often patronized by the in-
satiably thirsty white middle class. And the rents tended to run
considerably lower.

This was the dispersed and highly status-bound social situation as recently as 1950. At that time most Southerners could
see a racial crisis approaching, and for them the problems inherent in the residential pattern were immediately clear. In almost no direction away from the major public schools could
one walk without encountering at least a strip of Negro housing and a collection of school-age children. Central High
School received all white children in grades 9 to 12 who lived
east of The Creek (on the map, 9.1). Rebel High (No. 4)
was for all white children in grades 9 to 12 who lived west of
The Creek, including some areas not shown on the map. Washington High School (No. 2) was exclusively for the Negro children in grades 7 to 12 from the entire city and surrounding
county. Note how perilously close were Negro families, with
eligible children, to both of the white high schools, most particularly to Central, where virtually all of the children of upper middle- and middle-class families attended. Note also how
far a good half the Negro children commuted to Washington

High and also how many of them actually crossed the paths to Rebel and Central in the course of commuting. The same problem obtained for the junior highs (No. 3 and 7) and elementary schools (No. 5, 6, 7). Another junior high and elementary complex was similarly situated in an unmapped area east of The River.

THE PLAN

Into this situation stepped the Iron City Planning Commission in 1951. The Commission's first step was a thorough analysis of housing, land use, economic facilities, and deterioration. In 1952 they produced a handsome and useful Master Plan, the emphasis of which was upon the need for measures ". . . for arresting beginning blight and correcting advanced blight." On the basis of the master plan, a more intensive investigation was ordered, toward ultimate production of a Rehabilitation Plan to guide actual implementation and financing. The result was a careful study published in a very professional three-color, glossy-paper, fully illustrated booklet, *Iron City Redevelopment.* This plan centered upon three areas in which blight had made urban redevelopment necessary. On the map these are designated A, B, and E. Area E the plan identified as "occupied by Negroes, but the number is too few to justify provision of proper recreational, school, and social facilities. . . . The opportunity to reconstitute the area as a residential district in harmony with its surroundings was the main reason for its selection as the number one redevelopment site." The second area on the map, B, was chosen because "a relatively small amount of housing—standard and substandard —exists there"; therefore it would serve "as a companion project to . . . [Area E] . . . thus affording home sites for those occupants of [Area E] who are not eligible for relocation in public housing or who, for reasons of their own, prefer single-family or duplex dwellings." Area A, as shown by the intensive survey and the maps published with the Plan, contained as much dilapidated and blighted housing as Area E; but Area A was not designated an urban redevelopment area in the Plan. Although "blighted and depreciating," it was the "center part of the area . . . growing as the focal point of Negro life." Along the Main Street of this area, extending into area B, the Plan proposed the building of an auditorium, a playfield, and other public facilities "to serve [Iron City's] Negro community." Sites were inserted for the three Negro churches to be removed by the redevelopment of Area E.

The Plan was clearly a Negro removal plan. All of the projects proposed in the Plan are explicit on this point, as the selection of quotes from the document clearly demonstrates. The underlying intent of the Plan can be further identified, if need be, in the inconsistencies between the design for Area E and that for Area A. The latter possessed as much blighted housing as Area E, and yet the standard of blighting was not applied to it. There the Plan called for intensification of use rather than renewal.

THE PLAN IS IMPLEMENTED

Even before the completion of *Iron City Development*, implementation projects had begun in Iron City. These were expanded as financing allowed. The first steps, quite rationally, were toward expansion of housing replacements for those families to be displaced by renewal. Consistent with the types of people to be most affected by the Plan, those first steps were the construction of public housing. There had been some public housing construction under depression legislation, but it is of no concern here. Iron City built four public housing projects under the Housing Act of 1949. On the map they are the actual letters A, B, C, and D, and these designations have been placed as close as possible to their actual locations within each area.

Each public housing project was placed carefully. Project A was built in the middle of the largest Negro area. Project B was built in a sparse area, about 50 per cent Negro, but marked out in the Plan as the area for future expansion of the Negro community. (In the Plan, the proposed sites for the three new "colored churches" and the "colored auditorium" were strung along the area around Project B.) Project C, an exclusively white project, was built literally on top of the Negro area around it. While it is the smallest of the projects, as measured by the number of housing units, the structures were so designed to be spread over the entire 8-square-block area. It was, according to the executive director of the Greater Iron City Housing Authority, "a rather unique design, known in the architectural trade as a crankshaft design; thus providing both front and rear courtyards." This project was cited professionally as an outstanding example of good design and utility. And no wonder. Its maximum utilization of space, although it was a low-rent project, made it a combination of public housing and

TABLE 9.1

PUBLIC HOUSING PROJECTS IN IRON CITY

PROJECT	SIZE (NO. OF UNITS)	% NEGROES IN PROJECT	COMPOSITION OF ORIGINAL AREA	DEVELOPMENT COST
A	160	100	Negro	$1,491,000
B	224	100	Mixed	$2,491,000
C	146	0	Negro	$1,595,000
D	220	0	Negro	$2,300,000

slum (and Negro) removal project par excellence. Project D was also built on top of a blighted Negro neighborhood. However, although it is a relatively large project it did not alone eliminate every Negro in the area.

By 1955 the public housing projects had been completed and were occupied. From the start there was never any controversy over the racial distribution. The Plan was being implemented smoothly and in every respect. Projects A and B were 100 per cent Negro; Projects C and D were 100 per cent white. Meanwhile, but at a slower pace, renewal of the central city had begun. It was not until 1956 that implementation projects were fully designed. Two areas were marked out in the Plan for intensive renewal, the shaded Areas around B and E. The important one was Area E, a 56-acre area relatively tightly packed with rickety frame houses, outside toilets, corn and potato plots, and Negroes. In the official Plan proposals, Area E in-

cluded the unconnected Negro neighborhood just north of The
Circle as well as the entire shaded area due east of The Circle.
Area B, as noted before, was relatively sparse. A few shacks
needed removing, and in some of those shacks were white unemployables.

Within three years the two urban renewal projects were declared 100 per cent accomplished. In the official report to the
Urban Renewal Administration (HUD) the results were as
shown in the following table:

TABLE 9.2

ACCOMPLISHMENT	ACTIVITY	FOR AREA E	FOR AREA B
100%	Land Acquisition, No. of Parcels Acquired	168	39
100%	No. of Families Relocated	176	24
100%	No. of Structures Demolished (Site Clearance)	236	33

In Area E, every trace of Negro life was removed. As the executive director of the Greater Iron City Housing Authority
put it, "In this project, all of the then existing streets were
vacated and a new land-use map was developed." One entirely
new street was put in, several of the narrow lanes (e.g., "St.
James's Alley") were covered over, and through connectors
were built for a dead-end street or two.

All of Area E has become prime property. Most of the area
was zoned for single-family residences, and, as of mid-1967, the
boom in construction of houses in the $25,000–$40,000 range
in the area was still in progress. One large supermarket and
several neighborhood businesses are operating on renewal land
purchased from the Authority. A 95 per cent white elementary
school, with lighted ballfield and large playground, occupies
most of the eastern section. It is a consolidation of elementary
schools No. 5 and No. 6, which no longer exist. With the 95 per
cent white junior-high (No. 3), an impressive campus resulted.

Area B also enjoys a new elementary school, with fieldhouse, lighted ballfield, tennis court, and playground. The city also built a swimming pool in this area, but it and the original municipal pool on The River had been closed for several years to avoid integration of public facilities. As mentioned earlier, three of the redevelopment sites in Area B were set aside for the three churches demolished in the redevelopment of Area E. Each of the churches ultimately chose locations elsewhere in the Negro community. Except for the 224 units of public housing, most of the relocating Negroes chose the more densely populated and blighted Area A. Area B remains underutilized. The major part of Area B extends north of Project B toward the mountain, where although "some of the terrain is steep," reports *Iron City Development,* "much of it is gently rolling and well drained. . . . In most southern cities there is a scarcity of vacant land located close to schools and churches and shopping districts and served by city utilities and transportation, land that is suitable and desirable for expansion of Negro neighborhoods or creation of new ones. [Area B] is such an area." But apparently the Negroes did not agree, and most of the area remains a graded but raw expanse of red southern earth on the side of the mountain. This is the one part of the Plan that went wrong; this was the voluntary part of the Plan, *the part unfinanced by Federal agencies.*

The result, despite frustrated expectations in the north part of Area B, was overwhelming success for the Plan. Well before the 1960 Census the large Negro area in Area E had been reduced to 5.1 per cent of the entire census tract, and this was comprised of a few shanties behind the bottling works and the western edge of the Area along The River. In Area C, the removal process immediately around Central High was complete with Public Housing Project C. After 1960 some 10 per cent of the area was still nonwhite, but other families continued to move out. Removal from Area D was approaching totality. By 1964, removal from all areas west of The Creek was given further assistance by the completion of one federally supported arterial running east-west through the city, and the inauguration of Iron City's portion of the new north-south Interstate

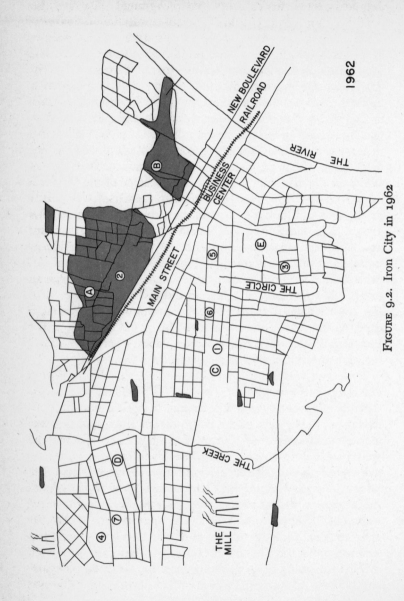

FIGURE 9.2. Iron City in 1962

Highway. That brought the nonwhite proportion in the western sectors of the city down to about 3 per cent.

This is how the situation stood by the end of 1967: west of The Creek and north of Main Street (all around Area D), there remained six Negro families. When a nearby textile mill was closed down some years before, they, as employees, were given the right to buy their houses, and they have chosen to remain. West of The Creek and south of Main Street (the area including The Mill) fewer than 5 per cent of the housing units were occupied by Negroes. Virtually every one of these houses is located in isolated and sparse sections along The Creek and behind The Mill, where one can still plant a plot of sorghum, catch a catfish, and, undisturbed, let a 1948 Chevrolet corrode into dust. East of The Creek and south of Main Street, closer to the center of things, the 1960 distribution of Negroes continues to be reduced. Every last shack is gone from Area E and the entire central area of the white city. Three small pockets remain in the western portion near Area C, and that is all that remains in all of the white city. The last remaining Negro neighborhood of any size, a group of shanties running along The River south of Main Street, was removed by the construction of a city hall–police department–YMCA complex. Area B remains completely nonwhite and underdeveloped. Area A now fills the entire triangle pointing north. It is a ghetto.

THE SECRET OF SUCCESS

The Plan enjoyed strong consensus among officials and white citizens. It enjoyed at least the acquiescence and tacit consent of the Negroes, who were, in any case, tenants whose landlords were white. But the Plan would have had little chance of success, consensus or not, without outside financial assistance. The assistance came from Federal programs. It was allocated, and continues in 1967 to be allocated, by Federal agencies whose personnel could and did have access to the Renewal Plan, the Master Plan, and all the project plans. Nothing was kept a secret in Iron City. What we have seen here is an honest, straightforward job of physical and social planning. And despite Iron City's open approach to *apartheid,* Federal assistance was never in question. Relative to Iron City's size, and especially the size of its annual public sector budget, Federal aid was quite substantial. And the results were dramatic. Perhaps only New Haven, Connecticut, a town famous for redevelopment, has had a higher per capita success ratio.

Direct Federal assistance for public housing in Iron City amounted to slightly over $280,000 for fiscal 1966. Each year since the completion of the four projects the city received about the same, or perhaps a slightly smaller amount. The figure varies and cannot be broken down among the four projects, because it is computed on the basis of the "development costs" (given above) and granted as a lump sum. The Public Housing (recently changed to Housing Assistance) Administration of HUD is authorized by law to grant *each year* to any housing authority the difference between expenses (governed by development costs) and income from public housing. Such a subsidy arrangement enabled authorities like Iron City's to borrow from private banks and to refinance through sale of relatively cheap housing authority bonds. What is even more significant is that under the formula, Iron City is authorized to receive a maximum grant of nearly $305,000 per annum. It is a point of pride at the Greater Iron City Housing Authority that the full amount available under the law was never needed or requested. At a minimum estimate of $250,-000 per year, Federal grants to help carry the public housing have amounted to $3,000,000. And federal public housing grants are neverending. Each year the total to Iron City goes up another $250,000 or more.

Federal assistance was also indispensable for the urban renewal projects in the Plan. Between 1957 and 1961, by which time virtually everything but land disposition was completed, Iron City received just short of $1,600,000 from the Federal government under the urban redevelopment laws. This amounts to a Federal subsidy of $400,000 per annum.

This Federal assistance of at least $300,000 for each year since 1954 or 1955, and of at least $700,000 during the years of peak planning activity (1957–62), constitutes the secret of the Plan's success. *It amounts to almost exactly 20 per cent of Iron City's total annual government budget.*

To this should of course be added an undetermined amount of Federal highway assistance which helped remove Negroes from the western edge of Iron City. There are also FHA and VA, which have been helping provide financing for the lovely homes being built in Area E. At this writing it has not yet been possible to determine whether Federal community facilities funds helped remove the Negroes from The River, where now stands the new city hall complex. It has also not been possible to determine whether the local banks balked at extending FHA and VA homeowner credit to Negroes for building on the mountainside north of Area B. But these facts would affect the meaning of the case only marginally.

IMPLICATIONS

First, the case bears out the contentions of two decades that slum removal means Negro removal. It supports the even more severe contention that the ultimate effects of Federal urban policies have been profoundly conservative, so much so as to vitiate any plans for positive programs of integration through alteration of the physical layout of cities.

Second, it supports the general thesis of this book, that policy without a rule of law will ultimately come to ends profoundly different from those intended by their most humanitarian and libertarian framers. It supports, still further, the contention of the book that some of the most cherished instruments of the positive state may be positively evil, and that the criterion by which this evil outcome can be predicted is absence of public and explicit legislative standards by which to guide administrative conduct.

Third, the case supports, especially by virtue of the explicitness of the racial policy, the main contentions of Part III. It shows precisely how and why Federal policy is ill-equipped to govern the cities directly. The case confirms beyond doubt the contention that the present disorder in the cities is properly explained by the failure of government and politics rather than by the inferiority of Negro adjustment. The case shows how national legitimacy can be tarnished to the degree that it is loaned to the cities for discretionary use, and how a crisis of public authority was inevitable as long as the virtue made of an untutored political process ended in the abuses cataloged in Iron City. In sum, it helps show why liberal governments cannot achieve justice.

Every Negro in Iron City knew what was happening. Every Negro in Chicago and New York and Cleveland and Detroit knows the same about his city too, but since these northern Negroes are not so docile, does that leave any possibility that Federal imperium was used completely differently outside the South? True, planning authorities would never so deliberately pursue racial planning. True, few social plans could be as extensive or as successful as Iron City's. Nonetheless, misuse of Federal programs in ways indistinguishable on principle from Iron City has been widespread and undeniable.

Martin Anderson, for example, estimated in 1964 that about two-thirds of all people displaced from urban renewal homes were Negroes, Puerto Ricans, or members of some other minority group.[2] In public housing the record is even more somber, first, because the pattern is even clearer, and second, because these projects stand as ever-present symbols of the acts of discrimination by which they were created.[3] As of 1965, only three of New York City's 69 public housing projects were officially listed as all-nonwhite or all-white in occupancy, but 10 of Philadelphia's 40 projects were all-nonwhite, and 21 of Chicago's 53, 5 of Detroit's 12, 4 of Cleveland's 14, and all of Dallas' 10 projects were listed as either all-nonwhite or all-white.[4] The rest of reality is hidden, because the Public Housing (renamed Housing Assistance) Administration defines an "integrated project" as one in which there are "whites and more than one nonwhite, including at least one Negro family."[5] Not only is it impossible to determine the real number of truly integrated projects; this system of reporting, as permissive as the law itself, was ideally suited for local racial policies

[2] Martin Anderson, *The Federal Bulldozer* (Cambridge: M.I.T. Press, 1964), pp. 6–8.

[3] See James Baldwin's observations, quoted at the beginning of Part III.

[4] Source: Public Housing Administration (HUD), *Low-Rent Project Directory,* December 31, 1965.

[5] *Ibid.,* p. v.

and local individual racial prejudices.[6] Until July, 1967, the agency even followed a rule of "free choice" allowing eligible tenants to wait indefinitely for an apartment, which allowed them also to decline a vacancy on racial grounds. Thus, while the whole story cannot be told from official statistics, every urban Negro knows it.

The Civil Rights Act of 1965 was supposed to have put an end to such practices, but there is little evidence that it can or will improve the situation in public housing in particular or city housing in general. It was not even until July of 1967 that the rule of "free choice" was replaced with a "rule of three," plan whereby an applicant must take one of the first three available units or be dropped to the bottom of the eligible list. All this has produced so far is undeniable testimony that the practices all along had constituted a "separate but equal" system of federally supported housing. As of June, 1967, therefore, following three years under the 1964 Civil Rights sections and following more strenuous efforts by the Johnson Administration, 2 of Detroit's 5 segregated projects became "integrated," by virtue of the fact that in each case exactly one white family had moved into a totally black project. At the same time at least 11 of New York's projects were classified as "integrated" when in fact fewer than 15 per cent of the units were occupied by families of some race other than the 85 per cent majority in that project.[7]

A month after the belated 1967 directive on public housing, the Federal Housing Administration (FHA) instituted a *pilot* program to increase FHA support for housing finance in "economically unsound" areas. This was an official confession that for 33 years FHA has insured over $110 billion of mortgages to help whites escape the city rather than build it. This step and others like it will not erase the stigma of second-class citizenship placed upon the residents of Federal housing programs

[6] *Cf.* a study by Bernard Weissbrourd which concluded: ". . . most cities have followed a deliberate program of segregation in public housing. . . ." *Segregation, Subsidies and Megalopolis* (Santa Barbara: Center for the Study of Democratic Institutions, 1964), p. 3.

[7] Source: Computer printouts provided by the Housing Assistance Administration.

nor remove the culpability of Federal power in the American local government policy of *apartheid*. These remedial steps came five years after President Kennedy's famous "stroke of the pen" decision aimed at preventing discrimination in publicly supported housing, and three years after the first applicable civil rights act. But all of the efforts surely suggest that mere remedy is never enough for bad organic laws, because bad organic laws literally possess congenital defects.

Better not to have had the housing at all than to have it on the Iron City pattern and at the expense of national legitimacy. Some would argue that the problem was actually one of mere timidity and that the answer is a proper expansion of public housing.[8] Judging from the patterns reviewed here, more could hardly have been better. Other writers and officials, including highly placed officials, have proposed solutions ranging from semipublic [9] to private [10] financing of public, low-cost housing. These proposals focus on the mere details of financing and offer further examples of the ignorance present liberals have of the implications of forms of law and administration for the achievement of simple, ordinary justice. Regardless of the means of financing, these programs will produce no lasting social benefit without a rule of law that states unmistakably what is to be achieved and what is to be forbidden. That is the moral of the Iron City story.

How to Approach the Revolution—Through Law

A new approach requires rejection of most of the policy that is being implemented or proposed today. If the new approach appears radical that is only because it opposes prevailing orthodoxy. If it appears reactionary that is only because it seeks to revive something old, for it seeks to combine the old liberal's concern for equality with the old conservative's con-

---

[8] *Cf.* Michael Harrington, *The Other America* (New York: Macmillan, 1962), pp. 139 ff.

[9] President Johnson, for example.

[10] Senators Charles Percy and Robert Kennedy, for example.

cern for legality. Since the one was impossible without the other, both were replaced by the self-defeating ideal of equity. To oppose mere equity is to seek something which is actually neither radical nor reactionary but simply imperative—a moral revival in public policy.

What must first be rejected, if the foregoing analysis has any value at all, is the Federal approach to society through economics and public works. Without this rejection there will be no chance to regain the moral posture with which the revolution was begun a decade or more ago. If proper standards of administration had been applied from the beginning—to everything from integrated transportation to integrated races, from clean air and water to safe streets, from who shall pay taxes to who shall be poor—there might have been some hope. But after more than 20 years of permissiveness and misuse, no mere salvage operation on public housing, urban redevelopment, and, more recently, New Welfare, will work. Elimination of practically all of the economics-public works approach, and limiting what is left of it to a role of implementing socially significant policies, would cut out a great deal of Federal activity. However, a moral posture toward the revolution requires less activity and more authority.

Policies and proposals involving structural reform must also be rejected. The various commonplaces that parade under the banner of metropolitan government are weakest of all. Metropolitan government based on a federal or confederal principle—where all existing governments in a metropolis maintain their identities and are given representation in some larger council—simply institutionalizes the stalemate that already exists in the region. If, on the other hand, metropolitan government were seriously tried on a unitary principle—where all autonomy within the region is eliminated—the new government would indeed then have reach and resource commensurate with its problems. But any State or central city with power to achieve that would then not need it, because there would already be sufficient power without bothering with the new level at all. Thus, the federal principle is feasible but ineffective; the unitary principle is quite effective but almost completely unfeasible. A third popular structural reform, more or less opposed to both of the others, is decentralization toward smaller and smaller units of self-government within the metropolis. The renewed and intensified cries for decentralization in the past decade—this time by the sentimental left rather than the right—provide further testimony to growing distrust of duly constituted authorities. But they provide no constructive direction for new uses of authority or new structures of authority. A time when national standards and local realities are almost completely out of joint is hardly a time for decentralization—or else Iron City is completely unique. Some day, when accepted moralities are enacted into law, decentralization of their implementation will be both possible and desirable. But until that time decentralization is only carte blanche for vested interests. What was true in the South when the social revolution of our time was initiated in 1954 remains true in all its ramifications in all parts of the country during the second decade of the revolution.

The most recent effort, open housing legislation, must also be rejected, although it warrants close attention for the future. Supreme Court decisions as old as 1937 and as recent as 1968 indicate that this type of law is constitutional—Federal law and the State and local versions of it. But it is not good legislation, for several reasons. First, the law will not work. Its claim to obedience is too weak for the behavior it seeks to alter, and the requirements for enforcement are too complex unless there is a manifold increase in the Federal police. Upon matters of ownership of personal property, government at all levels in the United States has its weakest claims, because ownership of personal property is historically remote from the obligations of individual citizenship. Exchange of personal property more frequently involves clear citizen obligations, but nonetheless the strong property tradition in this country will render such legislation as nugatory as liquor prohibition laws. This alone does not mean the laws should not be tried, but they run an enormous risk of inflating hopes that cannot be satisfied. Other approaches should be exhausted first.

A second argument against open housing legislation is that,

insofar as it is seriously implemented, it is a rather drastic measure to take before less drastic measures have been exhausted. This type of legislation involves a drastic change in the relations of citizens to government for which Americans have not been sufficiently educated. The social revolution of our time already involves the gigantic task of reeducation toward the universalization of the values concerning the human relations of Americans. In certain realms the citizen already knows he is obliged to be universalistic and he may already feel guilty that he is not. These realms are numerous and ripe for vigorous application of law. Public authority should prove successful there before turning to realms where the citizen is still almost certain to feel that he has the right to be particularistic in his associations.

Third, and most compelling, the open housing legislation will not work, or will work only as a war of attrition, because it will have to be applied to offenders least willing to abide by law and most willing to resist by organized and violent means. Correlatively, such legislation tends then to exempt those who are most responsive to lawful direction and most responsible for the abuses which have made modern urban life so desperate. In short, this is a law against the white lower classes that tends almost completely to exempt the higher classes. The framers of this legislation have succeeded in redistributing responsibilities where they have failed to redistribute rights or wealth, for open housing legislation must necessarily apply in those neighborhoods in which Negro families can afford to take advantage of the law. True, Negroes ought to be able to buy or rent where they can afford. But why deliberately seek to pursue the revolution through the white lower classes? If we truly seek to bring about a revolution through law, we should at least exhaust first of all the possibilities of pursuing it through those people in the community most likely to respect the law, to obey the law, and perhaps ultimately to come to see the actual necessity of eliminating all differences in human relationships due solely to indefensible and outmoded social criteria.

Also to be rejected are the prospective and seemingly bold

proposals for what might be called New New Welfare—that is, schemes for guaranteed incomes, including the Negative Income Tax. If the method of guarantee is a nondiscretionary negative income tax scheme, like the first and most famous proposed by Professor Milton Friedman, it constitutes simply a bit of reform of Old Welfare. If the scheme is built on a discretionary distribution system it merely constitutes a large expansion of New Welfare.[11] But either way these are welfare and antipoverty plans and they do not get at the question of who shall be poor any better than Old or New Welfare. *Welfare approaches are simply not appropriate for the revolution of our time.*

Rejection of so many existing commitments and proposals does not seriously reduce options for the future. It only suggests that the best approaches to the revolution have not yet been tried. New approaches must simply face the real flaws of the old, learn from those flaws, and depart from them. The old approaches failed and will continue to fail because they fail to take into account the fundamental demands of citizenship. The new approaches must depart directly from a clear notion of citizenship. The old approaches failed and will continue to fail because they either seek to avoid the revolution altogether or deliberately pursue it through the wrong classes. The new approaches must be developed out of an awareness that revolution is what is being dealt with; that requires some revolutionary thinking, and revolutionary thinking means thought about social structure and social classes. Finally, the old approaches fail because they leave untouched the very local political structures that isolate those who seek the revolution from the channels through which a legitimate revolution could take place. Therefore, the new approaches must seek to destroy some of the old political structures, particularly the corporate city.

FEDERAL POWER, CITIZENSHIP, AND THE REDISCOVERY OF THE CITY

Rejection of so many Federal activities does not severely reduce the Federal role but only reduces it to those things for

[11] For an excellent brief analysis of the problems, see Sar Levitan, "The Pitfalls of a Guaranteed Income," *Reporter*, May 18, 1967.

which it can be particularly effective. To be effective and to avoid tarnishing national legitimacy, the Federal role must be limited to those practices for which it is possible to develop a clear and authoritative rule of law, enacted democratically and implemented absolutely. These criteria eliminate most of the legislation of the past 20 years, but in so doing they reveal the true accomplishments of that period and the actual readiness of the Federal system to deal with the revolution. We are left with an impressive and comprehensive body of civil rights law, the immense power of the Federal purse, a widespread and intense desire to do something constructive with the revolution. These need only be combined, properly directed, and carried to absolute finality.

Federal dictation? In a way, yes. But that is true of democracies. When a democratic government is given power through a democratic process—and no one can deny that civil rights powers were granted democratically—unexceptionable implementation should no longer be in doubt. Moreover, in a crisis the choice is no longer between some dictation and none but between dictation by law or dictation by the mob. In fear for the liberal's constituency there has been an effort to avoid dictation in northern cities by buying off the Negro masses. To try to buy off the masses is to risk creating a mob. When society has become illegitimate, as American society has for Negroes, and when there is already a mob, as is the incipient case in every ghetto, the offer of deals will not disperse a mob but only demoralize it.

Impractical? It is interesting how liberals talk practicalities only when the hour of reckoning has arrived in their own constituencies; but there is in fact nothing impractical about the enforcement of good laws like civil rights. If middle-class mothers in Queens or Cicero or Berkeley have no respect for law, they can be garrisoned far more easily than the angry mob in Little Rock, the lumpenproletariat of Meridian, or the mindless rioters of Newark. Moreover, new legislation of this type offers few of the technical problems of the welfare and public works type, although technicality is what tends to get the most attention, if we can judge by all the research into civil disorder conducted in the past several years. "Problem-finding" is the essence of good law, just as it is of good science, and this is a role in which the most qualified are the educated amateurs and unspecialized philosophers. For, "in the Solution of Questions, the Maine Matter was the *well-stating of them;* wch requires motherwitt, & Logick . . . ; for let the question be but well-put, it will work almost of itselfe." [12]

Most of the problems of how Federal power can deal with the revolution through law can be properly solved by rediscovery of the city. Rediscovery is required on two levels. One level is socio-economic. The other level is philosophic and constitutional. Both operate as powerful guides to good public policy.

Socio-economically, the city is obviously something far larger than the corporate city. Only policies that deal with this true city will be effective in guiding the revolution. Sometimes only the Federal government is extensive enough to produce effective policy for the true socioeconomic city, but that option is limited, as already suggested, by the awesome problem of regional variation. The other level is the State, although at this stage of the game use of this level may require the holding of the nose. But there are no other alternatives in the United States. No law is worthy of the name unless applied by a sovereign, and Federal and State governments are the only sovereigns relevant to the revolution of our time. We may dream of the central city "getting together" with its satellites, or we may dream of good will bringing about uniform remedial action throughout the metropolis. But if there is no polity there will not be any policy. No local government has the jurisdiction for the revolution. It is not sovereign. The corporate city is an anachronism, and it has been for thirty years.

Since that which we conventionally designate the city really does not exist, we must define a new city. This is the philosophic dimension. The city is citizens. The city is the public character or the public dimension of people. In a democratic system citizenship is the only thing people absolutely, involun-

[12] John Aubrey, a seventeenth-century publicist, quoted in Robert Merton, "Notes on Problem-Finding in Sociology," in *Sociology Today* ed. Merton *et al.* (New York: Basic Books, 1959), p. ix. (Emphasis in original.)

tarily, and perpetually have in common. And it is in regard to this public dimension of people and things that government has its really effective claim. Through schemes of corporatism, syndicalism, interest group representation, and participatory democracy, liberals, in the name of liberalism, have sought to obliterate the distinction between public and private. The concept of citizenship restores that distinction and defines clearly where are the best opportunities to guide the revolution.

This definition goes to the core of a vital and practical constitutional point. In the United States there are two kinds of citizenship. There is national citizenship—that bundle of immunities and obligations relative to Federal power. And there is State citizenship—one's public character created by the constitutional grant of power to each State. This is one more type of citizenship than is found in most countries, but what is significant here is that there are only two and not three. *There is no city citizenship. Constitutionally, therefore, there is no corporate city.* The city is citizens. It is the State, or the Federal government, in relation to people. The corporate city is an aggregation of people which the State saw fit to render into an administrative structure. The corporate city is truly a creature of the State. The corporate city may have traditions and may enjoy the (ever-weakening) loyalty of its residents. The corporate city may indeed perform vital functions in the core and at the fringes of metropolis. But the corporate city as a public entity with absolute claims upon citizenship need not exist *except at the convenience of the State,* notwithstanding any law or State constitution to the contrary. And the corporate city is no longer a convenience.

The fiction of a third citizenship residing in the corporate city, as though it were a city-state, has been cultivated in the United States for three-quarters of a century. Home Rule it is called, and it was allowed to convey the totally erroneous impression that a corporate city could be made into a sovereign body. Thus, Home Rule is not only inconvenient, it is unconstitutional, because it permanently delegates (therefore alienates) State powers to some part within the State. Home Rule may have been a practical necessity in the early days of urban growth when the physical and social city was so far out of joint with the rest of the State. However, as the physical and economic distinctions between rural and urban disappear, the political distinction of a conventional city from the rest of the State becomes meaningless. And as the country at large comes to espouse certain values without regard to region or rural-urban differences, the political distinction of a city from the rest of the State becomes an unadulterated evil. The grant of Home Rule was once a grant of autonomy. Now it is simply a barrier to the peaceful resolution of revolutionary forces.

Rediscovery of the city therefore means rediscovery of the State as well as clarification of Federal roles. It is difficult to ponder the State as the key to the future, but the desirability of the State increases as other approaches are tried and found wanting. Some object on the mere practical grounds that State social policy is politically unrealistic, that States are remote and corrupt, that States have insufficient power or responsibility for such important tasks, and that State policy constitutes only an imposition upon local efforts. These objections, as well as others, all sound hauntingly familiar to anyone who lived through the period prior to the enactment of the first Federal civil rights bills, when southern leaders pleaded so eloquently the same cases against Washington.

By simple use of grant-in-aid and tax-rebate powers the Federal government could put starch in the character of State politics. A properly moral and legal attitude toward power could render the Federal government capable of overcoming rural conservatism and suburban reactionism and fear in the State legislatures. After that, literally with the stroke of a pen States could proceed in the one single action the present revolution begs for: *the destruction of the corporate city.* This would simplify immensely the expansion of the rights of man in the United States.

Old Welfare is standing proof of the power of Federal resources when used to attain legal and clearly defined purposes —just as New Welfare, urban renewal, and public housing represent the weakness of Federal power when used diffusely and without clear legal focus. States must be offered the choice, in other words, of maintaining or not maintaining membership in the industrial prosperity club, the key to which belongs to the Federal revenue system. No aids of any sort would ever again be forthcoming without actual proof, before the fact, that State programs deal with the rights of citizens. The technique itself is not new; it is only being put to new purposes. Such was intended in parts of the 1964 and 1965 civil rights acts, but for several important reasons they have not worked. One of those reasons is lack of will, but there are other hindrances even when the will exists. Most important is the fact that most of the substantive legislation to which the civil rights acts would apply is not sufficiently clear, and most of the precedent is weighted toward continuing to enable cities to carry out their local policies. Next, even if the purpose in the Federal legislation is spelled out clearly and an effort is made to apply antidiscrimination standards to it, the implementation of real social goals in cities will be hopeless as long as the city is defined as the corporate city. A Federal law that requires corporate central cities to solve important problems involving human rights is requiring the impossible of those cities and at the same time is reinforcing the irresponsibility of the satellite cities. Therefore the Federal government has no choice but to establish destruction of city boundaries as a clear goal, and the States must implement the goals with all the fervor of revival, because the future of State government, as well as the health of the society after the revolution, depends heavily upon the severing of these shackles. There are obviously other areas in need of Federal action, and there are methods of action other than grant-in-aid, tax-rebate, and other fiscal devices. However, a good legal purpose enforced by fiscal power has the advantage of keeping involvement of Federal sovereignty safely remote from tarnishing and unsavory relationships with local governments, without in fact destroying all hope of some regional and local variation.

BREAKING THE CYCLE: THE CASE OF EDUCATION

Education serves as the best single example of the practical application of these principles, because it is the one most important area for implementing them. Education alone might break the cycle of dual status even if all other reforms and improvements failed to take place.

The public schools are clearly public property. They can be possessed by no one but the State (or Federal) system. They cannot be the property, therefore, of the corporate cities or of the local school districts. They cannot be the property of, or subject to proprietary control by, any individuals or organizations, for individuals have no relation to the schools except in the capacity of their citizenship. Even a child of five is a citizen in the degree to which he must be educated—and these obligations do not change if the child is in what is called a private school. In any case, neither he, nor the neighborhood homebodies, the races, the PTA's, the unions, nor, indeed, the professional educators can sustain any proprietary claim. All these traits, while admirable to be sure, are traits of human beings and are totally irrelevant to school life, school districting, school eligibility, school organization, school purposes. Their claim, far from being proprietary, is no stronger a claim than that of the bricks or slates that comprise the physical school. If educational reform is to come, if education is to be made the key instrument in the revolution, the corporate school district with vested neighborhood rights must fall along with the rest of the old trappings of corporate city-hood. Real equality in education will die inside the conventional city and its conventional school district boundaries.

A "school district" is a useful administrative convenience. But if it is composed of citizens it can be of any shape, any size, any character. It can obviously be designed without regard to preexisting corporate boundaries. Why does one fiction have to recognize another? Federal legislation must provide simply the incentives for States to create socially meaningful districts. This is the concrete and practical way by which the Federal system can destroy an important barrier to justice.

Note on the accompanying map of Metropolitan Chicago how easily a few oval-shaped, relatively compact new school districts could accommodate the ghetto population. On the corporate Chicago part of the map, at the center near the lake,

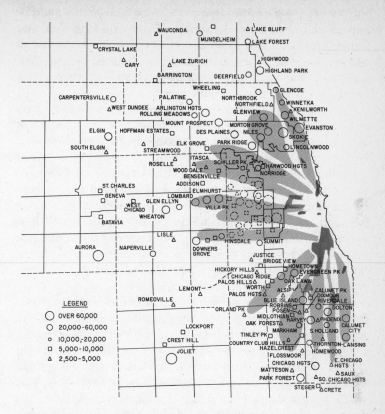

FIGURE 9.3. Chicago: Distribution and Proposed Redistribution of Negro School Children

the key Negro ghettoes are sketched out roughly. An oval reaching upward through Evanston and Kenilworth toward Glencoe in the north could easily accommodate a large proportion of the northernmost ghetto and the northern part of the next ghetto. A north-easterly and somewhat larger oval-shaped school district running toward Morton Grove and Glenview could easily accommodate the remainder of the second ghetto. Another just to the south and west of that one, running toward Des Plaines, could accommodate a large part of the school population of the West Side ghetto. A goodly proportion of the remainder of the schoolchildren of the West Side ghetto could be spread and shared among school districts running due west and slightly north and south of due west. Parents in the largest ghetto, the South Side ghetto, could be required to send their children to one of several school districts flanking outwards toward the south quadrant of the map.

No child would have to spend more than 30 to 40 minutes commuting each way in order to reach the outer fringes of each school district. And that is hardly any distance at all when compared to the distances children had to travel in the days of the old consolidated county school districts and in the days before school buses. A mere 20-mile commute from the northern Negro sections could reach Glencoe and environs. A mere 20-mile commute from the West Side ghetto reaches Glenellyn. A mere 20-mile commute from the very center of the South Side ghetto could reach any one of several prosperous and desirable South Side suburbs. Once corporate boundaries are disregarded the choices become amazingly easy.

Most of the burdens of such a plan fall upon Negro children, but of course this is one of the advantages of such an approach, since they and their families have most to gain from it. First, no plan of this sort will work without the use of benign quotas, or positive discrimination. In the 1960 Census 23.6 per cent of the population of the city of Chicago was nonwhite, while 3.1 per cent of the Chicago suburban population was nonwhite. The disparity in the distribution of nonwhites has probably become far greater in the years since that last official census, but the Negro population of the entire greater Chicago area is still around 15 per cent. If that is the case, the rule for redistricting the whole area would be simply that every school shall immediately be constituted with a student body of no larger or smaller than 15 per cent Negro students—give or take some practical "tolerance limit." Next, obviously this means that almost all the traveling would be done by the residents of the ghetto. Evanston's nonwhite population in 1960 was 12 per cent—surely larger since 1960. However, the more typical suburbs were Glencoe, with 6.5 per cent nonwhites, Kenilworth (Senator Percy's home town), with 1.3 per cent nonwhites, and Morton Grove, with 0.7 per cent. On the South Side, Chicago Heights was composed of 19 per cent nonwhites, but the more typical suburb was Flossmoor, with 0.6 per cent. Among 147 suburban towns of more than 2,500 population in the Chicago area in 1960, only 9 exceeded 15 per cent nonwhite populations, and 4 of these are virtually all-Negro suburbs whose children would also have to be bused.

But is all this really a basis for objecting to the plan? Many whites will object, as they already have, to modest busing experiments. But their practical arguments are extremely weak, and their claim to constitutionally vested rights in their present school situations has been shown to be illusory. Many Negro parents also fear such a system, but they must balance their fears against present educational opportunities that doom their child far more certainly than commuting. *Separate schools are inherently unequal.* To this dictum the Supreme Court should have added: *in the North too.* Ghetto schools are perpetuating the inferior culture that second-class citizenship created, and the cycle can be broken only by abandonment of those schools. The only real problem is whether the Negro community itself is as yet mature enough to accept positive discrimination. The hope is that they are already so accustomed to being singled out that a little more, especially if benign instead of malicious, will not hurt. It must be done, if the cycle of black poverty and the cycle of white fear and guilt shall ever be broken.

Another source of opposition is influential but almost completely illegitimate and most harmful. This source is Black Power, Black Nationalism, Black Separatism. One may indeed sympathize with the frustration these movements express. One may almost justifiably patronize them by seeing there an expression of new-found identity. But their expressions have no status as policy. Their suffering gives them cause, but cause does not define rights or specify remedies. Legal support for their separatism, in any form, is as evil as was legal prohibition of their integration. Both run against the very fiber and fabric of citizenship and statehood. Separatists are in effect demanding two legal systems at the very time when the nation is in agony trying to create one.

HOUSING, ON A METROPOLITAN SCALE

One of the subsidiary advantages to an educational scheme cutting across all existing boundaries is its immediate effect upon housing pressures. The white homeowner in Cicero is less likely to feel the urge to move or fear a potential decline in property values in face of the first Negro neighbor if he knows that the school situation for his children will not change appreciably. Hidebound school districts and residential requirements leave frightened residents almost no choice but to remove themselves totally from the area, even at the risk of great financial loss. Hidebound school districts are surefire ways of making certain that the main burden of revolution will be borne by the lower- and lower-middle-class whites. To spread that burden into the school systems all over the area is to extend to these frightened city residents the right to remain where they are. This is bound to stabilize neighborhoods.

However, there are also more direct housing policies one can easily perceive once the principle of citizenship is used to define the city. Why have Federal-local programs been contained within the central regions of corporate cities? Some tax base has been restored, but most of the projects have proven irrelevant, some quite harmful, to progress against the ghettoes. There is absolutely no reason why Federal and State powers of eminent domain cannot be used to create low- and middle-income integrated housing outside and directly across corporate boundaries. Most of the suburbs immediately outside Paris, for example, are working-class suburbs, a fact that contributes not only to a superior distribution of population but also to a far superior distribution of industry. Since fewer workers possess automobiles, their commutation requirements have even helped keep the Paris public transportation systems solvent.

If a 15 per cent benign quota in publicly supported housing were enforced in every community throughout each American metropolis, would white families move in? Would such projects impair property values in the nearby high-value areas? These questions are irrelevant, but the answers are simple. If rentals were reasonable enough no suburban housing would ever remain long unoccupied. This will be made more certain insofar as there is no decrease in the amount of subsidy suburbanites receive in the form of improved commuting facilities. As to the second question, there would probably be some immediate decline of property values, because suburbanites are terror-stricken. But that would pass. Meanwhile, suburbanites have already been enjoying for far too long an unearned increment on their properties due to the irresponsible and exploitative relation they have established with the central city. Again, what would the Kenilworth house be worth in South Dakota? How much value does a new, 90 per cent federally-supported arterial add to nearby suburban property? *The private profit from public facilities must be calculated in social terms.* The unearned increment Henry George wanted to tax was once due to the impersonal forces of population concentration. The unearned increment of today is far more frequently due to very deliberate acts of public policy—from the corporate boundaries, the public facilities and arterials, all the way over to tax breaks for property ownership and mortgage insurance, just to dot the i's and cross the t's. Upon this unearned increment the public need has an overwhelmingly justifiable claim.

CITIZENSHIP: PUBLIC MORALITY

Education and housing schemes for the metropolis are tremendously attractive because they face the key problems of the era directly, yet they are simple to enact and easy to understand. There are no special technicalities or eventualities that interfere with the making of real law, with real standards to guide the engineers and school administrators who must implement the programs. But the strongest advantage of all in such programs is that they put some kind of meaningful morality into the relationship between the Federal government and the local revolution. Despite what social science may say, politics is morality. Politics is the making of choices between good and bad, choices of priorities among competing good things. Democracy appeals because its emphasis on method keeps private moralities in check. But that does not mean that moral choice is not involved. Pretending that it is not was the beginning of the rise of cynicism and the decline of legitimacy. Marx believed that the seeds of revolution, alienation, were implanted the moment when a "cash nexus" was established between a person, his employer, and their product. In the modern state, alienation may have begun with the establishment of a cash nexus between a citizen and his government.

Public morality is a behavioral fact. Its basis is citizenship, and its influence and its limits can be studied like any other political phenomenon. Only time will test out the most important hypotheses, but certain of the tendencies of this cash nexus can be perceived now, just as social scientists were able to perceive certain tendencies in the economic system long before those tendencies reached maturity. At the most general level, the absence of public morality or citizenship will almost certainly yield Two Nations. All industrial states successfully met this problem when it manifested itself in the polarization of economic classes. The United States is the first country to face the problem in racial and ethnic terms. The policy choices may be more agonizing this time because popular majorities do not fall easily on the side of change. But the obligations of citizenship and the results of not obeying them are about the same.

The suburbs, legally separating themselves from American life, represent a failure of citizenship. Negroes who prefer to remain apart in the ghetto represent an escape from citizenship. Congress, in spreading the obligations of citizenship to uncertain realms before successfully exhausting Federal powers over certain realms, is deranging citizenship. The President, in calling forth these obligations when he cannot forcefully implement his own, is demoralizing citizenship. Programs erasing the obligations by buying off demands that they be fulfilled are destroying citizenship.

If the revolution is to be directed away from the Two Nations the notion of citizenship must be restored and the strongest and most authoritative of laws must be applied to it. An easy and effective place to begin is with complete destruction of the fiction of local citizenship and the sanctity of local corporate boundaries. Long ago the Supreme Court ruled that parties "cannot remove their transactions from the reach of dominant constitutional power by making contracts about them." [13] A corporate charter is merely a contract, and no contract is protected from State power, especially when it involves practices that are illegal or contrary to public policy. It is clear that the corporate city is contrary to public policy. Its destruction may be the first step toward real progress in the North, just as destruction of State segregation laws was the first step toward liberation of the South. Citizenship simply puts an end to segregation in all its forms. The policies of interest-group liberalism only serve to make segregation a little easier to abide.

[13] Chief Justice Hughes in *Norman v. Baltimore and Ohio Railroad Co.*, 294 U.S. 240 (1935).

PART IV

BEYOND LIBERALISM

"The law detains both man and woman
Who steal the goose from off the common
But lets the greater felon loose
Who steals the common from the goose."

Anon.

CHAPTER 10

TOWARD JURIDICAL DEMOCRACY

Assume that all developments of ideology, public philosophy, and public policy are part of some irresistible historical process. Epochs have no alternatives. Interest-group liberal ideology merely reflects the realities of power and rationalizes them into public policies. Criticism is irrelevant. All literature is a gigantic act of memorialization.

Fortunately, the influence of history and power over the human element is merely an hypothesis. To deny it is to wait for the long run. But to accept it is to confirm it. Ultimately, denial is the only choice, because acceptance is no test of hypothesis at all. History is much like a prison or a ghetto. It is difficult to escape, but the captive may succeed—unless he does not try. The only test of a deterministic hypothesis is whether real-world attempts to deny it fail.

THE END OF LIBERALISM: THE INDICTMENT

The corruption of modern democratic government began with the emergence of interest-group liberalism as the public philosophy. Its corrupting influence takes at least four important forms, four counts, therefore, of an indictment for which most of the foregoing chapters are mere documentation. Also to be indicted, on at least three counts, is the philosophic component of the ideology, pluralism.

SUMMATION I: FOUR COUNTS AGAINST THE IDEOLOGY

(1) Interest-group liberalism as public philosophy corrupts democratic government because it deranges and confuses expectations about democratic institutions. Liberalism promotes popular decision-making but derogates from the decisions so made by misapplying the notion to the implementation as well as the formulation of policy. It derogates from the processes by treating all values in the process as equivalent interests. It derogates from democratic rights by allowing their exercise in foreign policy, and by assuming they are being exercised when access is provided. Liberal practices reveal a basic disrespect for democracy. Liberal leaders do not wield the authority of democratic government with the resoluteness of men certain of the legitimacy of their positions, the integrity of their institutions, or the justness of the programs they serve.

(2) Interest-group liberalism renders government impotent. Liberal governments cannot plan. Liberals are copious in plans but irresolute in planning. Nineteenth-century liberalism was standards without plans. This was an anachronism in the modern state. But twentieth-century liberalism turned out to be plans without standards. As an anachronism it, too, ought to pass. But doctrines are not organisms. They die only in combat over the minds of men, and no doctrine yet exists capable of doing the job. All the popular alternatives are so very irrelevant, helping to explain the longevity of interest-group liberalism. Barry Goldwater most recently proved the irrelevance of one. The *embourgeoisement* of American unions suggests the irrelevance of others.

The Departments of Agriculture, Commerce, and Labor provide illustrations, but hardly exhaust illustrations, of such impotence. Here clearly one sees how liberalism has become a doctrine whose means are its ends, whose combatants are its clientele, whose standards are not even those of the mob but worse, are those the bargainers can fashion to fit the bargain.

Delegation of power has become alienation of public domai
—the gift of sovereignty to private satrapies. The political barriers to withdrawal of delegation are high enough. But liberalism reinforces these through the rhetoric of justification and
often even permanent legal reinforcement: Public corporations
—justified, oddly, as efficient planning instruments—
permanently alienate rights of central coordination to the
directors and to those who own the corporation bonds. Or, as
Walter Adams finds, the "most pervasive method . . . for
alienating public domain is the certificate of convenience and
necessity, or some variation thereof in the form of an exclusive
franchise, license or permit. . . . [G]overnment has become
increasingly careless and subservient in issuing them. The net
result is a general legalization of private monopoly. . . ."[1]
While the best examples still are probably the 10 self-
governing systems of agriculture policy, these are obviously
only a small proportion of all the barriers the interest-group
liberal ideology has erected to democratic use of government.

(3) Interest-group liberalism demoralizes government, because liberal governments cannot achieve justice. The question
of justice has engaged the best minds for almost as long as
there have been notions of state and politics, certainly ever
since Plato defined the ideal as one in which republic and justice were synonymous. And since that time philosophers have
been unable to agree on what justice is. But outside the ideal,
in the realms of actual government and citizenship, the problem is much simpler. We do not have to define justice at all in
order to weight and assess justice in government, because in
the case of liberal policies we are prevented by what the law
would call a "jurisdictional fact." In the famous jurisdictional
case of *Marbury v. Madison* Chief Justice Marshall held that
even if all the Justices hated President Jefferson for refusing to
accept Marbury and the other "midnight judges" appointed by
Adams, there was nothing they could do. They had no authority to judge President Jefferson's action one way or another because the Supreme Court did not possess such jurisdiction over
the President. In much the same way, there is something about

[1] Adams and Gray, *op. cit.*, pp. 47–48.

liberalism that prevents us from raising the question of justice at all, no matter what definition of justice is used.

Liberal governments cannot achieve justice because their policies lack the *sine qua non* of justice—that quality without which a consideration of justice cannot even be initiated. Considerations of the justice in or achieved by an action cannot be made unless a deliberate and conscious attempt was made by the actor to derive his action from a general rule or moral principle governing such a class of acts. One can speak personally of good rules and bad rules, but a homily or a sentiment, like liberal legislation, is not a rule at all. The best rule is one which is relevant to the decision or action in question and is general in the sense that those involved with it have no direct control over its operation. A general rule is, hence, *a priori*. Any governing regime that makes a virtue of avoiding such rules puts itself totally outside the context of justice.

Take the homely example of the bull and the china shop. Suppose it was an op art shop and that we consider op worthy only of the junk pile. That being the case, the bull did us a great service, the more so because it was something we always dreamed of doing but were prevented by law from entering and breaking. But however much we may be pleased, we cannot judge the act. We can only like or dislike the consequences. The consequences are haphazard; the bull cannot have intended them. The act was a thoughtless, animal act which bears absolutely no relation to any aesthetic principle. We don't judge the bull. We only celebrate our good fortune. Without the general rule, the bull can reenact his scenes of creative destruction daily and still not be capable of achieving, in this case, aesthetic justice. The whole idea of justice is absurd.

The general rule ought to be a legislative rule because the United States espouses the ideal of representative democracy. However, that is merely an extrinsic feature of the rule.[2] All

[2] As argued in Chapter 5, there is a high probability that efforts to make rules will lead to the legislature. A general rule excites continuous efforts at reformulation, which tend to turn combatants toward the levels of highest legitimacy and last appeal. Contrary to the fears of

that counts is the character of the rule iself. Without the rule we can only like or dislike the consequences of the governmental action. In the question of whether justice is achieved, a government without good rules, and without acts carefully derived therefrom, is merely a big bull in an immense china shop.

(4) Finally, interest-group liberalism corrupts democratic government in the degree to which it weakens the capacity of governments to live by democratic formalisms.[3] Liberalism weakens democratic institutions by opposing formal procedure with informal bargaining. Liberalism derogates from democracy by derogating from all formality in favor of informality. Formalism is constraining; playing it "by the book" is a role often unpopular in American war films and sports films precisely because it can dramatize personal rigidity and the plight of the individual in collective situations. Because of the impersonality of formal procedures, there is inevitably a separation in the real world between the forms and the realities, and this kind of separation gives rise to cynicism, for informality means that some will escape their collective fate better than others. There has as a consequence always been a certain amount of cynicism toward public objects in the United States, and this may be to the good, since a little cynicism is the father of healthy sophistication. However, when the informal is elevated to a positive virtue, and hard-won access becomes a share of official authority, cynicism becomes distrust. It ends in reluctance to submit one's fate to the governmental process under any condition, as is the case in the United States in the mid-1960's.

Public officials more and more frequently find their fates paradoxical and their treatment at the hands of the public fickle and unjust when in fact they are only reaping the results of their own behavior, including their direct and informal treatment of the public and the institutions through which

pluralists, the statement of a good rule can produce more flexibility and more competition than the avoidance of the rule. These tendencies are still further developed under proposals for reform.

[3] One aspect of this was dealt with at some length at the end of Chapter 3. Another was dealt with at the end of Chapter 6. Here, at the risk of some repetition, the various aspects of it are put together.

they serve the public. The more government operates by the spreading of access, the more public order seems to suffer. The more public men pursue their constituencies, the more they seem to find their constituencies alienated. Liberalism has promoted concentration of democratic authority but deconcentration of democratic power. Liberalism has opposed privilege in policy formulation only to foster it, quite systematically, in the implementation of policy. Liberalism has consistently failed to recognize, in short, that in a democracy forms are important. In a medieval monarchy all formalisms were at court. Democracy proves, for better or worse, that the masses like that sort of thing too.

Another homely parable may help. In the good old days, everyone in the big city knew that traffic tickets could be fixed. Not everyone could get his ticket fixed, but nonetheless a man who honestly paid his ticket suffered in some degree a dual loss: his money, and his self-esteem for having so little access. Cynicism was widespread, violations were many, but perhaps it did not matter, for there were so few automobiles. Suppose, however, that as the automobile population increased a certain city faced a traffic crisis and the system of ticket fixing came into ill repute. Suppose a mayor, victorious on the Traffic Ticket, decided that, rather than eliminate fixing by universalizing enforcement, he would instead reform the system by universalizing the privileges of ticket fixing. One can imagine how the system would work. One can imagine that some sense of equality would prevail, because everyone could be made almost equally free to bargain with the ticket administrators. But one would find it difficult to imagine how this would make the total city government more legitimate. Meanwhile, the purpose of the ticket would soon have been destroyed.

Traffic regulation, fortunately, was not so reformed. But many other government activities were. The operative principles of interest-group liberalism possess the mentality of a world of universalized ticket fixing: Destroy privilege by universalizing it. Reduce conflict by yielding to it. Redistribute power by the maxim of each according to his claim. Reserve an official place for every major structure of power. Achieve order by worshiping the processes (as distinguished from the forms and the procedures) by which order is presumed to be established.

It these operative principles will achieve equilibrium—and such is far from proven [4]—that is all they will achieve. Democracy will have disappeared, because all of these maxims are founded upon profound lack of confidence in democracy. Democracy fails when it lacks confidence in its own authority.

Democratic forms were supposed to precede and accompany the formulation of policies so that policies could be implemented authoritatively and firmly. Democracy is indeed a form of absolutism, but ours was fairly well contrived to be an absolutist government under the strong control of consent-building prior to taking authoritative action in law. Interest-group liberalism fights the absolutism of democracy but succeeds only in taking away its authoritativeness. Whether it is called "creative federalism" by President Johnson, "cooperation" by the farmers, "local autonomy" by the Republicans, or "participatory democracy" by the New Left, the interest-group liberal effort does not create democratic power but rather negates it.

SUMMATION II: THREE COUNTS AGAINST
THE INTELLECTUAL COMPONENT

It ought to be clear from many sources that liberal leaders operate out of a sincere conviction that what they do constitutes an effort to respond to the stress of their times in ways best calculated to further the public interest. If the results are contrary to their hopes, it is because their general theory of cause and effect must be wrong. Everyone operates according to some theory, or frame of reference, or paradigm—some generalized map that directs logic and conclusions, given certain facts. The influence of one's paradigm over one's decisions is enormous. It helps define what is important among the multitudes of events (i.e., it "sets one's attention"). And it literally programs one toward certain kinds of conclusions. Men are un-

[4] *Cf.* David Easton, *The Political System* (New York: Alfred A. Knopf, 1953), Chapter 11; *cf.* also Easton, *A Systems Analysis of Political Life* (New York: John Wiley, 1965), Chapter 2.

predictable if they do not fully understand their own theory, and no theory is explicit enough on all issues to provide predictable guidance. But no thinking man operates without one. Pragmatism is merely an appeal to let theory remain implicit. The truth lies in Lord Keynes's famous aphorism, quoted earlier. History influences one's choice of paradigm. But one's paradigm influences what aspects of history will be most influential—unless everything is already locked in a predetermined secular trend.

Interest-group liberals have the pluralist paradigm in common, and its influence on liberal policy and liberal methods of organization has obviously been very large and very consistent. Discrediting the pluralist component of interest-group liberalism has been one of the central purposes of this volume, in the hopes that a change of theory can have some small impact on history. Nothing seems to be more evident than the observation that present theory is inappropriate for this epoch. Among the many charges made against pluralism, the following three seem relevant to a final effort at discrediting the entire theoretical apparatus.

(1) The pluralist component has badly served interest-group liberalism by propagating and perpetuating the faith that a system built primarily upon groups and bargaining is perfectly self-corrective. This is based upon assumptions which are clearly not often, if ever, fulfilled—assumptions that groups always have other groups to confront them, that "overlapping memberships" will both insure competition and keep competition from becoming too intense, that "membership in potential groups" or "consensus" about the "rules of the game" are natural and inevitable, scientifically verifiable phenomena that channel competition naturally toward a public interest. It is also based on an impossible assumption that when competition does take place it yields ideal results. As has already been observed, this is as absurd as a similar assumption of laissez-faire economists about the ideal results of economic competition. One of the major Keynesian criticisms of market theory is that even if pure competition among factors of supply and demand did yield an equilibrium, the equilibrium could be at some-

thing far less than the ideal of full employment. Pure pluralist competition, similarly, might produce political equilibrium, but the experience of recent years shows that it occurs at something far below an acceptable level of legitimacy and at a price too large to pay—exclusion of Negroes from most of the benefits of society.

(2) Pluralist theory is outmoded and unrealistic in still another way comparable to the rise and decline of laissez-faire economics. Pluralism has failed to grapple with the problem of oligopoly or imperfect competition as it expresses itself in the political system. When a program is set up in a specialized agency, the number of organized interest groups surrounding it tends to be reduced. Generally it tends to be reduced precisely to those groups and factions to whom the specialization is most salient. That in turn tends to reduce the situation from one of potential competition to potential oligopoly. That is to say, one can observe numerous groups in some kind of competition for agency favors. But competition tends to last only until each group learns the goals of the few other groups. Each adjusts to the others. Real confrontation leads to net loss for all rather than gain for any. Rather than countervailing power there will more than likely be accommodating power.

Galbraith has assumed that each oligopoly will be checked by an oligopsony—an interest from the opposite side of the market rather than a competitor for a share in the same market. This notion of countervailing power—competition between big labor and big industry, big buyers against big sellers, etc.—was to explain economic and political phenomena. But not only is this new kind of confrontation an unfounded assumption. It was to be created by public policy: ". . . the support of countervailing power has become in modern times perhaps the major peacetime function of the Federal government." [5] Countervailing power, in old or new form, can hardly be much of a theory of the way the industrial state nat-

[5] Galbraith, *American Capitalism, op. cit.,* p. 136. *Cf.* Anshen and Wormuth, *op. cit.,* p. 18 and p. 132. For the best case of accommodation, see any study of the cigarette industry, especially Chapter 10 of *The Structure of American Industry,* ed. Walter Adams (New York: Macmillan, 1961).

urally works if it requires central government support. And it hardly warrants government support if its consequences, as already proposed, do not produce the felicitous results claimed for them.

(3) Finally, the pluralist paradigm depends upon an idealized and almost totally miscast conception of *the group.* Laissez-faire economics may have idealized the firm and the economic man but never to the degree to which the pluralist thinkers today sentimentalize the group, the group member, and the interests. Note the contrast between the traditional American notion of the group and the modern pluralist definition. Madison in Federalist 10 defined the group ("faction") as "a number of citizens, whether amounting to a majority or minority of the whole, who are united and actuated by some common impulse of passion, or of interest, *adverse to the right of other citizens, or to the permanent and aggregate interests of the community.*" (Emphasis added.) David Truman uses Madison's definition but cuts the quotation just before the emphasized part.[6] In such a manner pluralist theory became the complete handmaiden of interest-group liberalism, in a sense much more than laissez-faire economics was ever a handmaiden to big capitalism. To the Madisonian, and also to the early twentieth-century progressive, groups were necessary evils much in need of regulation. To the modern pluralist, groups are good; they require accommodation. Immediately following his definition in Federalist 10, Madison went on to say: "The regulation of these various interfering interests forms the principal task of modern legislation. . . ." This is a far cry from Galbraith's "support of countervailing power," or Schlesinger's "hope of harnessing government, business and labor in a rational partnership . . . ," or the sheer sentimentality behind the notion of "maximum feasible participation," and "group representation in the interior processes of. . . ."

A revived feeling of distrust toward interests and groups would not destroy pluralist theory but would only prevent its remaining a servant of a completely outmoded system of public endeavor. Once sentimentality toward the group is de-

[6] Truman, *op. cit.*, p. 4.

stroyed, it will be possible to see how group interactions might fall short of creating an ideal equilibrium. Such distrust of prevailing theory might then lead to discomfort with the jurisprudence of delegation of power, for it too rests mightily upon an idealized view of how groups make law today. In such a manner the theoretical foundations of interest-group liberalism can be discredited. Some progress will then have been made toward restoration of an independent and legitimate government in the United States. Until that occurs, liberalism will continue to be the enemy rather than the friend of democracy.

The Ends of Juridical Democracy: Proposals for Radical Reform

These proposals are written for the time when men of influence come to see that the Consensus of 1937 is finished. At the moment they continue to search for distant sociological causes of American distress. But ultimately they must come to see that they and their belief system constitute the pathology. When this is fully realized, all leaders—the ins as well as the outs—will begin to search for new goals rather than merely to express dissatisfactions. This basic shift of attitudes will be fruitless unless it yields fundamental institutional change. To accomplish that they will need a new paradigm. And, since a good cry is half the battle, I offer Juridical Democracy as the candidate. The following proposals provide the platform for such a movement. As is true of all radical platforms, each proposal is deceptively simple, each would be enormously effective, each would be politically extremely difficult to accomplish. However, as is also true of radicalism in America, once the first step is taken, the rest suddenly seems no longer radical.

RESTORING RULE OF LAW

The first and most important step would be the easiest to accomplish but would probably excite the strongest opposition and fear if anyone ever took it seriously. This is mere revival of the still valid but universally disregarded *Schechter* rule. To accommodate interest-group liberal programs the Supreme Court created a basic line of jurisprudence by giving official and complete faith and credit to all expressions formally passed along by the legislature. The Court's rule must once again become one of declaring invalid and unconstitutional any delegation of power to an administrative agency that is not accompanied by clear standards of implementation.

Restoration of the *Schechter* rule would be dramatic because it would mean return to the practice of occasional Supreme Court invalidation of congressional acts. Nothing is more dramatic than the confrontation of these two jealous Branches, the more so due to its infrequent occurrence in recent years. But there is no reason to fear judicial usurpation. Under present conditions, when Congress delegates without a shred of guidance, the courts usually end up rewriting many of the statutes in the course of "construction." Since the Court's present procedure is always to try to find an acceptable meaning of a statute in order to avoid invalidating it, the Court is legislating constantly. A blanket invalidation under the *Schechter* rule is a Court order for Congress to do its own work. Therefore the rule of law is a restraint upon rather than an expansion of the judicial function.

There is also no reason to fear reduction of government power as a result of serious application of the Schechter rule. Fortunately, interest-group liberals have less to fear from the rule-of-law requirement than they might have thought. Rather than study the problem they have simply allowed their defenses against rule of law to be defined by the fact that it has been the nineteenth-century liberals who have championed its cause.[7] But the laissez-faire hope that such a requirement would help keep government small is based on a misunderstanding of the principle or upon some definition of it quite different from the one employed all through this volume. Historically, rule of law, especially statute law, is the essence of positive government. A bureaucracy in the service of a strong

---

[7] See, for example, F. A. Hayek's superb essay "The Rule of Law," in his *Road to Serfdom* (Chicago: University of Chicago Press, 1944).

and clear statute is more effective than ever. Granted, the rule-of-law requirement is likely to make more difficult the framing and passage of some policies. But why should any program be acceptable if the partisans cannot fairly clearly state purpose and means? We ask such justification even of children. It may also be true that requirement of rule of law will make government response to demands a bit slower and government implementation of goals less efficient. Good statistical analysis of the record would probably not support such a hypothesis; but even if the hypothesis were fully confirmed, one must still ask, What good is all our prosperity if we cannot buy a little more law with it?

RULE OF LAW BY ADMINISTRATIVE FORMALITY

The Schechter rule, even forcefully applied, could not eliminate all vagueness in legislative delegation of power. Ignorance of changing social conditions is important, although it is a much over-used congressional alibi for malfeasance in legislative drafting. It is also true that social pressure for some kind of quick action prevents a full search for a proper rule in a statute once in a great while. But fortunately reform can be realistic, because there is a perfectly acceptable way to deal with the slippage within the dictates of rule by law. This is the simple requirement for early and frequent *administrative rule-making*.[8]

Most of the administrative rhetoric in recent years espouses the interest-group liberal ideal of administration by favoring the norm of flexibility and the ideal that every decision can be bargained. Pluralism applied to administration usually takes the practical form of an attempt to deal with each case "on its merits." But the ideal of case-by-case adjudication is in most instances a myth. Few persons affected by a decision have an opportunity to be heard. And each agency, regulatory or non-regulatory, disposes of the largest proportion of its cases with-

[8] I am grateful to Professor Kenneth C. Davis for forcefully urging this dimension upon me and for providing the best possible guidance in his *Administrative Law Treatise* (St. Paul: West Publishing Company, 1958), especially pp. 9–53 and 144 ff. of the 1965 *Supplement*. See also Friendly, *op. cit.*, pp. 141 ff.

out any procedure at all, least of all a formal adjudicatory process. In practice, agencies end up with the worst of case-by-case adjudication *and* of rule-making. They try to work without rules in order to live with the loose legislative mandate. They then treat their cases in practice as though they were operating under a rule. For example, most of the applications to the Civil Aeronautics Board are disposed of without hearings, even where applicants are entitled to them.[9] The so-called flexibility of a case approach is an unconvincing rationalization. Bargaining is involved, but it is reserved for leaders in the field who will not accept mere processing.

In contrast, treatment of the same cases by a real administrative rule has most of the advantage claimed for the case-by-case approach, yet possesses few of the disadvantages. Davis observes that rule-making is especially superior to formal adjudication or informal bargaining when more than a handful of parties will be affected. A rule can be general and yet gain clarity through examples drawn up with known cases in mind. It was precisely this ability to perceive the public policy implications in complex phenomena that underlies reliance on expert agencies. The rule can be further refined by taking large numbers of potential cases into account. And even with this specificity the rule can become a known factor in every client's everyday life. In contrast, there is an implicit rule in every bargained or adjudicated case, but it cannot be known to the bargainer until he knows the outcome, and its later application must be deciphered by lawyers representing potential cases.

All these are important advantages to clients. But most important of all are the improvements rule-making would bring to administration and to legislative-administrative relationships. First, administrators should want to make rules deliberately focusing broad delegations of power, because broad delegations are a menace to formal organization and to the ideal of the Neutral Civil Servant. The pluralistic principle impairs the rational ordering of tasks and the routinization of routines. Broad discretion makes a politician out of a bu-

[9] Davis, *Supplement,* p. 151.

reaucrat. Many bureaucrats are good politicians, but when such skills and talents become the prime criterion of appointment and promotion they tend to negate the original *raison d'être* and justification of administrative independence—expertise.

Rule-making would improve the administrative process still further by making administrative power more responsible as well as more efficient. When an agency formulates a rule, it is indeed formulating legislation. But it is not usurping legislative power this way any more than the Supreme Court would be usurping power if it went back to declaring bad delegations unconstitutional. When an agency formulates a rule it is merely carrying out what Congress delegated to it and what was expected of all such agencies by the Administrative Procedure Act passed by Congress.[10] Moreover, formulation of a rule will most likely lead the agency back to Congress more frequently. This is part of what was referred to as "bargaining on the rule" in Chapter 5. In contrast, as argued earlier, "bargaining on the decision" is more likely to keep the political process down on the line far away from political responsibility. Thus it seems clear that avoidance of rule-making is more of a usurpation than rule-making. When there are good administrative rules, legislative evaluation of whole programs becomes possible; Congress need no longer depend wholly upon piecemeal committee oversight and narrow appropriations subcommittee scrutiny. Still further administrative responsibility is secured by the fact that rule-making early in the life of a statute brings on some judicial evaluation before the agency is too committed to its own existence or before some flaw in the agency's makeup becomes too demoralizing to the clientele.

In a sense, Woodrow Wilson was correct when he argued in 1886 for centralized administration as a necessity for modern democracy. He was also probably correct in observing that large delegations of power end up more responsibly adminis-

[10] 60 Stat. 237 (1946), Sec. 2(c) and Sec. 3(a): "Every agency shall separately state and currently publish in the Federal Register . . . (3) substantive rules as authorized by law and statements of general policy. . . . No person shall in any manner be required to resort to organization or procedure not so published."

tered than small delegations. But his recommendations must be understood in the proper context. Broad delegation to Wilson must have meant well-guided delegation. Otherwise centralization and responsibility would be impossible; for broad, unguided delegation means the very opposite of centralization. On the other hand, centralization does not have to mean stern, hierarchical subordination, as in the classic Prussian system. Administrative centralization and responsibility can be achieved by centralization around rules: *Lesser authority can be subject to higher authority through criteria relevant to the programs themselves.*

An illustration from the judicial process may serve better than abstract elaboration of the point. Is a leading opinion by the Supreme Court a centralizing or a decentralizing force in judicial administration? Obviously it is both, in the best sense of both terms. A strong and clear ruling is an act of centralization by the Supreme Court. Yet at the same time it leads to significant decentralization of caseload and a good deal of self-administration by lower courts and counsel. To look at it in a slightly different way, an area with good leading opinions is an area of "easy law" in which there are few appeals to the top; nonetheless the area is centralized too, in the sense that each decision in each lower judicial unit becomes more consistent with all other comparable decisions, because the clear rule is a good criterion, departures from which are easily detectible by higher courts and clients. In contrast, the Supreme Court can inundate itself in areas of "hard law" where it cannot or will not enunciate a leading opinion expressing good governing rules. In such an area there is even greater centralization, but in the worse sense of the word because responsibility can be maintained only through regular, bureaucratic supervision (in judicial administration this takes the form of appeals and certiorari).

In 1958 Professor Davis concluded his analysis of delegated legislation with the widely-quoted observation that the typical statute was telling the agency, "Here is the problem; deal with it." Seven years later, following a period of unprecedented government expansion. Davis went further: "Sometimes [the statute] has not even said 'Here is the problem.' It does less than that. It says, instead: 'We the Congress don't know what the problems are; find them and deal with them.' " [11] To Davis, the period between 1958 and 1965 had "passed without a significant development in the law of delegation." [12] This is a strong sign of retrogressive tendencies. But they can be reversed when and as the need for reversal has been perceived. The advantages to a more formal and rule-bound administrative process ought to be obvious to anyone not blinded by an ideology framed for a period when perhaps we could not afford legality. But now, when legality and efficiency tend to go together, it would be foolish not to grasp them.

THE SENIOR CIVIL SERVICE VERSUS THE OMBUDSMAN

Efforts to make a virtue of loose administration are known by many labels and are all doomed to dismal failure. At this point further critical commentary is hardly necessary on the administrative or political implications of such notions as interest representation, participatory democracy, community action, and the like. However, there is one other, a technique that at first seems appealingly different as a means of making administration more responsible and legitimate while yet allowing it to remain unbound by rules. This is the Ombudsman.[13] This device was in use for a century in its home country, Sweden, before its recent flush of popularity in the United States and elsewhere. The Ombudsman is a man and an office whose responsibility has generally been to respond to complaints of maladministration.

At first glance the Ombudsman may appear as the knight in shining armor, but that is unfortunately not at all the case. The idea of the Ombudsman has appealed to mayors and reformers in many American cities and to many serious observers of American national problems, as well as to thoughtful dissidents in the U.S. and many other countries, because there is a wide-

[11] Davis, pp. 43–44 of 1965 Pocket Part.
[12] *Ibid.*, p. 54.
[13] For an excellent brief treatment, comparing this device to the French Conseil d'Etat, see Andrew Shonfield, *Modern Capitalism* (New York: Oxford University Press, 1965), pp. 421 ff.

spread expectation that government power is inevitably mal-
administered. But the Ombudsman would improve little and
would in fact interfere with substantial progress during the
course of the experiment. First, to handle the complaint load in
a single American city today would require an office of many
hundreds of assistants, clerks, and perhaps even a few assistant
Ombudsmen.[14] Its size would vitiate its purpose. We would
soon have to have an auxiliary Ombudsman just to handle
complaints against the Ombudsman. Second, the Ombudsman
would relieve the administrative process precisely where pressure is needed to expose problems that need central agency attention. Third, the Ombudsman would be a redundancy. He
would perform functions that would duplicate congressional
committees, courts, political parties. Fourth, and most important, he would not do the one thing the system really needs
having done: He would not give agencies any more law or
justification. Our problems go beyond the Ombudsman. We
must reinstate a legitimate regime before we again concern
ourselves with the details of equity.

A far more meaningful administrative reform in the United
States would be the fostering of a truly independent and integrated administrative class—a Senior Civil Service. A profession of public administration, as distinct from a career within a
specific agency, is vital to the proper centralization of a democratic administrative process. The independent Senior Civil
Servant can be designed for weak loyalty to any one agency.
He comes closer to the intellectual who prefers to generalize,
yet he is an activist. The makings of a Senior Civil Service lie
already within the grasp of the Civil Service Commission if it
will but perceive the opportunity in its interrelated Bureau of
Executive Manpower, its Executive Assignment System and its
Executive Seminar Centers. Through these units, recruitment
of such a class out of the ranks, rather than through an Oxford
or an École Nationale d'Administration, would provide a balance of legal and technological considerations. If such a class
were combined with court-imposed, Congress-imposed, and

[14] Shonfield reports an average of only 1,000 complaints per year in
all of Sweden. (*Op. cit.*, p. 423.)

administratively-imposed standards of law, the administrative process would inevitably be more centralized without any loss of real pluralism in the larger system. Centralizing through law and formalizing through administrative recruitment would only centralize the places where groups must seek access. This would serve all the better to insure that conflicting groups be thrown together in public competition rather than kept apart within the almost secret confines of their respective programs.

If adopted, all of the foregoing proposals would definitely increase formalism, and yet they would also contribute to real competition. They would help restore emphasis upon the competition component rather than the group component of the pluralist paradigm. Inevitably this increases the frequency of congressional as well as presidential opportunities to enter the act. The price is a certain additional instability and perhaps in the short run a bit less efficiency. But due process and legitimacy are after all system values of some importance. Moreover, this type of instability was precisely what was supposed to make a pluralistic system work. It is distressing how many 1930's left-wing liberals become 1960's interest-group liberals out of a concern for instability.

RESTORE REGIONAL GOVERNMENT: HOW TO SEE VIRTUE IN THE STATES

Part of the reform program bears some resemblance to an old-line constitutional argument, for restoration of the rule of law provides a basis for establishing some practical limitations on the scope of Federal power. If an applicable and understandable set of standards must accompany every Federal program, Federal power could not extend to those objects for which no general rules are either practicable or desirable. Thus, where regional or local variation is desired, the Federal government is not even the appropriate unit. Unconditional rebates would be infinitely preferable. When regional variation is not desirable it is usually because some problem uniformly distributed across the country has been identified and is well known—as for example civil rights, military service, tax liability, access to the airwaves, obligations of contracts, free speech and petition—in which case there is no barrier, except fear, to prevent enactment of statutes in which clear and effective standards can accompany delegations of vast public power.

It matters little whether the delegation is to a Federal agency or to a State government, so long as standards flow with delegations. And in many, if not most, of our contemporary social problems State government would be superior to Federal units. This argument is not based on mere antiquarian admiration of federalism or fear of federal domination. It is based on an appreciation of the practical advantages of differentiation of functions. State governments have been systematically weakened by Home Rule, by Federal absorption of tax base, by the poor reputation given them by the abuses of southern State governments, and by the expansion of direct Federal-local relations. Now that cities have proven that they cannot cope with urban problems, even with Federal help, we have, in any case, no other place but the States to turn to. But relying on the State need not be thought of as an act of desperation. As already argued, the State possesses all the powers of its cities plus the advantage of containing most of the metropolitan realities that are beyond the reach of cities.

The proposition that the State may be the only governmental unit capable of coping with contemporary problems can be better appreciated by French and British scholars and planners, who feel seriously weakened by not having an established unit of government at a regional level. Perhaps we have held on to our old model long enough for it to appear suddenly as the latest fashion. If so, it provides the further benefit, without extra charge, of restoring the practice of approaching persons through their citizenship, of defining persons according to their rights and obligations rather than according to their location in a group, a class, or a race.

FISCAL POLICY AS AN INSTRUMENT OF CONTROL: TOWARD AN EXPANSION

Limiting Federal power to programs for which it can provide acceptable standards of law is a limitation that could turn the Federal government toward far greater use of its fiscal and

monetary techniques. (For simplicity, I shall refer to the category as fiscal.) This would be a very good reform in itself.
Manipulating the entire system in order to influence conduct
may sound insidious at first glance. The citizen may not know
he is being manipulated. He may fear manipulation as he fears
subliminal advertising. But that is a mistaken notion. Most fiscal techniques are very noticeable at the time of their adoption
and tend only afterwards to recede into the subliminal. That,
in fact, is the most outstanding advantage of the typical fiscal
techniques. They are very noticeable in the threat but, once in-
stalled, tend to become part of a person's *modus operandi*. Fiscal techniques, in sum, tend to be administered according to
clear general rules about which a person can learn and to
which he can adjust. They tend to affect large aggregates of
persons. Fiscal techniques cut across organized groups. It is
difficult to imagine adoption of a major fiscal activity that is
not the occasion of considerable debate and publicity. These
actions range from an announced deliberate budget deficit to a
decision to cut taxes at an unusual time, from the mere administrative decision to change slightly the Federal Reserve dis-
count rate to a decision to alter the price of gold (devalua-
tion), from decisions to manipulate aggregates of industry (investment tax credit) to decisions to redistribute regional
wealth (block grant-in-aid criteria).

Fiscal policies immediately possess broad and noticeable social significance. They are once or twice removed from constituencies at the level of formulation, yet they engage the best of
constituency behavior in comparison to subsidy policies. Although at first glance subsidy and porkbarrel programs may
appear closer to the public and the people, it is well known
that legislative action on subsidy policies is contained almost
completely inside the committee system, insulated from the
parliamentary level of Congress as well as from the President.[15] Fiscal policies are a great deal more public. Using
amending activity as a measure of open parliamentary creativity vis-à-vis committee control, note on the Table the dramatic

[15] For the best case study of this, see Arthur Maass, *Muddy Waters*
(Cambridge: Harvard University Press, 1951).

contrast between action on subsidy and porkbarrel bills as compared to fiscal and other "redistributive bills." There is no question that political processes are far more exposed to public view on the latter than on the former.

TABLE 10.1

LEGISLATIVE CREATIVITY OF CONGRESS
ON SUBSIDY BILLS AND FISCAL BILLS *

	(1) AVERAGE NO. OF AMENDMENTS PROPOSED PER BILL	(2) % PASSED	(3) % SIGNIFICANT AMENDMENTS PASSED OVER OBJECTIONS OF SPONSORING COMMITTEE	(4) SCALE SCORE SUMMARY OF 8 ATTRIBUTES OF AMENDMENTS	
				House	Senate
Subsidy and Porkbarrel Bills (N = 22)	5.8	41.8	0	1.09	2.12
Fiscal and Redistributive Bills (N = 25)	9.1	61	24	1.81	4.50

* Sources: L. John Roos (Unpublished Master's thesis, University of Chicago, 1968); and my forthcoming *Arenas of Power*. The bills included: (1) all bills in 87th Congress, 1st Session, that received roll call votes in House and Senate, and (2) 13 major bills since 1948 on which major case studies were published. Mr. Roos worked out an ingenious scaling device based upon 8 possible amending actions on a bill. Bills were then scaled along these 8 attributes, which included Columns 1, 2, and 3 on the table plus 5 others. For Column 4, Coefficients of Reproducibility averaged over 95, indicating excellent scales. The scores on Column 4 can be interpreted as follows: The higher the score the easier it was for the parliamentary body of Congress (the floor) to take some legislative functions back from its Committees. In other words, only on distributive bills can it truly be said that "congressional government is committee government." For a full discussion of the categories, see my "American Business," *op. cit.*

Most of the implementation of fiscal policy is purely executive, but that too accords with the classic democratic formalisms.[16] Most fiscal policy implementation is in fact controlled at the very highest reaches of the executive—the President acting in concert with the Budget Director and Council of Economic Advisers, the Secretary of the Treasury, the top echelons of the Federal Reserve System. This too is a tremen-

[16] In contrast, congressional-committee meddling in public works, procurement, natural resources, etc., is notorious, but fortunately this pattern is not universal.

dously attractive feature of fiscal policy—a model of responsibility in comparison both to subsidy programs and to regulatory programs. It is all the more attractive because these decisions, unlike regulatory decisions, can be translated into rates through which very small changes can bring about large changes in behavior. As a result, fiscal policy is really the only type of policy that can achieve a high degree of rationality through the incremental approach so dear to pluralists.

Fiscal policy is not a panacea, for only rarely is a fiscal technique appropriate as a direct replacement for a subsidy or a regulatory policy. Each may be desirable or undesirable on its own terms, the criteria being need, result, and, above all, the accompaniment of a good general rule.[17] A negative income tax, for example, might well become a good addition to or replacement for Old Welfare, but that involves substitution of one fiscal technique for another. Meanwhile, neither the negative income tax, Old Welfare, or New Welfare can adequately fight civil wrongs. For that, only a stiff regulatory statute with inviolable standards and strong enforcement will work. However, fiscal policy, although not a panacea, is an area where federal expansion is most desirable.

A TENURE-OF-STATUTES ACT

The final proposal for reform is for a statute setting a Jeffersonian limit of from five to ten years on the life of every organic act. As the end of its tenure approaches, an agency is likely to find its established relations with its clientele beginning to shake from exposure, new awareness, and competition. This may ultimately be the only effective way to get substantive evaluation of a program and an agency. There is a myth

---

[17] It is my opinion that subsidy policies are inherently amoral because it is almost impossible to formulate general rules for them. The great advantage of subsidy is the very absence of moral considerations. This makes techniques of subsidy ideal for nation-building, when co-optation may be the only important criterion until a regime is well established. In mature nations the virtue of such policies seems to disappear. But these are only opinions at this point. They will be documented in a later volume, *Arenas of Power.*

that programs are given evaluation at least once a year through a normal appropriations process that extends through the Executive Office of the President to the two appropriations committees of Congress and their specialized subcommittees. However, these yearly evaluations get at only the marginal and incremental aspects of most programs. Substantive questions are most often treated as off limits; while individual members of Congress often ask substantive questions, they are likely to be disregarded or ruled out of order. Here indeed is a good illustration of the distinction between functional and sub-stantive accountability. The very cost-consciousness and care for detail that makes appropriations review functionally rational is the source of its weakness as a means of achieving any substantive conclusions. Those who prefer formulation and evaluation of laws by democratic institutions rather than by courts should strongly favor statutory tenure.

THE FUTURE AS JURIDICAL DEMOCRACY

When this inquiry was undertaken several years ago the prob-lem of interest-group liberalism seemed limited to a few areas, and the chances for changing the practices of politicians and beliefs of intellectuals regarding those areas seemed slim. Fur-ther familiarity revealed that a far wider range of government had been affected by interest-group liberalism but that never-theless it had become possible to be optimistic about the prospects for reform.

The interest-group liberal phenomenon no longer appeared limited after the discovery that pluralistic government de-pended upon policy without law and that underlying pluralist political theory provided reasoning for the necessity and the justification of policy without law. This meant that mere group representation was not the only manifestation of the new liberal state. It could often be merely a byproduct of a far broader phenomenon. This also meant that the ideology of interest-group liberalism was not actually confined to a few in-tellectuals who were influencing the verbalisms of a few

Democratic Party politicians. It meant, rather, that this ideology had long since escaped its earlier confines and had become the new public philosophy. While fortunately it was not applied with 100 per cent consistency to all actions of government, it is nevertheless clear that interest-group liberalism had become the public philosophy, that it clearly dominated all other ideologies. It had its controlling establishments in both major political parties. It had its own jurisprudence. The Supreme Court was seeing to its enforcement with almost total consistency.

At this advanced stage in the failure of interest-group liberalism to cope with the problems of our time, it is possible nevertheless to be optimistic, because interest-group liberalism combines all of the worst traits of pluralist society and is therefore weak enough to be subject to radical reform and even, perhaps, complete replacement as public philosophy. Interest-group liberalism arose out of weakness. It was the New Deal rationalized. It was making the best of one of our worst periods of history by buying time and support with sovereignty. Big rationalizations are durable, and in the 1960's interest-group values are applied almost habitually even in periods of national strength. Yet one can be optimistic if the practical alternative, juridical democracy, can be shown to combine all the best traits of the pluralist society:

(1) Interest-group liberalism cannot plan. Juridical democracy can. Law is a plan. Positive law guides and moves in known ways. Its flexibility is not a flabby bargain but its capacity to be changed in known ways. That is also the basis of the superior rationality and administrative efficiency of juridical democracy.

(2) Interest-group liberalism cannot achieve justice. Juridical democracy can, because its actions can be judged. Requirement of a rule of law leads to a justice-oriented politics just as automatically as the requirement of unguided delegation leads to a pluralistic, bargain-oriented politics. The juridical approach to politics produces increments of justice just as surely as the interest-group liberal approach produces increments of equilibrium. And yet, while pluralism eliminates justice from all

consideration, the juridical approach does not eliminate pluralist patterns or principles. The juridical approach does not dictate a particular definition of justice, of virtue, or of the good
life. It is not popular totalitarianism in disguise. The juridical
principle can convert a consumer economy into a just society
without altering in any way the virtue of consumption or the
freedom to consume. It does not reduce the virtue of political
competition but only makes access to some areas a bit more
difficult to acquire.

(3) Interest-group liberalism weakens democratic forms.
Juridical democracy strengthens them. Rule of law may have
become unpopular to contemporary liberals because of a widespread idea that it operates as a "check against democracy."
The truth lies almost altogether the other way. The decline of
Congress, supposedly the popular branch, began with the expansion of delegation of power. The emergence of control by
congressional committee absolutely parallels those developments. Congress is at its classic best when a proposed bill em-
bodies a good rule. Good recent cases include Landrum-Griffin,
the 1962 Trade Act, Medicare, and Civil Rights. Taking 10
years to pass a good civil rights law is no reflection on Congress as a parliamentary body but only upon the frailty of the
urban-liberal forces in the country until 1964. (For examples,
see Chapters 7 and 9.) The role of the Supreme Court is in-
structive here. Congress did not become a real parliament on
civil rights until it had a rule of law to debate, *and that was a
rule forced upon it by the Supreme Court's exercise of its
power to declare legislative acts unconstitutional.* Rule of law
is no check against democratic forms. The one will not endure
without the other.

(4) Interest-group liberalism also weakens democratic
power. Juridical democracy strengthens it. Here too its reputation as a check against government contributed to the contemporary unpopularity of the juridical principle. But again, most
of the evidence lies the other way. No government is more
powerful than one whose agencies have good laws to implement. Much is spoken and written of the problem of "bureau-

cratic power" and how to keep it under presidential control or how to be sure it is effective. But nothing serves better to direct bureaucracy than issuing it orders along with powers. One can hardly avoid being impressed with how effective a clear statute or a clear presidential order is. Students of Congress are struck by how effective a hearing or threatened investigation can be. Such orders and inquiries are least effective upon agencies that traditionally operate in the absence of rules of law—for example, the Corps of Engineers, the Armed Services, the public works and other subsidizing agencies. A grant to an agency of powers without rules or standards leads to the bargaining, the unanticipated commitments, and the confusions that are the essence of the illegitimate state. Juridical democracy tends to reduce the inconsistency between power and legitimacy.

(5) Finally, interest-group liberalism produces an apologetic political science. Juridical democracy produces an independent and critical political science. Interest-group liberalism's focus on equilibrium and the paraphernalia of its establishment is apology. The focus on the group is a commitment to one of the more rigidified aspects of the social process and is, therefore, another kind of apology. Stress upon the incremental is also apology. The separation of facts from values is apology.

Is the apologetic a price required for science? Most assuredly the price need not have been paid. There is no denying that modern pluralistic political science brought science to politics. And that is a good thing. But it was pluralism and not science that required the absolute separation of facts and values. Pluralism required the separation because it could not live with the fact that governments make actual substantive choices. In embracing facts it embraced the ever-present. In thus embracing science from this viewpoint it took rigor without relevance. Juridical democracy need be no less scientific in its tendency to work toward fusion of facts and values. All that really amounts to in practice is a fusion of political behavior, public administration, and public law. Rules of law and their

consequences—rights, justice, legitimacy—are just as susceptible of scientific generalization as their behavioral equivalents—
bargaining, equilibrium, and opinions.

Juridical democracy could produce a superior science of
politics because it allows rigor but is no enemy of relevance.
The juridical approach permits apology. It simply does not
make apology obligatory. The juridical principle does not destroy the idea of equilibrium. It simply does not indoctrinate
students into believing that equilibrium is the only goal of the
political system. The juridical principle does not erect barriers
to the scientific study of behavior. It only insists that political
behavior not destroy the scientific study of other dimensions of
the polity. The juridical principle treats pathology and physiol-
ogy as equal sciences and insists further that neither is impaired by efforts to define a healthy body.

Quite properly, *The End of Liberalism* concludes with an
academic issue, for this may turn out to be the most important
issue of all—the influence of theories and the insidiousness of
theories that mask outmoded ideologies. But it would be
wrong to leave the impression that political science created
interest-group liberalism or that political scientists will produce
the future of theory beyond liberalism. The political theories
that regimes and revolutions are made of are not written in
academe. Theories are only systematized and propagated
there. In the United States the history of political theory since
the founding of the Republic has resided in the Supreme
Court. The future of political theory probably lies there too. A
Court that can make a regime of interest-group liberalism can
also unmake it. The Court has not done so, and so it surrounds
itself in suspense: Is the Republic or is it not in good hands?

Index

Acheson, Dean, 163, 177
Adams, Walter S., 66, 90, 289
Administrative Procedure Act, 95, 301
Administrative process, 23, 29, 31–33, 38–39, 44, 49, 50, 51, 52–53, 76, 94, 96, 127; abstract categorization as regulatory standard, 135–38, 140–42, 143, 154–55; and capitalist ideology, 27–28; concrete categorization as regulatory standard, 133–35, 143; constitutional issues, 130–32; defined, 27, 30, 31; delegation of power and, 132–36; early implementation of, 128–29; expansion and development of, 133–43; Ombudsman and, 303–4; private, 33–41; question of legislative standards, 133–34, 144, 146–56, 299–305, 306, 312; regulation of the economy by, 133–43, 146–54; need for Senior Civil Service, 304–5
AFL-CIO, 40, 66, 116
Agricultural Stabilization and Conservation Service, 109, 112
Agriculture, 80, 87, 91, 102, 103, 140, 289; credit associations, 109–10; early development of, 104–6; Federal expenditures on, 110; New Deal legislation concerning, 106; political autonomy and power, 104, 108, 112–15, 123–24; prices, 103, 104, 107, 109, 112, 113, 114, 141; self-governing programs and institutions, 65, 102–4, 106–12; 123–24; wheat-cotton bill of 1964, 103–4
Agriculture, Department of, 75, 108, 109, 110, 112–13, 114, 115, 123, 164, 288
Alinsky, Saul, 242

American Farm Bureau Federation, 88, 108
American Medical Association, 37, 64–65
Anderson, Clinton P., 112
Anderson, Martin, 264
Anfuso, Victor, 112
Appalachia program, 81–82, 120
Area Redevelopment Administration, 120
Armed Forces, 167, 168, 169, 170, 173, 178–79
Arnold, Thurmond, 66
Atomic Energy Commission, 170–73; and the Presidency, 171–73

Bargaining, decision-oriented, 147–48, 149–53; rule-oriented, 147–48, 149–53, 301; see also Liberalism, interest-group
Bauer, Raymond, 36
Bell, Daniel, 34
Bendix, Rinehart, 33–34
Benson, Ezra Taft, 113
Bentley, Arthur F., 49
Berle, Adolph, 217
Binkley, Wilfred, 74–75
Black Americans, 191–92, 194–95, 205, 206–7, 240, 241, 242, 244–45, 246, 247, 248–49, 250–56, 269, 271, 277–80, 282, 283, 295
Brogan, Denis, 185
Brown, Ralph S., 171
Brown v. Board of Education, 68
Bruce, David, 164
Bruce, Howard, 164
Bryan, William Jennings, 105
Bryce, Lord, 128–29
Budget, Bureau of, and War on Poverty, 231, 232
Business, Federal regulation of, 80–81, 82, 83, 105, 106, 129–43, 146–54; and Liberal-Conservative dialogue, 65–67

315